William Walter Merry

Selected Fragments of Roman Poetry

William Walter Merry

Selected Fragments of Roman Poetry

ISBN/EAN: 9783337007324

Printed in Europe, USA, Canada, Australia, Japan

Cover: Foto ©Thomas Meinert / pixelio.de

More available books at **www.hansebooks.com**

OF

ROMAN POETRY

FROM THE EARLIEST TIMES OF THE REPUBLIC

TO THE AUGUSTAN AGE

EDITED, WITH INTRODUCTIONS, HEADINGS, AND NOTES

BY

W. W. MERRY, D.D.

RECTOR OF LINCOLN COLLEGE, OXFORD

SECOND EDITION, REVISED

Orford

AT THE CLARENDON PRESS

1898

Oxford
PRINTED AT THE CLARENDON PRESS
BY HORACE HART, M.A.
PRINTER TO THE UNIVERSITY

PREFACE

This little volume is an attempt to meet a difficulty which is often felt by young students of Roman poetry,—the want of a convenient handbook, containing a sufficiently representative selection from the fragments which have been preserved of the epic, dramatic, and satiric poets of Rome, from the earliest times of the Republic to the Augustan age.

From the Comedies of Plautus and Terence we can learn all that we require of the Fabulae Palliatae, as exhibited on the stage. But to form any idea of Roman Tragedy, or of the peculiarly national Praetextae and Togatae (or Tabernariae), we must make the best use we can of the remains of Pacuvius and Accius, of Atta, Titinius, and Afranius. Nor shall we appreciate the growth of the Epic, which culminates in Virgil, nor of the Satire as presented to us by Horace and Juvenal, without some study of the fragments of Livius, Naevius, and Ennius, of Lucilius and Varro.

But this implies access to a good many books, which are not always easily procurable; and, even then, unless we have some clue to their connection, the scattered fragments are often unintelligible. The object of this volume is to supply such a clue. No doubt there is a constant danger of suggesting a fanciful explanation;

and the endeavour to work isolated lines into the plot of a play or the subject of a satire may be, here and there, nothing better than a piece of misplaced ingenuity. But so much has been done for the interpretation of Ennius by Vahlen and L. Müller, and for the remains of Roman Tragedy and Comedy by O. Ribbeck, that, with such experienced guides, one may hope to have gone not very far astray. Besides the collections of fragments edited by Ribbeck (which are indispensable to every student of the Roman drama), there are two other books by the same scholar—*Die römische Tragödie*, and *Geschichte der römischen Dichtung*—which are very helpful. For the Saturae of Lucilius, the notes in Wordsworth's *Fragments and Specimens of Early Latin* are most valuable, as far as they go. The Saturae Menippeae of Varro have been adapted from Riese's edition, with some aid from Bücheler. For the remains of other poets, constant use has been made of E. Bährens' *Fragmenta Poetarum Romanorum*. But no attempt has been made in the present volume to present a critical text, or to settle questions of metrical arrangement. The editor has endeavoured to avail himself of the best sources; and he will be amply satisfied if he shall have succeeded in making the study of these Fragments more easy and more interesting.

W. W. M.

OXFORD, *September*, 1891.

THE Second Edition has been carefully revised, and some necessary corrections made.

W. W. M.

OXFORD. *August*, 1898.

CONTENTS

	PAGE
Carmen Saliare	1
Carmen Fratrum Arvalium	2
Vaticinia, Sententiae, Praecepta	2
Scipionum Elogia	4
Livius Andronicus:	
Odisia	7
Tragoediae	10
Ex incertis fabulis	12
Cn. Naevius:	
Tragoediae	14
Praetextae	19
Naevii et Metellorum altercatio	20
Palliatae	21
Ex incertis fabulis	24
Bellum Punicum	25
Q. Ennius:	
Annales	31
Tragoediae	48
Saturae	64
Ambracia	65
Epicharmus	65
Hedyphagetica	66
Epigrammata	67
M. Pacuvius:	
Tragoediae	68
Praetexta	90
Caecilius Statius:	
Palliatae	92

	PAGE
Aquilius:	
Boeotia	102
Licinius Imbrex:	
Neaera	103
Titinius:	
Togatae	104
Sextus Turpilius:	
Palliatae	108
L. Accius:	
Tragoediae	112
Praetextae	139
Fragmenta	143
C. Lucilius:	
Saturae	146
T. Quinctius Atta:	
Togatae	159
L. Afranius:	
Togatae	161
Pompilius:	
Epigramma	171
Valerius Aedituus:	
Epigrammata	172
Q. Lutatius Catulus:	
Epigrammata	173
Porcius Licinus	174
Volcatius Sedigitus:	
Poetarum comicorum aestimatio	176
In Terentium	176
Hostius	178
A. Furius Antias	179

	PAGE		PAGE
Cn. Matius:		C. Iulius Caesar:	
Ilias	180	Iudicium de Terentio	245
Mimiambi	180	P. Terentius Varro Atacinus:	
Laevius:			
Erotopaegnia, &c.	182	Argonautae	246
Sueius:		Chorographia	248
Moretum, &c.	186	Ephemeris	248
Novius:		Publilius Syrus:	
Atellanae	187	Mimus	250
Pomponius:		Sententiae	251
Atellanae	190	C. Helvius Cinna:	
M. Terentius Varro:		Ludicra	253
Saturae Menippeae	196	Propempticon Pollionis	253
Ex libro imaginum	223	Zmyrna	254
M. T. Cicero:		Epigramma	254
Marius	225	Populares Versus	255
Limon	226	C. Licinius Macer Calvus:	
De consulatu suo	226	Epithalamia	257
Ex Graecis conversa	230	Io	257
Epigramma, &c.	236	Ludicra	258
Decimus Laberius:		L. Varius Rufus:	
Mimus	237	De Morte	259
M. Furius Bibaculus:		M. Tullius Laurea:	
Ludicra	242	Epigramma	260
Annales	243		

FRAGMENTA SELECTA.

AXAMENTA,

OR

CHANTS USED IN RITUAL.

CARMEN SALIARE.

These fragments may, perhaps, be arranged into rude Saturnians; but the language is hardly intelligible, in spite of ingenious conjectures. In Horace's time (*Ep.* 2. 1. 85) the 'Saliare carmen Numae' was a puzzle; and Quintilian (*Inst. Or.* 1. 6. 40), acknowledges that the priests themselves did not understand the words.

I.

Dívum em pa cánte, divúm deo supplicáte.

[Varro, *L. L.*, 7. 26, 27.]

By *em pa* Havet understands *eum patrem*. Others read *empta* for which Bergk proposes *tmpli* and Bährens *parentem*; *cante* = canite; *divum deo*, i. e. Ianus (Macrob. *Sat.* 1. 9).

II.

In Terent. Scaur. (2661 P.) two lines of a Salian hymn are given thus:

Cume ponas Leucesiae praetexere monti
quot ibet etinei (? eunei) de is cum tonarem.

This is unintelligible. Bergk ingeniously refers the end of the first line, *praetexere monti*, to a gloss in Festus (p. 205 *prae tet tremonti* = praetremunt te. The lines may, perhaps, with a few slight alterations be printed

Cume tonas Leucetie prae tet tremonti
Quot ibi te viri audeïsunt tonare.

Cume = cum; *Leucetie* = lord of light (Macrob. *Sat.* 1. 15); *audeïsunt* = audierunt. Bergk daringly gives the second line as 'quom tibi cunei deestumum tonaront,' 'when thy bolts thunder on the right.'

CARMEN FRATRUM ARVALIUM.

An inscription from the Acts of the Arval Brotherhood, found in Rome in A. D. 1778. The actual copy of the old Latin, more or less correct, apparently belongs to the time of Elagabalus.

1. Enós Lasés iuváte (*ter*)
    Neve lúe rúe Mármar sins incúrrere in pléores (*ter*).
    Satúr fu fére Mars limén salí sta bérber (*ter*)
    Semúnis álternei ádvocápit cónctos (*ter*).
5. Enós Marmór iuváto (*ter*)
    Triúmpe (*quinquies*).

l. 1. *enos* = nos; with the form cp. E-castor; *Lases* = Lares. l. 2. *lue* = luem; *rue* = ruem, i. e. ruinam; *sins* = sines, 'thou must not suffer'; as *advocapit* l. 4 = advocabitis. l. 3. *fu* = esto, 'be satiate, fierce Mars!' *limen sali* = 'leap over, or cross (thy temple's) threshold'; *sta berber* (verbera? 'stop thy scourging'; or (addressed to each dancing priest) 'leap on the threshold! halt! smite (the ground).' l. 4. *semunis* (se-homo, homōnes) = 'superhuman powers.'

The form of the chant printed here, as adopted by Mommsen, may be taken as giving its general sense and character. But it is impossible to recover the original words with any certainty. The inscription itself is defaced, and carelessly cut, the spelling of the same words varying in different lines.

In the second line Havet would read 'ne velucre (= volueris) Marmars incurrere,' taking *sins* as a mistaken product of the final *s* of *Marmars*, and the initial syllable of *incurrere*. For *limen sali* he prints *nive* (= neve) *ensalli* (= insili), i. e. 'and leap not upon us.'

VATICINIA, ETC.

INCERTI AUCTORIS VATICINIUM.

During the siege of Veii (B.C. 395), commissioners came from Delphi 'sortem oraculi adferentes congruentem responso captivi vatis' (Liv. 5. 16 . The utterance of the oracle, as given in Livy, may possibly be arranged, with some alteration, in Saturnian measure, which Bährens thus gives ; referring the legend about the prophecy to the age of Naevius and Livius Andronicus :

Románe, aquám Albánam | cáve lacú tenéri,
cave ín maré manáre | flúminé sinás suo.
emíssa agrós rigábis | dissipátam rívis
exstíngues : túm tu insíste | aúdax hóstium múris.
memór quam pér tot ánnos | óbsidés úrbem,
ex eá tibí his fátis | núnc datám victóriam,
duéllo perfécto dónum | pórtato ámplum víctor
ad meá templá, sacráque | pátria quórum cúra est
omíssa, ut adsolet, | endóstauráta fácito.

APPII CLAUDI SENTENTIAE.

Appius Claudius Caecus, censor B. c. 312, consul 307, 296, was the ' great patrician . . . with whom begins the first attempt at Latin prose-composition and at art-poetry,' Teuffel, *R. L.*, § 90.

I.

. . . . .[1] qui, ánimi | cómpotém esse,
ne quíd fraudís pariát | feróciá stuprique.
[Festus, stuprum pro turpitudine.]

II.

Amícum cúm vidés | oblísceré[2] misérias,
inimícis si es comméntus, | nec libéns aéque.

[Priscian, s.v. commentus = σεσοφισμένος, i. e. 'if deceived by foes.']

[1] Bährens suggests that the gap may be thus filled up [?] *Iudicis ae|qui*, 'it belongs to a just judge.'
[2] *obliscere*, Fleckeisen. *obliviscere*, codd.

III.

Est únus quísque fáber | ipse suaé fortúnae.

[Pseudo Sallust, *De Ord. Rep.* 1. 1. 2.]

MARCII VATIS PRAECEPTA.

'Marcius the prophet' lived some time before the second Punic War (Cic. *De Div.* 1. 50. 115; Liv. 25. 12, &c.).

I.

Postrémus dícas, prímus | táceas ⏑⏑⏑⏑.

[Isidon. 6. 8. 12.]

II.

Ne níngulús medéri | quéat ⏑⏑⏑⏑.

[Paulus, 176, ningulus = nullus.]

III.

Quamvís noventium[1] | dúonum negumáte.

[Festus, 165, negumate = negate.]

INCERTI SENTENTIAE.

I.

Religéntem ésse opórtet | róligiósus nó seis.

[Aul. Gell. 4. 9. 1.]

II.

Est péssimúm malúm | consílium cónsultóri.

[Aul. Gell. 4. 5. 5.]

EPITAPHIA.

SCIPIONUM ELOGIA.

From the monument of the Scipios, near the Appian Way.

I.

Epitaph on L. Cornelius Scipio Barbatus, consul 98, censor 290 B. C.

---

[1] *noventium* = nuntium for MSS. moventium. Büchl.

EPITAPHIA.

1. Cornéliús Lucíus Scípió Barbátus,
   Gnaivód patré prognátus fórtis vír sapiénsque,
   quoiús formá vírtutei parísuma fúit,
   consól censór aidílis quei fuit apúd vos,
5. Taurásiá Cisaúna Sámnió cépit
   subigít omné Loucánam ópsidésque abdoúcit.

   l. 2. *Gnaivod* = Gnaeo.   l. 3. *parisuma* = parissima.   l. 5. *Taurasia[m], Cisauna[m], Samnio* = 'in Samnium.'

II.

L. Cornelius L. f. Scipio, consul 259, censor 258 B. C.
(The Italic letters show where the stone has been broken away.)

1. Honc oíno ploirumé coséntiónt Románe
   duonóro óptumó fuíse virô *virôro*
   Lucíom Scipióne. Filiós Barbáti
   consól censór aidílis híc fuét *apúd vos.*
5. hec cépit Córsica Aleriáque urbe *pugnandod*
   dedét Témpestátebus aíde *móretod vólam.*

   l. 1. *oino* = unum; *ploirume* = plurimi (as in *Romane*).   l. 2. *duonoro* (as in ll. 3, 5, 6 with final *m* dropped.   l. 4. *fuet* (as *dedet*) perf. indic.   l. 6. *aide* = aedem; *moretod* = merito.

III.

P. Cornelius P. f. Scipio, son of Scipio Africanus maior, B. C. 204-164.

1. Quei ápice insígne Diál*is* fl*ámin*ís gesístei
   mors pérfec*it* tua ut éssent ómniá brévia,
   honós famá virtúsque glória átque ingénium;
   quibús sei in lónga lícuisét tibe útier víta,
5. facilé factéis superáses glóriám maiórum.
   quaré lubéns te in grémiu, Scípió, récipit
   terrá, Publí, prognátum Públió, Cornéli.

   l. 1. *apice, insigne,* with final *m* dropped.   l. 3. *famā,* nom., as *terrā.*   l. 7. *Publi, Corneli,* vocatives, while *prognatum* takes up *te.*

IV.

L. Cornelius Scipio Cn. f. Cn. n. This Scipio, a son and a grandson of a Gnaeus, is not otherwise known.

1. Magná sapiéntia multásque vírtútes
   aetáte quóm párva pósidét hoc sáxsum,
   quoieí vitá defécit nón honós honóre.
   is híc sitús quei núnquam víctus ést virtútei.
5. annós gnatús vigínti ís *Díteist mandátus*,
   ne quaíratís honóre queí minus sít *mandátus.*

l. 1. *magna*, accus. 1. 2. *quom*, prep.=cum. 1. 3. *honos, honore*(m), in double sense, 'worth' and 'preferment.' 1. 4. *virtutei*, abl. 'in goodness.' 1. 5. *Ditei est* (Diti, Dis) ; al. *leto est* ; or *loceis*='resting-place.' 1. 6. *honore*(m), 'ask not about his office, seeing that none was assigned him.' He died too young.

V.

Cn. Cornelius Cn. f. Scipio Hispallus, second cousin of Scipio Africanus major ; praetor in B. C. 139. With the exception of a few verses of Ennius, these are the earliest elegiacs preserved.

1. Virtutes generis mieis moribus accumulavi,
   progenie mi genui, facta patris petiei.
3. Maiorum optenui laudem ut sibei me esse creátum
   laetentur, stirpem nobilitavit honos.

l. 1. *mieis*=meis, monosyllable. 1. 2. *progenie'm*) *mi* : if this reading be right, *progenie* must be pronounced as three syllables ; al. *progeniem genui*, ib. *petiei*, 'have sought to attain,' 'have ensued.' l. 4. *honos*, 'office.'

LIVIUS ANDRONICUS.

(Circ. 284-204 A.C.).

ODISIA.

1. Virúm mihi, Caména | ínsecé versútum.
   [Od. 1. 1.]
2. Patér nostér, Satúrni | fílié, *rex súmme*.
   [Od. 1. 45, 85.]
3. Meá puér, quid vérbi | éx tuo óre súpera fugít?
   [Od. 1. 64.]
4. ⏑‒ neque ením te oblítus, | Lértié, sum, nóster.
   [Od. 1. 65.]
5. Argénteó polúbro | aúreó eclútro.
   [Od. 1. 136.]
6. Tuquó mihí narráto | ómniá disórtim.
   [Od. 1. 169.]
7. Quae haec daps est? qui festus | diés ⏑ ‒ ⏑ ‒ ⏑.
   [Od. 1. 225.]
8. *Medm* mátrem prócitum | plúrimí venérunt.
   [Od. 1. 248.]
9. *Aut* ín Pylúm advéniens | aút ibí omméntans.
   [Od. 2. 317.]

l. 1. *insece* = ἔννεπε.   l. 5. *polubro*, 'basin'; ib. *eclutro* = ἐκλούτρῳ, 'bath.'   l. 8. *procitum* (procieo), 'to woo': Paul. 225.   l. 9. *ommentans*, fr. *mento*, frequent. of *maneo*.

10. . . . . . túmque rémos
    iussít religáre strúppis . . .
    [Od. 2. 422.]

11. Ibídemqué vir súmmus | ádprimús Patróclus.
    [Od. 3. 110.]

12. Quandó diés advéniet, | quém profáta Mórta est.
    [Od. 2. 99; 3. 227.]

13. Atquó escás habeámus | *rúsus* méntiónem.
    [Od. 4. 213.]

14. Partim erránt, nequeínont | Graéciám redíre.
    [Od. 4. 495.]

15. Sanctá puér Satúrni | máximá regína.
    [Od. 4. 513.]

16. Apúd nimphám Atlántis | filiam Cálipsónem.
    [Od. 4. 557.]

17. Igitúr demúm Ulíxi | fríxit praé pavóre
    cor.
    [Od. 5. 297.]

18. Celsós ocrís arváque | Néptuni ét mare mágnum.
    [Od. 5. 411.]

19. Utrúm genuá amplóctens | vírginem oráret.
    [Od. 6. 142.]

20. Ibí manéns sedéto, | dónicúm vidébis
    me cárpentó vehéntem | én domúm venísse.
    [Od. 6. 295.]

21. Simúl ac dácrimas de óre | noégeó detérsit.
    [Od. 8. 88.]

22. Namqué nihílum peíus | mácerát homónem
    quamdó mare saévom : | víres et cuí sunt mágnae,
    toppér *virim* confríngent ínportúnae | úndae.
    [Od. 8. 138.]

l. 10. *struppis* = τροποῖς.   l. 12. *Morta*, one of the Parcae, goddess of death (Aul. Gell. 3. 16. 11).   l. 13. *escas*, genitive : *rusus* = rursus. l. 18. *Neptuni*. So Bähr. for cod. *pulvia*.   l. 21. *noegeo*, Fest. 174 'amiculi genus praetextum purpura.'   l. 22. *topper* = toto opere, 'thoroughly.'

LIVIUS ANDRONICUS.

23. *Venit* Mercúrius cúmque eo | fíliús Latónas.
 [*Od.* 8. 322.]

24. Nexábant múlta intér se | fléxu nódórum dubió.
 [*Od.* 8. 378.]

25. Nam divíná Monétas | filiá dócuit.
 [*Od.* 8. 480.]

26. . . . inférnus an supérus tíbi fert díus | fúnerá, Ulíxes?
 [*Od.* 10. 64.]

27. Toppér facít homónes | út priús fuérunt.
 [*Od.* 10. 395.]

28. Toppér cití ad aédis | vónimús Círcae;
 duóna eórum sérvae | pórtant ád náves.
 milía aliá vína | ísdem inseriúntur.
 [*Od.* 12. 17.]

29. . . . parcéntes | praémodum—
 [*Od.* 12. 321.]

30. . . . síc quoque fítum est.
 [*Od.* 13. 40.]

31. . . . affátim édi, bibí, lusí.
 [*Od.* 15. 373.]

32. Quom *rém* eám audívi | paucís gavísi.
 [*Od.* 16. 92.]

33. . . . vecórde et málefícá vacérra.
 [*Od.* 17. 248.]

34. Vestís pullá purpúrea | ámpla . . .
 [*Od.* 19. 225.]

35. . . . dusmóso in lóco.
 [*Od.* 19. 439.]

l. 23. *Latonas*, genitive. l. 25. *Monetas* = Μνημοσύνης. l. 30. *fitum est* = fit; so fitur, potestur. l. 32. *gavisi* = gavisus sum. l. 33. *vacerra*, 'log,' 'block.' Cod. *recordia*. l. 35. *dusmoso* = dumoso.

36. Cum sócios nóstros Cíclops | ímpiús mandísset.
[*Od.* 20. 19.]

37. Inqué manúm surémit | hástam . . .
[*Od.* 21. 433.]

38. . . . at céleris
hastá voláns perrúmpit | péctóra férro.
[*Od.* 22. 91.]

39. Carnís vinúmque quód | libábant, ánclabátur.
[*Od.* 23. 304.]

40. Dequé manibús dextrábus | . . .
[*Od.* 24. 534.]

l. 37. *suremit*. Paul. in Fest. 299. suremit = sumpsit. l. 39. *anclabatur* (anculus, ancilla) = ministrabatur.

TRAGOEDIAE.

ACHILLES.

The words in this fragment may be supposed to be uttered by Achilles, after the offer of reparation described in Hom. *Il.* 9.

Sí malos imitábo, tum tu prétium pro noxá dabis.
[Nonius, *s. v.* pretium : imitat.]

AEGISTHUS.

The play opens with the preparations of the Greek host for their return from Troy (I). On the smooth seas of their homeward voyage, they watch the dolphins playing round the ships (II); and a chorus of thanksgiving is raised to the gods (III).

Agamemnon is seen taking his seat at the banquet (IV); and then being stabbed and falling to the ground (V). Electra speaks bitterly to her mother over her father's corpse VI; and Aegisthus orders her (or, perhaps, Cassandra) to be dragged away from the altar at which she had taken refuge (VII).

I.

nam ut Pérgama
accénsa et praeda pér participes aéquiter
partíta est.

[Nonius, s. v. aequiter.]

II.

Tum autém lascivum Nérei simúm pecus
ludéns ad cantum clássem lustratúr. . . .

[Nonius, s. v. lustrare : pecus.]

III.

Solémnitusque deó litat laudém lubens.

[Nonius, s. v. solemnitus.]

IV.

in sedes cónlocat se régias :
Clutëméstra iuxtim, tértias natae óccupant.

[Nonius, s. v. iuxtim.]

V.

Ipsús se in terram saúcius fligít cadens.

[Nonius, s. v. fligi.]

VI.

Iamne óculos specie lactavisti optábili?

[Nonius, s. v. lactare : species.]

VII.

Quin quód parere míhi vos maiestás mea
procát toleratis témploque hanc dedúcitis?

[Nonius, s. v. procare = poscere.]

AIAX MASTIGOPHORUS.

The lament of Teucer over man's ingratitude.

Praestátur laus virtúti, sed multo ócius
vérnó gelu tabéscit.[1]

[Nonius, s. v. gelu, neutr.)

ANDROMEDA.

A flood is sent by Neptune upon the land of Cepheus because of Cassiopea's reckless boast about her daughter's beauty, to the disparagement of the Nereids.

Cónfluges ubí conventu cámpum totum inúmigant.

[Nonius, s. v. confluges.]

EQUUS TROIANUS.

This play probably follows the same lines as the *Sinon* of Sophocles. The scene may be the appearance of Cassandra, firebrand and axe in hand, to destroy the Wooden Horse, while she prays Apollo that her prophetic words may find credence.

Dá mihi hasce opes
quás peto, quás precor :
pórrige ! opitula !

[Nonius, s. v. opitula.]

INO.

See inf. under Laevius, page 183.

EX INCERTIS FABULIS.

I.

Florem anculabant Líberi ex carchésiis.

[Pauli Fest. s. v. anclare = haurire. See note on l. 39, p. 10, inf.]

---

[1] Cp. Soph. *Ai.* 1266 Φεῦ· τοῦ θανόντος ὡς ταχεῖά τις βροτοῖς | χάρις διαρρεῖ, καὶ προδοῦσ' ἁλίσκεται.

II.

The next fragment may possibly be referred to the *Aegisthus*, sup.; in which case 'the toothless infant whom the mother reared with the support of her milk' will be Orestes.

Quem ego néfrendem alui lácteam immulgéns[1] opem.

[PAULI FEST. *s. v.* nefrendes.

---

[1] Cp. Aesch. *Choeph.* 897 πρὸς ᾧ σὺ πολλὰ δὴ βρίζων ἅμα | οὔλοισιν ἐξήμελξας εὐτραφὲς γάλα.

CN. NAEVIUS.

(Circ. 264-194 A.C.).

TRAGOEDIAE.

AESIONA.

AESIONA (better known to us in the Greek form, Hesione), the daughter of Laomedon, was rescued from a sea-monster by Hercules and Telamon, who were to claim the maiden on their return from Colchis.

But Laomedon, with his usual bad faith, broke his promise, and this fragment may contain the threat of Hercules or Telamon, that the father shall be chastened not with mere words (*lingua*), but with the sword-blade (*lingula*).

Né mihi gerere mórem videar língua verum língula.
[AUL. GELL. 10. 25.]

ANDROMACHA.

THE advice of a mother to her son.

Quod tú, mi gnate, quaéso ut in pectús tuum
demíttas, tanquam in físcinam vindémitor.
[SERV. *in Verg. Georg.* 1. 266.]

DANAE.

ACRISIUS immures his daughter Danaë in a brazen tower, but Iupiter finds means to enter the stronghold. He may be supposed to be speaking confidentially to Mercury, before the maiden is imprisoned (I'), extolling her beauty, and acknowledging the mastery of Love (II). Acrisius accuses Danaë, and all other women, of incontinence (III, IV); and justifies her punishment (V). Danaë is banished from her home by her angry father (VI; and all that 'shower of gold' has profited her nothing (VII). In her distress she prays Iupiter to give her a sign from heaven (VIII : and her prayer is granted (IX).

I.

Contémpla placido fórmam et faciem vírginis.

[Nonius, s. v. contempla.]

II.

Omnés formidant hómines eius valéntiam.

[Nonius, s. v. valentia.]

III.

Desúbito famam tóllunt si quam sólam videre in via.

[Nonius, s. v. desubito.]

IV.

Eam cómpotem scis núnc esse inventám probri.

[Nonius, s. v. compotem, in mala parte.]

V.

Quin ut quisque est méritus praesens prétium pro factis
    ferat.

[Nonius, s. v. pretium.]

VI.

. . . indigne éxigor patria innocens.

[Nonius, s. v. exigor.]

VII.

Mále parta male dilábuntur.

[Cic. Phil. 2. 27.]

VIII.

Mánubias[1] suppétiat prone . . .

[Nonius, s. v. manubiae.]

[1] *manubiae*, in the technical language of the augurs, meant 'flashes of lightning.' Serv. *in Verg. Aen.* 2. 259.

IX.

Suo sónitu claro fúlgorivit Iúppiter.
[NONIUS, *s. v.* fulgorivit.]

HECTOR PROFICISCENS.

THE main subject of this play was the setting out of Hector to battle. Proud of his father's praise (I , he designs to burn the Greek fleet, and leave not one man alive (II). See Hom. *Il.* 8. 132, 173; 12. 73.

I.

Laétus sum laudári me abs te, páter, a laudató viro.
[CIC. *Tusc. Disp.* 4. 31; 5. 12; *Ad Fam.* 15. 6.]

II.

Túnc ipsos adóriant, ne qui hinc Spártam referat núntium.
[PRISCIAN, 8. p. 801 P. *s. v.* adorio.]

IPHIGENIA.

THIS fragment is apparently taken from an Iphigenia in Tauris. The prayer, 'that the North Wind may spread his wings and waft me home,' may be uttered by Orestes or by his sister, or by one of her home-sick maidens, weary of their life in Scythia.

Pásso velo vicinum, Aquilo, méd in portum fór foras.
[NONIUS, *s. v.* passum = extensum.]

LYCURGUS.

WE are told by Sophocles (*Antig.* 955 foll.) how Lycurgus, son of Dryas, the haughty king of the Edoni, sought to stop the revels of the Bacchanals; and how Dionysus punished him for his insolence. The play of Naevius follows the general outline of the *Bacchae* of Euripides; and the fate of Lycurgus corresponds with that of Pentheus, as there described. The king's watchmen report the appearance of the Wine-god's Maenads, trampling down the crops, and chanting wild songs (I-III). He orders his guards to draw them into the deep forest; to trap them there like birds in a snare, and to put them to death (IV-VI). But they suspect the king's intention: 'he means to hunt them down, and to conduct the revellers from his groves, with savage vengeance as their guerdon' (VII). But the king's behest shall not stop them! (VIII). Then the guards bring the Wine-god before the king, who questions them as to the capture (IX). He threatens his prisoner; but is warned not to try conclusions with him (X, XI). Lycurgus and Liber proceed to altercation (XII, XIII); meanwhile the guards return and report in amaze the sportive fearlessness of the Bacchae (XIV XVI). Then Liber calls down fire from heaven, and all the king's palace bursts into flame, brilliant as a flower (XVII, XVIII); while a loud voice is heard, summoning Lycurgus forth (XIX).

I.

Alté iubatos ángues inlaesáe ferunt.

[Nonius, s. v. angues.]

II.

Líberi sunt; quáque incedunt ómnes arvas ópterunt.

[Nonius, s. v. arvas, *femin.*]

III.

suavisonúm melos.

[Nonius, s. v. melos.]

IV.

Vos quí regalis córporis custódias
agitátis, ite actútum in frundiferós locos,
ingénio arbusta ubi náta sunt, non óbsita.

[Nonius, s. v. ingenio = sua sponte.]

V.

dúcite
eó cum argutis línguis mutas quádrupedes.

[Nonius, s. v. mutus.]

VI.

Sublíme in altos sáltus inlicite ínvios
ubi bípedes volucres líno linquant lúmina.

[Nonius, s. v. inlicere.]

C

VII.

Ut ín venatu vítulantes éx suis
lucís nos mittat poénis decoratás feris.
[NONIUS, *s. v.* vitulantes = gaudentes.]

VIII.

pérgite
thyrsígerae Bacchae Bácchico cum schémate.
[NONIUS, *s. v.* schema.]

IX.

Dic quó pacto eum potíti, pugnan án dolis?
[NONIUS, *s. v.* potior *cum accus.*]

X.

Ne ílle mei feri íngeni [iram] atque ánimi acrem acrimóniam.
[NONIUS, *s. v.* acrimonia.]

XI.

Cáve sis tuam conténdas iram cóntra cum ira Líberi.
[NONIUS, *s. v.* contendere = comparare.]

XII.

'Oderunt di hominés iniuros.' 'Egone an ille iniúrie fácimus?'
[NONIUS, *s. v.* iniurie = iniuriose.]

XIII.

Síc quasi amnis céleris rapit, sed támen inflexu fléctitur.
[NONIUS, *s. v.* amnis, *femin.*]

XIV.

Iam íbi nos duplicat ádvenientis máximus timós pavos.
[NONIUS, *s. v.* timos = timor.]

XV.

Námque ludere út lactantes ínter sese vídimus
própter amnem, aquám creterris súmere ex fonte . . .
[Nonius, s. v. creterra.]

XVI.

síne terrore pécua ut ad mortém meant.
[Nonius, s. v. pecua.]

XVII.

. . . ut vídeam Volcani ópera haec flammis fieri flora.
[See Aul. Gell. 3. 9. 3.]

XVIII.

Longé lateque tránstros nostros férvere.
[Nonius. s. v. fervĕre.]

XIX.

Proinde húc Dryante régem prognatúm patre
Lycúrgum cette!
[Nonius, s. v. cette = cedite, date.]

PRAETEXTAE.

ALIMONIUM REMI ET ROMULI, SIVE ROMULUS, SIVE LUPUS.

The title of the play is uncertain and the scanty remains leave the subject hopelessly obscure. Perhaps the Veientine king Viba visits Amulius, but is coldly received. He is questioned, somewhat contemptuously, as to the troubles in the state of Veii (I, II).

I.

Réx Veiens regém salutat Víba Albanum Amúlium cómiter seném sapientem. 'Cóntra redhostis?' 'Mín salust?'

[FESTUS, *s. v.* redhostire = referre gratiam.]

II.

'Cedo quí rem vestram públicam tantam ámisistis tám cito?'

'provéniebant orátores noveí, stulti adulescéntuli.'

[CIC. *Cat. Mai.* 7. 20.]

CLASTIDIUM.

THIS play recounts the victory of Marcellus over the Gallic chieftain, Virdumarus, whom he attacked while besieging the Roman dependency, Clastidium, and stripped him of the 'spolia opima.'

Vita ínsepulta laétus ín patriám redux.

[VARRO, *L. L.* 9. 78.]

The *Clastidium* may have been acted on the occasion of Marcellus' triumph, or at the funeral games after his death; or, perhaps when Claud. Marcellus dedicated the temple to Virtus, which his father had vowed seventeen years before.

NAEVII ET METELLORUM ALTERCATIO.

Naevius maintained that the consulships of the Metelli had fallen to them by *luck*, and not by merit; with a possible further meaning of 'to our misfortune.'

'Antiquum Naevii est :

    Fató Metélli Rómae cónsulés fiunt.

Cui tunc, Metellus consul iratus versu responderat senario hypercatalecto, qui et Saturnius dicitur :

    Dabúnt malúm Metélli Naóvio poétae.'
[PSEUDASCON. in Cic. Verr. Act. 1. 10.

There is a particular force in the word *malum*, which has a special reference to a flogging, such as might be administered to slaves. Cp. PLAUT. *Rudens*, 4. 4. 81 ; TERENT. *Adelph.* 4. 45 ; LIVY, 4. 49, 50.

PALLIATAE.

ARIOLUS.

ACCORDING to Aul. Gellius (3. 3.), the 'Ariolus' and 'Leo' were the titles of two plays written by Naevius while in the prison, to which he had been brought by his *superbia Campana*. He is said by means of these plays to have made the *amende honorable* to the powerful personages whom he had offended ; and so 'a tribunis plebis exemptus est.' But if the first fragment has any meaning to us, it would seem that the 'hungry lion, in whose jaws you would put the curb—at your peril,' was none other than Naevius himself, in anything but a submissive mood. The second fragment contains a joke at the favourite viands of some of the Italian towns—a stew of the inside of a sow after farrowing, for the Lanuvini : and 'Praenestinae nuces' (Cato, *R. R.* 8), for the guests from Praeneste.

I.

Deprándi item leóni si obdas óreas.
[FESTUS, 182 M, oreae, freni quod ori inferuntur.]

II.

'Quis heri ápud te?' 'Praenestíni et Lanuvíni hóspites.'
'suópte utrosque décuit acceptós cibo;
altrís inanem vúlvulam madidám dari,
altrís nuces in próclivi profúndier.'

COLAX.

In the prologue to the *Eunuchus*, Terence alludes to the *Colax* of Naevius and of Plautus, as introducing the characters of the parasite and the swashbuckler. But Menander was the original inventor of these characters; and it is from Menander, and not from his own Latin predecessors, that Terence has borrowed them, as he warmly insists.

We have here the parasite and the swashbuckler on the stage together. The soldier in his conceit claims to be Hercules, and demands his usual tithe: the parasite jokingly retorts that he has practically given it already, as he has appropriated to his own use the dainties provided for someone else's table; and this may be looked upon as the public feast which was regularly offered to Hercules as his tithe.

Qui décumas partis? quántum mi aliení fuit
pollúxi tibi iam públicando epulo Hérculis
decumás.

[Priscian, *s. v.* pollucere.]

TARENTILLA.

In the play of the 'Girl of Tarentum' we have a prologue, the single remnant of which is thus interpreted by Mommsen (*H. R.*, B. 3, cap. 14): 'the position of the poet under the sceptre of the Lagidae and Seleucidae is enviable as compared with his position in free Rome' (I). The plot describes the adventures of two young men who are paying a visit to Tarentum, where they are feasting (II), and flirting, with at least one very facile damsel (III). Suddenly their fathers appear on the scene (IV). The young men pay them the best welcome they can (V); but they meet with a rude rebuff (VI), and a stern lecture; after which they are straightway sent home (VII).

I.

Quae ego ín theatro meís probavi plaúsibus
ea nón audere quémquam regem rúmpere!
quantó libertatem hánc hic superat sérvitus.

[CHARIS. 2. p. 192 P, *s. v.* quanto.]

II.

Úterubi cenatúri estis? hícine an in triclínio?

[CHARIS. 2. p. 198 P, *s. v.* utrubi.]

III.

                        quasi pila
in choro ludéns datatim dát se et communém facit.
álii adnutat, álii adnictat, álium amat, alium tenet.
álibi manus est óccupata, álii percellit pedem,
ánulum dat álii spectandum, a labris alium ínvocat,
cum álio cantat, át tamen alii suó dat digito lítteras.

[ISIDOR. *Orig.* 1. 25, Ennio locum adscribens.]

IV.

. . . ubi isti dúo adulescentés habent,
qui hic ánteparta pátria peregre pródigunt?

[CHARIS. 2. p. 189 P, *s. v.* peregre.]

V.

Sálvi et fortunáti sitis dúo duum nostrúm patres!

[CHARIS. 1. p. 102 P, *s. v.* duum.]

VI.

Ei ef! etiam aúdent me coram ápparere . . . ?

[CHARIS. 2. p. 213 P, *s. v.* ei, ei.]

VII.

Prímum ad virtutem út redeatis, ábeatis ab ignávia,
dómo patres patriam út colatis pótius quam peregrí
    probra.
[CHARIS. ut sup. IV.]

TUNICULARIA.

It is not easy to understand the picture here given, but it would seem that Theodotus, who is engaged on some trumpery decoration for the altars at the Compitalia—a sketch of the Lares dancing, roughly washed in with a 'bull's-tail' for a brush—is so profoundly impressed with the importance of his work that he shuts himself up in his studio, and keeps out the prying public by a screen of mats. The reading 'oppeilans ... aras' = 'blocking up the altars,' is a conject. of Bücheler. The MSS. give 'compellas,' for which Ribbeck substitutes 'compiles' = 'you may pilfer from.'

            Theodotum
Compíles *nuper* qui áris Compitálibus
sedéns in cella círcumtectus tégetibus
Larés ludentes péni pinxit búbulo.
            [FESTUS, p. 230 M, penem = caudam.]

EX INCERTIS FABULIS.

I.

SEE Aul. Gell. 7. 8. 5: 'Scipionem istum, verone an falso incertum, fama tamen, cum esset adulescens, haud sincera fuisse, et propemodum constitisse hosce versus, a Cn. Naevio poeta in eum scriptos esse.'

Etiám qui res magnás manu saepe géssit glorióse,
  cuius fácta viva núnc vigent, qui apud géntes solus
        praéstat,
eùm suus patér cum pállio úno ab amíca abdúxit.
            [AUL. GELL. *l. c.*]

II.

See Fronto (*Epist.* 2. 10. p. 33): 'Haec enim olim incommoda [sc. subsentatorum doli] regibus solis fieri solebant; at enim nunc adfatim sunt qui et

regum filiis

linguis faveant átque adnutent, *haut animis* subsérviant.'

III.

Líbera linguá loquemur lúdis Liberálibus.

[Festus, *s. v.* Liberalia = Liberi festa.

IV.

Perhaps this fragment gives a description of the actual prison into which Naevius was thrown; but it is more likely the picture of an *ergastulum*.

Tantum íbi molae crepitúm faciebant, tíntinnabant cómpedes.

[Paulus, *s. v.* tintinnire, -are.]

BELLUM PUNICUM.

Book I.

(The invocation.)

Novém Iovís concórdes fíliaé soróres,
Musás[1] quos mémorant Grái quásque nós Casmónas.

[1] This line has also been referred to Ennius, in the hexametrical form, 'Musas quas Grai memorant, nos Casmenarum. . . .'

(*Anchises learns from the auspices the impending fate of Troy.*)

Postquám avés aspéxit ín templó Anchísa
sacra ín mensá Penátium órdiné ponúntur.
tum víctimam ímmolábat aúreám púlchram.

[Prob. *Ad Verg. Ecl.* 6. 31.]

(*Aeneas and Anchises leave Troy with their wives,*)

ámborúm uxóres
noctú Troiád exíbant cápitibús opértis,
flentés ambaé abeúntes lácrimís cum múltis.

[Servius Dan. *Ad Verg. Aen.* 3. 10.]

. . . . . .

eorúm sectám sequúntur múlti mórtáles.

[Id. *Ad Verg. Aen.* 2. 797.]

(*carrying treasures from the city.* Cp. Aen. 2. 763 *foll.*)

Ferúnt pulchrás cretérras[1] aúreás lepístas[2] ;

[Caes. Bass., &c.]

pulchráque ex aúro *téxta* véstemqué citrósam[3].

[Macrob. *Sat.* 3. 19. 5.]

(*Before sailing Anchises addresses the God of the Sea.*)

Senéx fretús pietátei tum ádlocútus súmmi
deúm regís frátrem Neptúnum régnatórem.
marúm[4].

[Prisc. 770, *s.v.* marum.]

(*Venus appeals to Iupiter on behalf of the storm-tost Trojans.*)

Patrém suúm suprémum óptumúm adpéllat:
summé deúm regnátor, quíanam mé genuísti?

[Varro, *L. L.* 7. 51 ; Fest. 237.]

---

[1] *creterras* = crateras.
[2] *lepistas* = (λεπαστάς) 'goblets.'
[3] *citrosam*, acc. to Macrob. *l. c.* = the Homeric θυώδεα εἵματα.
[4] *marum* = marium, Prisc. 770.

(*Visit to the Sibyl, and (possibly) description of the Cumaean Temple.*)
Inerant signa expressa, quomodo Titanes
bicorpores Gigantes magnique Atlantes,
Runcus atque Porporeus filii Terras¹ . . .
[Prisc. 679, s. v. Terras.]

Book II.

(*Aeneas is questioned by Dido, or more likely) by Latinus, about his departure from Troy.*)
Blande et docte percontat Aenea quo pacto
Troiam urbem liquisset.
[Nonius, s. v. perconcta.]

(*Amulius discovers the parentage of the rescued twins.*)
Manusque susum ad caelum sustulit suas rex
Amulius divisque gratulabatur.
[Nonius, s. v. gratulari = gratias agere.]

(*Appearance of gods, perhaps to protect the Capitol.*)
⌣—⌣ prima incedit Cereris puer² Proserpina.
[Prisc. 697, s. v. puer.]

. . . .
deinde pollens sagittis inclutus arquitenens,
sanctus Delphis prognatus Pythius Apollo.
[Macrob. Sat. 6. 5. 8; cp. Verg. Aen. 3. 75.]

Book III.

(*Sacred ceremonies of the Fetials in proclaiming war.*)
Scopas atque verbenas³ sagmina sumpserunt.
[Paul. 320, s. v. sagmina.]

¹ *Terras*, gen.   ² *puer*, fem.
³ *verbenas*, prob. genitive with *sagmina*, or accus. pl. in appos. with *scopas* = 'twigs.'

    . . . . . .
Simul átrociá proícerent éxta ministratóres.

[NONIUS, s. v. atrox.]

(*Exploits of the Consul Marcus (al. Manius) Valerius in Sicily,*
B.C. 263.)

Marcús Valérius cónsul
partém exércití[1] in éxpedítiónem
ducít.

[CHARIS. 103, s. v. exerciti.]

Book IV.

(*Formation of Roman fleet and naval drill.*)

Ratem aérátám conférre quí queánt períte
per líquidum máre sedéntes átque soédántes[2].

[VARRO, L. L. 7. 23.]

(*Exploits of Atilius Regulus in Malta,* B.C. 257.)

tránsit Mélitam
exércitús Románus, ínsulám intégram
urít popúlatur vástat, rém hostiúm concínnat[3].

[NONIUS, s. v. concinnare.]

(*The next passages may refer to the disastrous defeat of Regulus near Clypea* (B.C. 255), *and the discussions in the Senate upon the relief of the garrison or the ransom of the prisoners. Others find in them an allusion to Atilius Calatinus, entrapped with his army into an ambush near Camarina, from which he was delivered by the gallantry of the tribune Calpurnius Flamma,* B.C. 258.)

Seséque veí[4] períre mávolúnt ibídem

[1] *exerciti*, gen. as from the O declension.
[2] *soedantes* = sudantes (the passage is almost hopelessly corrupt).
[3] *concinnat*, a sort of grim irony = 'arranges the foemen's affairs'; or, perhaps, 'secures the foemen's property.'
[4] *vei* = vi, Bährens, for *ei* or *i*.

quam cúm stupró[1] redíre ád suós populáres.

. . . . .

Sin íllos déserant fortíssimós virórum,
magnúm stuprúm pópulo fíerí per géntis.

[Fest. 317, s. v. stuprum.]

Book V.

(*Vahlen suggests that the following words may refer to the contemptuous action of Publius Claudius who, to defy the senate, named his own clerk Claudius Glicia as dictator. Glicia, though his appointment was immediately cancelled, appeared at the Great Games in his praetexta.*)

dictatór ubi cúrrum insédit
pervéhitur úsque ad óppidum[2].

[Varro, L. L. 5. 153.]

Book VI.

(*Commemorates the seventeenth year of the War, sc. 248 B.C. The Romans are supposed to be wearied by its length.*)

Iam séptimúm decimum ánnum ilicó[3] sedéntes

[Nonius, s.v. ilico.]

(*Aurelius Cotta and P. Servilius Geminus, the consuls, carry on war in Sicily.*)

Censét eó ventúrum óbviám Poénum.

[Nonius, s. v. censere.]

Book VII.

(*Hanno's fleet having been (B.C. 241) crushed near Lilybaeum, Hamilcar makes terms with C. Lutatius Catulus.*)

[1] *stupro* = 'dishonour,' Fest. 317.
[2] *oppidum*. 'In circo unde mittuntur equi, nunc dicuntur carceres, Naevius *oppidum* appellat.' Varro, L. L. 5. 153.
[3] *ilico* 'in eo loco,' Non. 325. 5.

Id quóque pacíscunt, moénia[1] ut sínt quae concilient
Lutátium: captívos plúrimós ídem
Siciliensés paciscit óbsidés ut réddant.

[Nonius, s. v. paciscunt.]

[1] *moenia*, perhaps = munia, 'duties,' i.e. 'terms' or 'conditions.' If *moenia* be taken in its ordinary sense, we must with Bährens suppose a lacuna.

Q. ENNIUS.
(239-169 A.C.)

ANNALES.

Book I.

Invocation of the Greek Muses.

Musae quae pedibus magnum pulsatis Olympum.
      [Varro, L. L. 7. 20.]

(The poem begins with the fall of Troy,)

Cum veter occubuit Priamus sub Marte Pelasgo.
      [Prisc. 607, s. v. veter.]

(and the landing of Aeneas in Italy:)

Est locus Hesperiam quam mortales perhibebant:
      [Macrob. Sat. 6. 1. 11.]
quam prisci casci populi tenuere Latini.
      [Varro, L. L. 7. 28.]

(The prophetic dream of Ilia the Vestal, daughter of Aeneas.)

Excita cum tremulis anus attulit artubus lumen,
talia commemorat lacrimans, exterrita somno:
'Euridica prognata, pater quam noster amavit,
vires vitaque corpus meum nunc deserit omne.
nam me visus homo pulcher per amoena salicta
et ripas raptare locosque novos; ita sola

postilla, germana soror, errare videbar
tardaque vestigare et quaerere te, neque posse
corde capessere, semita nulla pedem stabilibat.
Exin compellare pater me voce videtur
his verbis : 'o gnata, tibi sunt ante ferendae
aerumnae, post ex fluvio fortuna resistet[1].'
haec ecfatus pater, germana, repente recessit
nec sese dedit in conspectum corde cupitus,
quamquam multa manus ad caeli caerula templa
tendebam lacrimans et blanda voce vocabam.
vix aegro tum corde meo me somnus reliquit.
[Cic. De Div. 1. 20. 40.]

Ilia, condemned to be thrown with her twin boys into the Tiber, invokes the aid of Venus and the River-god.)

Te venerata precor Venus tu genetrix patris nostri ;
ut me de caelo visas rogitata parumper.
[Nonius, s. v. parumper.]

tuque pater Tiberine tuo cum flumine sancto !
[Macrob. Sat. 6. 1. 12.]

(*The Tiber stays his current, and the babes are left on dry land.*)

Postquam consistit fluvius qui est omnibus princeps
qui sunt Italia.
[Fronto, Ep. ad M. Anton. : Cic. Orat. 48.]

(*Romulus and Remus, before founding their city, observe the auspices.*)

Cum cura magna curantes, tum cupientes
regni, dant operam simul auspicio augurioque.

. . . . . .

hinc Remus auspicio se devovet, atque secundam
solus avem servat ; at Romulus pulcher in alto

---

[1] *resistet* = restituetur. Cp. Cic. Pro Mur. 39. 84.

quaerit Aventino, servat genus altivolantum:
omnibus cura viris uter esset induperator;
certabant urbem Romam Remoramne vocarent.
exspectant veluti consul cum mittere signum
volt, omnes avidi spectant ad carceris oras,
quam mox emittat pictis e faucibus currus:
sic exspectabat populus atque ora tenebat,
rebus, utri magni victoria sit data regni.
interea sol albus[1] recessit in infera noctis,
exin candida se radiis dedit icta foras lux,
et simul ex alto longe pulcherrima praepes
laeva volavit avis; simul aureus exoritur sol.
cedunt de caelo ter quatuor corpora sancta
avium, praepetibus sese pulchrisque locis dant.
conspicit inde sibi data Romulus esse priora,
auspicio regni stabilita scamna solumque.

[CIC. De Div. 1. 48.]

(*Remus laughs at his brother's caution in building a wall.*)

Iuppiter ut muro fretus magis quamde manus vi!

[FESTUS, 261, s. v. quamde.]

(*He leaps over it, and is slain by Romulus.*)

Non pol homo quisquam faciet impune animatus[2]
hoc quod tu: nam mi calido dabis sanguine poenas!

[MACROB. Sat. 6. 1. 15.]

(*The Rape of the Sabines.*)

Virgnes[3] nam sibi quisque domi Romanus habet sas[4].

[FEST. 325, PAULUS 324, s. v. sas.

[1] *sol albus* is generally taken of the 'moon': but cp. albicascit Phoebus (inf. Matii *Mimiambi*, page 1, 181).

[2] *animatus* = anima praeditus.

[3] *virgnes*: so Müller for *virgines*, comparing the form *Proserpna* (Naev. *Bell. Pun.* lib. 2). [4] *sas* = eas.

(Reconciliation of Romulus and Titus Tatius, perhaps by the pleading of Hersilia (Liv. I. 11.) who says:)

Aeternam scritote diem concorditer ambo.
[CHARIS. 177.]

. . . . . .

Accipe daque fidem foedusque feri bene firmum.
[MACROB. Sat. 6. 1. 13.]

(Titus Tatius was slain by some Laurentines, one of whom may have complained of his arrogance.)

O Tite tute Tati tibi tanta, tyranne, tulisti!
[PRISC. 947, s. v. tutĕ.]

(The Assumption of Romulus.)

Romulus in caelo cum dis genitalibus aevum
degit.
[SERV. in Verg. Aen. 6. 764.]

Book II.

(The Lament for Romulus.)

Pectora dia tenet desiderium: simul inter
sese sic memorant, 'o Romule, Romule die,
qualem te patriae custodem di genuerunt!
o pater, o genitor, o sanguen dis oriundum,
tu produxisti nos intra luminis oras.'
[CIC. De Rep. 1. 41.]

(Accession of Numa; his meetings with the nymph.)

Olli respondit suavis sonus Egeriai.
[VARRO, L. L. 7. 42.]

(War between Rome and Alba: the victory to be decided by the combat of Horatii and Curiatii.)

quianam legiones caedimus ferro?
[SERV. in Verg. Aen. 10. 6.]

(*The victorious Horatius excuses himself to his sister for the slaughter of her betrothed.*)

Adnuit sese mecum decernere ferro.
[Prisc. 882, s. r. adnūo.]

(*Treachery of Mettus Fuffetius, the Alban general, and his punishment by Tullus.*)

tractatus per aequora campi.
[Macrob. De Verb. 4. 651.]

(*His body is devoured by birds of prey.*)

Vulturus in spinis miserum mandebat homonem.
heu, quam crudeli condebat membra sepulcro!
[Prisc. 683, s. r. vulturus.]

(*Accession of Ancus Marcius,*)

Isque dies postquam Ancus Marcius regna recepit
[Serv. ad Verg. Aen. 3. 333.]

(*who founds the Port of Ostia.*)

. . . ut Tiberis flumen vomit in mare salsum,
Ostia munita est. idem loca navibus celsis
munda¹ facit, nautisque mari quaesentibus vitam
[Macrob. Sat. 6. 4. 3 : Fest. 258.]

Book III.

(*Descent of the eagle on Tarquin.* [Liv. 1. 34.])

Olim de caelo laevum dedit inclutus signum.
[Nonius, s. v. laevum.]

. . . .

et densis aquila pennis obnixa volabat
vento.
[Probus in Verg. Ecl. 6. 31.]

¹ *munda*, i. e. instructa.

(After the death of Ancus the people made Tarquin king.)
Postquam lumina sis[1] oculis bonus Ancus reliquit,
Tarquinio dedit imperium simul et sola regni.

[FESTUS, 301, s. v. sis.]

(Wars of Tarquin, and critical position of Etruria, perhaps before the battle of Eretum [Dion. 3. 59; 4. 3]*.)*
Hac noctu filo pendebit Etruria tota.

[MACROB. Sat. 1. 4. 18.]

(The remaining fragments may refer to the outrage on Lucretia, her appeal to heaven, and her suicide.)
Caelum suspexit stellis fulgentibus aptum.

[MACROB. Sat. 6. 1. 9.]

. . . . . .

Vosque Lares tectum nomen qui funditus curant.

[CHARIS. 238, 9.]

. . . . . .

Inde sibi memorat unum superesse laborem.

[AUL. GELL. 1. 22. 16.]

Book IV.

(Storming of Anxur [Livy 4. 59]*.)*
. . . Volsculus perdidit Anxur.

[PAULUS. 22.]

. . . .

Romani scalis summa nituntur opum vi.

[MACROB. Sat. 6. 1. 17; VERG. Aen. 12. 552.]

(Attack on the Capitol by the Gauls [*others refer this to* Book vii]*.)*
Qua Galli furtim noctu summa arcis adorti
moenia, concubia, vigilesque repente cruentant.

[MACROB Sat. 1. 4. 17.]

---

[1] *sis* = suis.

Book V.

Period of the Samnite Wars.

(Civitas sine suffragio [Livy 8. 14] *given to the Campani.*)

Cives Romani tunc facti sunt Campani.

[CENSORIN. De Metr. 2725.]

(*Minucia the Vestal* [Livy 8. 15] *buried alive for unchastity.*)

Cum nihil horridius unquam lex ulla iuberet.

[OROS. 3. 9. 5.]

(*Fierce contests between Romans and Samnites* [Livy 7. 33].)

Bellum aequis manibus nox intempesta diremit.

[ACRO ad Hor. Ep. 2. 2. 97]

Book VI.

(*War with Pyrrhus: importance of subject.*)

Quis potis ingentes oras evolvere belli?

[SERV. in Verg. Aen. 9. 528.]

(*The Tarentines defy Rome, and find a champion in Pyrrhus,*)

Navus repertus homo Graio patre Graius domo rex,
nomine Burrus, uti memorant de stirpe supremo.

[FEST. 169: NONIUS, s. v. stirpe, masc.]

(*who undertakes the war, encouraged by an ambiguous oracle.*)

Aio te Aeacida Romanos vincere posse.

[CIC. De Div. 2. 56. 116.]

(*The Romans enlist the lowest of their citizens.*)

Proletarius publicitus scutisque feroque
ornatur ferro, muros urbemque forumque
excubiis curant.

[AUL. GELL. 16. 10.]

(After the battle of Heraclea, Pyrrhus generously builds a pyre to burn the bodies of the fallen foe, as well as those of his own soldiers.)

Incedunt arbusta per alta, securibus caedunt:
percellunt magnas quercus, exciditur ilex,
fraxinus frangitur atque abies consternitur alta,
pinus proceras pervortunt: omne sonabat
arbustum fremitu silvai frondosai.

[Macrob. Sat. 6. 2. 27; Hom. Il. 23. 114.]

(But, in spite of his elephants,)

tetros elephantos,

[Isidor. Or. 10. 270.]

· · · · ·

It nigrum campis agmen.

[Serv. in Verg. Aen. 4. 404.]

(he fought with doubtful success, as he acknowledged by his inscription in the Temple of Tarentine Jove.)

Qui antehac invicti fuerunt, pater optime Olympi,
Hos et ego in pugna vici, victusque sum ab isdem.

[Oros. 4. 1. 14.]

(When Fabricius proposes to ransom the prisoners, Pyrrhus sends them back to Rome, as a free gift.)

Nec mi aurum posco nec mi pretium dederitis:
nec cauponantes bellum sed belligerantes
ferro, non auro, vitam cernamus utrique.
vosne velit an me regnare era quidve ferat Fors
virtute experiamur. et hoc simul accipe dictum:
quorum virtuti belli fortuna pepercit
eorundem libertati me parcere certumst.
dono ducite doque volentibus cum magnis dis.

[Cic. De Off. 1. 12. 38.]

(Cineas is sent by Pyrrhus to Rome to negotiate a peace. The blind old Appius fiercely protests.)

Quo vobis mentes, rectae quae stare solebant

antehac, dementes sese flexere viai?

[Cic. Cat. Mai. 6. 16.]

. . . . .

Orator sine pace redit regique refert rem.

[Varro, L. L. 7. 41.]

(*To this book belongs the Devotion of the youngest Decius, in the battle at Asculum* [Cic. Tusc. Disp. 1. 37].)

. . . divi hoc audite parumper,
ut pro Romano populo prognariter armis ,
certando prudens animam de corpore mitto.

[Nonius, s. v. praegnaviter.]

(*Battle of Beneventum, 274 B.C., and victory of the famous consul, M'. Curius* [Cic. De Rep. 3. 3].)

Quem nemo ferro potuit superare nec auro.

[Cic. l. c.]

Book VII.

(*First Punic War. The subject had been already treated of by Naevius: but his rude 'Saturnians' are uncultured in comparison with the Greek metre of Ennius.*)

scripsere alii rem
versibus, quos olim Fauni vatesque canebant,
cum neque Musarum scopulos quisquam superarat,
nec dicti studiosus erat.

[Cic. Brut. 19. 76; 18. 71; Orator, § 171.

(*Ennius was the first to attain to real philosophy.*)

Nec quisquam Sophiam, sapientia quae perhibetur,
in somnis vidit prius quam sam discere coepit.

[Fest. 325, s. v. sam = eam.]

(*He introduces the Carthaginians, a barbarous folk.*)

Poenos Didone oriundos.

[Prisc. 685.]

. . . .

Poeni suos soliti dis sacrificare puellos.
[FEST. 249, etc.]

(*against whom Rome declares war*.)
Appius indixit Karthaginiensibus bellum.
[CIC. De Inv. I. 19. 27.]

(*A stranded Carthaginian galley becomes a model for the hastily built Roman fleet*.)
Mulserat huc navim compulsam fluctibus pontus.
[PRISC. 870, s. v. mulceo.]

. . . .

et melior navis quam quae stlataria portat.
[PROB. ap. Vallam in Iuv. Sat. 7. 134.]

(*The Roman legionaries are put to naval drill*.)
. . . tonsamque tenentes
parerent, observarent portisculus signum
cum dare coepisset.
[NONIUS, s. v. portisculus.]

. . . .

poste recumbite, vestraque pectora pellite tonsis.
[FEST. 356, s. v. tonsa.]

(*The temple of Janus, which was closed in B. C. 235 for the second time since its foundation, was soon opened anew, when a quarrel broke out between Rome and the Ligurians*.)
postquam Discordia tetra
Belli ferratos postes portasque refregit.
[HOR. Sat. 1. 4. 60.]

(*War with Illyria, and triumph of M. Livius B C. 219*.)
Illyrii restant sicis sibunisque fodentes.
[PAULUS, 336, s. v. sibuna. Vid. ad VIII. p. 87 inf.]

. . . .

Livius inde redit magno mactatus triumpho.
[SERV. in Verg. Aen. 9. 641, s. v. mactus.]

Book VIII.

(Second Punic War to battle of Cannae. Formidable character of Hannibal.)

     . . . at non sic dubius fuit hostis
Aeacida Burrus.
[Oros. 4. 14. 3.]

(State of Society in time of war.)

     . . . si sunt proelia promulgata,
pellitur e medio sapientia, vi geritur res,
spernitur orator bonus, horridus miles amatur:
haud doctis dictis certantes, sed maledictis
miscent inter sese inimicitiam agitantes.
non ex iure manum consertum, sed magis ferro
rem repetunt, regnumque petunt, vadunt solida vi.
[Cic. Pro Mur. 14. 30; Aul. Gell. 20. 10.]

(Q. Fabius Maximus appointed dictator B.C. 217.)

Unus homo nobis cunctando restituit rem;
noenum rumores ponebat ante salutem;
ergo postque magisque viri nunc gloria claret.
[Cic. Cat. Mai. 4. 10.]

(Cautious advice of L. Aemilius Paulus against the rashness of C. Terentius Varro, his colleague.)

     praecoca pugnast:
certare abnueo: metuo legionibus labem.
[Noxius, s. v. praecoca.]

. . . multa dies in bello conficit unus:
et multae rursus fortunae forte recumbunt;
haudquaquam quemquam semper fortuna secutast.
[Macrob. Sat. 6. 2. 16.]

(Description of the confidential friend of Servilius Geminus. Under this character, Ennius was said (teste Aelio Stilone apud Aul. Gell. 12. 4) to have portrayed himself.)

aece locutus vocat, quo cum bene saepe libenter

mensam sermonesque suos rerumque suarum
materiem partit, magnam cum lassus diei
partem fuisset de summis rebus regundis
consilio indu foro lato sanctoque senatu;
cui res audacter magnas parvasque iocumque
eloqueretur, cuncta simul malaque et bona dictu
evomeret, si qui vellet, tutoque locaret,
prudenter quod dicta loquive tacereve posset;
quo cum multa volup ac gaudia clamque palamque;
ingenium cui nulla malum sententia suadet
ut faceret facinus levis aut malus; doctus, fidelis,
suavis homo, facundus, suo contentus, beatus,
scitus, secunda loquens in tempore, commodus, verbum
paucum, multa tenens antiqua sepulta, vetustas
maiorum veterum leges divomque hominumque,
quae faciunt mores veteresque novosque tenentem.
hunc inter pugnas compellat Servilius sic:
[AUL. GELL. 12. 4. 1.]

(*Some details from the battle of Cannae, e.g. the thick dust, the blinding sun, the hamstringing of the wounded* [Liv. 22. 46 f.].)

iamque fere pulvis ad caelum vasta videtur.
[NONIUS, *s. v.* pulvis, *fem.*]

. . . . . .

amplius exaugere obstipo lumine solis.
[FEST. 193, *s. v.* obstipum.]

. . . . . .

his pernas succidit iniqua superbia Poeni.
[FEST. 305, PAUL. 304.]

(*But the Romans obstinately hold out, saying,*)

Qui vicit non est victor nisi victus fatetur.
[SERV. *in Verg. Aen.* 11. 307.]

Book IX.

(Consulship of Cornelius Cethegus and P. Semp. Tuditanus B.C. 204)

Additur orator Cornelius suaviloquenti
ore Cetegus Marcus Tuditano conlega
Marci filius . . .
. . . is dictust ollis popularibus olim,
qui tum vivebant homines atque aevom agitabant,
flos delibatus populi suadaeque medulla.

[Cic. Brut. 15. 58, etc.]

Book X.

(Macedonian War to the battle of Cynoscephalae.)

Insece, Musa, manu Romanorum induperator
quod quisque in bello gessit cum rege Philippo.

[Aul. Gell. 18. 9. 2.]

(Consulship of Sext. Aelius Paetus and T. Quintius Flamininus, B.C. 198.)

Egregie cordatus homo catus Aelius Sextus.

[Cic. De Rep. 1. 18. 30 ; De Or. 1. 45. 198.]

(The Roman army, entrapped in a defile in Chaonia, is guided into safety by an Epirot shepherd, who thus addresses Flamininus:)

Sollicitari te Tite, sic noctesque diesque!

 .   .   .   .   .   .

O Tite, si quid ego adiuero curamve levasso,
quae nunc te coquit et versat in pectore fixa,
ecquid erit praemi?

[Cic. Cat. Mai. init.]

(The general watches his troops during the fight at Cynoscephalae.)

Aspectabat virtutem legionis suai,
exspectans si mussaret, quae denique pausa
pugnandi fieret aut duri *meta* laboris.

[Philargyr. in Verg. Georg. 4. 188.]

(*The remaining fragments of the book perhaps refer to a scene between Sophonisba and Masinissa.*)

Erubuit mulier ceu lacte et purpura mixta.

[Nonius, s. v. lacte.]

. . . .

           negro
corde, comis palmis late passis 'pater' . . .

[Nonius, s. v. passum.]

Book XI.

(*The exploits of Flamininus, and the submission of the haughty Philip.*)

Quippe solent reges omnes in rebus secundis —

[Fest. 257.]

Flamin'nus [Livy 33. 32] *proclaims at the Isthmian games the liberty of the Greek cities; and dwells upon the connection of Rome with Troy:*)

Contendunt Graios, Graecos memorare solent sos.

[Fest. 286, s. v. sos.]

. . . .

Quae neque Dardaniis campis potuere perire,
nec cum capta capi, nec cum combusta cremari.

[Macrob. Sat. 6. 1. 60.]

(*The scene changes to Rome, and the violent protest of Cato against the abrogation of Lex Oppia de cultu mulierum* [Livy 34 ad init.].)

      malo cruce fatur uti des
Iuppiter!

[Nonius, s. v. crux, masc.]

. . . .

Pendent peniculamenta unum ad quodque pedule.

[Nonius, s. v. peniculamentum.]

Book XII.

Perhaps alluding to the carousal of the Histri, after they had taken the Roman camp [Livy 41. 3¹.]

Omnes mortales victores cordibus imis
laetantes, vino curatos, somnus repente
in campo passim mollissimus perculit acris.

[Prisc. 647. s. v. acer et acris.]

Book XIII.

(The fear of the impending war with Antiochus, who appeared to be [Florus 1. 24. 43] *a second Xerxes or Darius.)*

Isque Hellesponto pontem contendit in alto.

[Varro. L. L. 7. 21.]

(Difference of opinion between Antiochus and Hannibal, who had originally urged the king to war.)

Hannibal audaci cum pectore de me hortatur
ne bellum faciam? quem credidit esse meum cor
suasorem summum et studiosum robore belli.

[Aul. Gell. 6. 2. 3.]

Book XIV.

(Battle of Myonnesus, in which M. Aemilius Regillus, B.C. 190, conquers Polyxenides, the commander of the fleet of Antiochus [Liv. 37. 28, etc.].)

Verrunt extemplo placidum mare marmore flavo,
caeruleum spumat sale conferta rate pulsum.

[Aul. Gell. 2. 26. 31.]

. . . . . .

Labitur uncta carina; volat super impetus undas.

[Macrob. Sat. 6. 1. 51.]

. . . .

Cum procul aspiciunt hostes accedere ventis
navibus velivolis.

[Ib. 6. 5. 10.]

(*Exhortation of Antiochus to his soldiers.*)

Nunc est ille dies cum gloria maxima sese
nobis ostentat, si vivimus sive morimur.

[Prisc. 880, *s. v.* moriri.]

(*His dismay at being defeated.*)

Infit 'o cives, quae me fortuna ferocem
contudit indigne, bello confecit acerbo!'

[Prisc. 891, *s. v.* contudit.]

Book XV.

(*Exploits of M. Fulvius Nobilior, who defeated the Aetolians, and stormed Ambracia.*)

Malos diffindunt, fiunt tabulata falaeque.

[Nonius, *s. v.* falae.]

· · · · · ·

Occumbunt multi letum ferroque lapique
aut intra muros aut extra praecipe casu.

[Prisc. 725, *s. v.* praecipis.]

Book XVI.

(*The poet approaches more recent times;*)

Quippe vetusta virum non est satis bella moveri.

[Fest. 257.]

(*Philip has grown too old to renew the war.*)

. . . post aetate pigret sufferre laborem.

[Nonius, *s. v.* **pigret**.]

· · · · · ·

Postremo longinqua dies confecerat aetas.

[Aul. Gell. 9. 14. 5.]

(*He dies, and receives a splendid burial.*)

Reges per regnum statuasque sepulcraquo quaerunt.
aedificant nomen, summa nituntur opum vi.
[Macrob. *Sat.* 6. 1. 17.]

(*Histrian War carried on by C. Claudius Pulcher against King Epulo, and taking of Nesactium* [Livy 41. 11].)

Quos ubi rex Epulo spexit de cotibus celsis.
[Fest. 330, s. v. spexit.]

(*Fight of the tribune Caelius, or, more likely, C. Aelius*, Livy 41. 4.)

Undique conveniunt velut imber tela tribuno:
configunt parmam, tinnit hastilibus umbo,
aerato sonitu galeae. Sed nec pote quisquam
undique nitendo corpus discerpere ferro:
semper adundantes hastas frangitque quatitque.
totum sudor habet corpus multumque laborat,
nec respirandi fit copia praepete ferro:
Histri tela manu iacientes sollicitabant.
[Macrob. *Sat.* 6. 3. 2 : cp. Hom. *Il.* 16. 102 foll.]

Book XVII.

(*Perhaps a reference to the exploits of Fulvius Flaccus in Celtiberia.*)

It eques, et plausu cava concutit ungula terram.
[Macrob. *Sat.* 6. 1. 22.]

 . . . . . .

Concurrunt veluti venti, cum spiritus austri
imbricitor aquiloque suo cum flamine contra
indu mari magno fluctus extollere certant.
[Macrob. *Sat.* 6. 2. 28.]

Book XVIII.

(To this book may be referred these general and personal sayings.)

Audire est operae pretium, procedere recte
qui rem Romanam Latiumque augescere vultis.
[PORPHYR. ad Hor. Sat. 1. 2. 37.]

* * * * *

Noenu decet mussare bonos qui facta labore
nixi militiae peperere perennia multo.
[PHILARG. in Verg. Georg. 4. 188.]

(The poet recalls the fact of his own citizenship, and weary with his task is glad to seek repose.)

Nos sumus Romani qui fuimus ante Rudini.
[CIC. De Orat. 3. 42.]

Sicut fortis equus, spatio qui saepe supremo
vicit Olympia, nunc senio confectus quiescit.
[CIC. Cat. Mai. 5. 14.]

TRAGOEDIAE.

ALCUMAEO.

ALCMAEON, after murdering his mother Eriphyle, for her treachery to her husband Amphiaraus, is pursued from land to land by the Furies, till he reaches the city of Psophis in Arcadia, where he finds purification at the hands of Phegeus the king. He marries the king's daughter Arsinoë; and here he is represented as appealing to her in his terror at the avenging deities (I, II).

I.

Múltimodis sum círcumventus mórbo exilio atque ínopia :
túm pavor sapiéntiam omnem mi éxanimato expéctorat.
mater terribilém minatur vítae cruciatum ét necem.
quaé nemost tam firmo ingenio et tánta confidéntia
quín refugiat tímido sanguen átque exalbescát metu.

[Cic. De Orat. 3. 58.]

II.

Unde haéc flamma oritur?
in caédem meam, in caedem ádsunt, adsunt, me éx-
    petunt!
fer mi aúxilium, pestem ábige a me.
flammíferam hanc vim, quae me éxcruciat.
caerúlea incinctae angui íncedunt
circúmstant cum ardentíbus taedis.
in me íntendit crinítus Apollo
arcum aúratum, luna ínnixus,
Diána facem iacit á laeva.

[Cic. Acad. Pr. 2. 28.]

ALEXANDER.

Hecuba, wife of Priam, having dreamed that she had brought forth a firebrand, her husband ordered that the son she bore should be put to death. But the servants spared his life, and certain shepherds having found him when he was exposed, he was rescued, and brought up under the name of Paris I); which was afterwards changed to Alexander, because of his prowess in the games (II, III). He is received into the king's palace, and Cassandra, terrified at the sight of him, prophesies the downfall of Troy (IV). She foretells the fatal 'Iudicium Paridis' V ; the death of Hector (VI); and the stratagem of the 'Wooden Horse' (VII).

E

I.

. . . máter gravida párere se ardentém facem
visást in somnis Hécuba: quo fató pater
rex ípse Priamus sómnio mentís metu
percúlsus, curis saúcius superántibus,
sic sácrificabat hóstiis balántibus.
tum cóniecturam póstulat, pacém petens,
ut se édoceret óbsecrans Apóllinem,
quo sése vertant tántae sortes sómnium.
ibi éx oraclo vóce divina édidit
Apóllo, puerum prímus Priamo quí foret
post ílla natus, témperaret tóllere[1]:
eum ésse exitium Troíae, pestem Pérgamo,

[Cic. De Div. 1. 21. 42.]

II.

Is habét coronam vítulans victória.

[Paulus, s. v. vitulans.]

III.

Quápropter Parím pastores núnc Alexandrúm vocant.

[Varro, L. L. 7. 82.]

IV.

Hec. Séd quid oculis rábere visa es dérepente ardén-
tibus?
úbi illa tua paulo ánte sapiens vírginalis modéstia?
Cass. Máter, optumárum multo mulier mélior múlierum,
missa sum supérstitiosis áriolatiónibus.
námque Apollo fátis[2] fandis démentem invitám ciet.
vírgines aequáles vereor: pátris mei, meum[3] factúm pudet,

---

[1] *tollere,* 'to acknowledge.'
[2] *fatis,* dative.
[3] *meum,* gen. plur.

óptumi virí[1], mea mater, tui me miseret, meí piget.
óptumam progéniem Priamo péperisti extra me, hóc
    dolet!
mén obesse, illós prodesse, me óbstare, illos óbsequi!
    ádest adest fax óbvoluta sánguine atque incéndio,
    múltos annos látuit: cives, férte opem et restinguite.
        iámque mari magnó classis cita
        téxitur, exitium éxamen rapit:
        ádveniet, fera vélivolantibus
        návibus complebít manus litora.
            [Cic. De Div. 1. 31.]

V.

                        eheu! videte
iúdicabit ínclutum iudícium inter deás tris aliquis:
quó iudicio Lácedaemonia múlier, Furiarum úna, ad-
    veniet.
            [Cic. De Div. 1. 50.]

VI.

O lúx Troiae, germáne Hector!
quid te ita . . . . contuó lacerato córpore,
miser, aút qui te sic tráctavere nóbis respectántibus?
            [Macrob. Sat. 6. 2. 18.]

VII.

Nam máximo saltú superabit grávidus armátis equus,
suó qui partu . . . pérdat Pergama árdua.
            [Macrob. Sat. 6. 2. 25.]

ANDROMACHA AECHMALOTIS.

Andromache laments the loss of Hector and Astyanax I); and
mourns over her city burned to the ground (II).

[1] *viri*, gen. sing. with *patris*; or voc. plur.

I.

Vidi videre quód me passa aegérrume,
Hectórem[1] curru quádriiugo raptárier,
Hectóris natum de muro iactárier.
[Cic. *Tusc. Disp.* 1. 44.]

II.

Quíd petám praésidi aút éxsequár? quóve núnc
aúxilió éxili aút fugaé fréta sím?
árce et úrbe órba súm. quo áccidám? quo ápplicém?
cui nec arae pátriae domi stant, fráctae et disiectaé iacent,
fána flamma déflagrata, tósti alti stant párietes
déformati atque ábiete crispa.

. . . .

O páter, o patria, o Príami domus,
saeptum áltisono cardíne templum!
vidi égo te astante ope bárbarica,
tectís caelatis lácuatis,
auro, ébore instructam régifice.
haec ómnia videi inflámmari,
Priamó vi vitam evítari[2],
Iovis áram sanguine túrpari.
[Cic. *Tusc. Disp.* 3. 19.]

CRESPHONTES.

Cresphontes, king of Messenia, espoused the cause of the people against the nobles, whose leader, Polyphontes, slew him, together with his two sons, forcibly taking to wife Merope, the widow of the murdered man. Merope's own father Cypselus was among the adherents of Polyphontes. We hear the protest of the nobles against the claims of the burghers (I); the altercation between Cypselus and Merope (II); and her grief at being debarred from paying funeral honours to her sons (III).

[1] *Hectorem.* For the quantity cp. Varro, *L. L.* 10. 70.
[2] *evitari,* with play on *vitam*; 'unlifed of his life.'

Q. ENNIUS.

I.

An ínter sese sórtiunt urbem átque agros?

[Nonius, *s. v.* sortiunt.]

II.

'Iniúria abs te adfícior indigná, pater.
nam si ímprobum esse Crésphontem tu exístimas,
cur me huíus locabas núptiis? sin ést probus,
cur tálem invitam invítum cogis línquere?'
'nulla te indigna, o náta, adficio iniúria,
si próbus est, bene locávi; sin est ímprobus,
divórtio te liberabo incómmodis.'

[Auct. *Ad Herenn.* 2. 24.]

III.

Neque térram inicere néque cruenta cónvestire córpora
mihi lícuit miserae, néque lavere lácrima salsa sánguinem.

[Macrob. *Sat.* 6. 2. 1: cp. Verg. *Aen.* 9. 486.]

HECTORIS LUTRA.

This play includes the whole of the action in the Iliad from the sally of Hector to the restoration of his corpse to his father, including the death of Patroclus. Hector comes boldly forth from the walls (I), and in the battle which ensues many are wounded, among them Eurypylus, who comes back to Patroclus, seeking the aid of a physician (II). Patroclus enquires eagerly about the fortune of the day (*ib.*). Achilles suffers Patroclus to take his place in the field, and the young man commits himself to the protection of heaven (III). News comes of the death of Patroclus, and Achilles steps forth in terrible anxiety from his tent (IV). He calls on each of the Myrmidones to find him armour for the fray, but no one is willing, as he bitterly acknowledges (V). When at last he rushes forth to war, all nature is hushed in awful expectancy (VI), as he drives his fiery steeds (VII), and checks their impetuous speed (VIII). The special scene which gives its name to the play is not preserved; we only have Priam crying on the Myrmidones for pity; and urging his plea for that justice which is better than all gallantry (IX, X).

I.

Hectór vi summa armátos educít foras,
castrísque castra iam últro conferre óccupat.

[Nonius, s. v. occupare.]

II.

Euryp. O Pátricoles, ad vós adveniens aúxilium et vestrás manus
petó, prius quam appetó malam pestém datam hostilí manu.

. . . . . .

neque sánguis ullo pótis est pacto prófluens consístere.

. . . . . .

si quí sapientiá mágis vestra mórs devitarí potest.
namque Aésculapi líberorum saúcii opplent pórticus:
non pótis accedi.

Patric. Cérte Eurypylus híc quidem. hominem exércitum [1]!

Euryp. Qui álteri exitiúm parat
eum scíre oportet síbi paratum péstem ut participét parem.

Patric. Eloquére, eloquere, rés Argivum praélio ut se sústinet.

Euryp. Non pótis ecfari tántum dictis, quántum factis súppetit.

[Cic. Tusc. Disp. 2. 16: cp. Hom. Il. 11. 804 foll.]

III.

. . . át ego, omnipotens Iúppiter,
téd exposco ut hóc consilium Achívis auxilí fuat!

[Nonius, s. v. fuam = sim.]

---

[1] exercitum, sc. malis.

IV.

Quid hoc hic clamoris, quid tumulti est?   nomen qui usurpat meum?

[Nonius, *s. v.* tumulti.]

V.

Qui cupiant dare arma Achilli, cunctent pugnam obbitere.

[Nonius, *s. v.* cunctant.]

VI.

Constitit, credo, Scamander, arbores vento vacant.

[Nonius. *s. v.* vagas (?).]

VII.

. . . sublimiter
quadrupedantes . . . flammam halitantes.

[Diomedes, *s. v.* halitare.]

VIII.

Adducit quadrupedem invitam indomitam iniugem,
evalida quoius tenacia infrenast nimis.

[Nonius, *s. v.* tenacia.]

IX.

per vos et vostrorum ducum
imperium et fidem, Myrmidonum vigiles, commiserescite.

[Nonius, *s. v.* commiserescere.]

X.

Melius est virtute ius: nam saepe virtutem mali
nanciscuntur: ius atque aequom se a malis spernit
procul.

[Nonius, *s. v.* spernere = segregare.]

HECUBA.

Hecuba, after the treacherous murder of her son Polydorus, makes a passionate appeal to heaven (I). When she hears that sentence has gone forth for the immolation of her daughter Polyxena, she entreats Ulysses to use his all-persuasive powers to prevent the sacrifice (II). But she feels that her supplication is all in vain (III). In her misery, she fain would take her own life, or share her daughter's death (IV, V). And, over the corpse of her murdered son, she beseeches Agamemnon to pity her, reminding him of the claim that Cassandra's surrender of herself has upon him (VI.

I.

O mágna templa caélitum, commíxta stellis spléndidis!

[VARRO, *L. L.* 7. 6 M.]

II.

Haéc tu etsi pervérse dices, fácile Achivos fléxeris:
nám opulenti cúm locuntur páriter atque ignóbiles,
eádem dicta eadémque oratio aéqua non aequé valet.

[AUL. GELL. 11. 4.]

[Cp. EUR. *Hec.* 293-295:

τὸ δ' ἀξίωμα, κἂν κακῶς λέγῃς, τὸ σὸν
πείσει· λόγος γὰρ ἔκ τ' ἀδοξούντων ἰὼν
κἀκ τῶν δοκούντων αὐτὸς οὐ ταὐτὸν σθένει.

Gellius, *l. c.*, while generally approving of the rendering, does not consider *ignobiles* and *opulenti* as a satisfactory translation of the Greek.]

III.

Heú, me míseram, intérii! pergunt lávere sanguen
sánguine.

[NONIUS, *s. v.* sanguen.]

IV.

... miseréte anuis
date férrum qui me animá privem!

[NONIUS, *s. v.* miserete.]

V.

Extémplo acceptam mé necato et fíliam.

[VARRO, *L. L.* 7. 13 M.]

VI.

Vide núnc meae in quem lácrumae guttatím cadunt.

[Nonius, s. v. guttatim.]

VII.

Quaé tibi in concubió verecunde ét modice morém gerit.

[Nonius, s. v. modice = modeste.]

[Cp. Eur. Hec. 829 :

Ἡ τῶν ἐν εὐνῇ φιλτάτων ἀσπασμάτων
χάριν τίν' ἕξει παῖς ἐμή, κείνης δ' ἐγώ;]

IPHIGENIA.

Agamemnon, in his tent, asks his old servant 'What of the night?' (I) [Cp. Eur. *I. A.* 6]. Instead of the Euripidean Chorus of maidens we have a Chorus of Achaean soldiers, fretting at the long delay (II). Then follows the altercation between Agamemnon and Menelaus : the former condemning the flight of Helen, and deprecating the sacrifice of Iphigenia (III, IV). [Cp. Eur. *I. A.* 328 foll.]. Agamemnon, realising that the sacrifice must proceed, laments the hard law that forbids kings to weep V. [Cp. Eur. *I. A.* 446]. Achilles sneers at the pretended prescience of Calchas (VI) [*I. A.* 956.] Iphigenia accepts her death, and surrenders herself for her country's weal (VII) [*I. A.* 1375 foll.].

I.

Agam.   Quid nóctis videtur in áltisono
        caelí clipeo ?

Senex.   superát temo[1]
        stellás cogens etiam átque etiam
        noctís sublime iter.

[Varro, *L. L.* 7. 73 M.]

II.

Otio qui néscit uti plús negoti habet
quam cum quis negótiosod útitur negótio.

---

[1] *temo*, sc. the constellation of the ἅμαξα, or septentrio.

nám cui quod agat ínstitutumst. núllo quasi negótio
id agit, id studét, ibi mentem atque ánimum delectát
    suum.
ótioso in ótio animus nóscit quid velit.
hóc idem hic est: enim néque domi nunc nós nec
    militiaé sumus:
ímus huc, hinc illuc: cum illuc véntumst, ire illínc lubet:
íncerte errat ánimus, praeter própter vitam vívitur.
                    [Aul. Gell. 19. 10. praeterpropter = 'outside.']

III.

Agam. Quís homo te exsuperávit usquam géntium
    impudéntia?
Menel. Quís ted autem málitia?
                    [Cic. Tusc. Disp. 4. 36.]

IV.

Agam. Égone plectar, tú delinques: tú pecces, ego
    árguar?
pró malefactis Hélena redeat, vírgo pereat ínnocens?
túa reconciliétur uxor, méa necetur fília?
                    [Rufinian, De Fig. Sent.]

V.

Plebés in hoc regi ántistat: largó licet
lacrumáre plebi, régi honeste nón licet.
                    [Hieronym. Epitaph. Nepot.]

VI.

Ástrologorum sígna in caelo quaésit, observát Iovis
cúm capra aut nepa[1] aut exoritur lúmen aliquod béluae.
quód est ante pedes noénu spectant: caéli scrutantúr
    plagas.
                    [Cic. De Rep. 1. 18.]

[1] *nepa*, the constellation of the Scorpion.

VII.

Acheróntem obibo, ubi mórtis thesauri óbiacent,
ut hóstium eliciátur sanguis sánguine.

[Fest. *De Praep. ob.*: Cic. *Tusc. Disp.* 1. 48.]

MEDEA EXUL.

Cicero (*De Fin.* I. 2. 4) quotes the Medea of Ennius as among those 'fabellas Latinas ad verbum e Graecis expressas.' This is certainly overstated.

I.

Nutrix. Utinám ne in nemore Pélio secúribus
caesa áccidisset ábiegna ad terrám trabes,
neve índe navis íncohandae exórdium
coepísset, quae nunc nóminatur nómine
Argó, quia Argiví ín ea delectí viri
vectí petebant péllem inauratam árietis
Colchís, imperio régis Peliae, pér dolum.
Nam númquam era errans méa domo ecferrét pedem
Medéa, animo aegra, amóre saevo saúcia.

[Cic. *De Inv.* I. 49, etc.]

[Cp. Eur. *Med.* 1–7 :

εἴθ᾽ ὤφελ᾽ Ἀργοῦς μὴ διαπτάσθαι σκάφος
Κόλχων ἐς αἶαν κυανέας Συμπληγάδας,
μηδ᾽ ἐν νάπαισι Πηλίου πεσεῖν ποτὲ
τμηθεῖσα πεύκη, μηδ᾽ ἐρετμῶσαι χέρας
ἀνδρῶν ἀριστέων, οἳ τὸ πάγχρυσον δέρος
Πελίᾳ μετῆλθον· οὐ γὰρ ἂν δέσποιν᾽ ἐμὴ
Μήδεια πύργους γῆς ἔπλευσ᾽ Ἰωλκίας,
ἔρωτι θυμὸν ἐκπλαγεῖσ᾽ Ἰάσονος.]

II.

(The next passage does not express the meaning of the corresponding words in Euripides. There, Medea excuses herself to the Corinthian dames for coming forth from her house; here Ennius

seems to represent the Corinthians as taunting Medea with her
exile from her country, while she defends herself.)

Quae Corinthi arcem áltam habétis, mátronae opuléntae
    óptimates!
múlti suam rem béne gessére et públicam patriá procul,
múlti, qui domi aétatem agérent, própterea sunt ín-
    probati.
[Cic. Ad Fam. 7. 6.]

[Cp. Eur. Med. 214 foll. :

    Κορίνθιαι γυναῖκες, ἐξῆλθον δόμων,
    μή μοί τι μέμψησθ'· οἶδα γὰρ πολλοὺς βροτῶν
    σεμνοὺς γεγῶτας, τοὺς μὲν ὀμμάτων ἄπο,
    τοὺς δ' ἐν θυραίοις· οἱ δ' ἀφ' ἡσύχου ποδὸς
    δύσκλειαν ἐκτήσαντο καὶ ῥᾳθυμίαν.]

III.

(From the same passage : Medea contrasts the life of a man with
that of a wife and mother.)

. . . nam tér sub armis málim vitam cérnere
quám semel modo párere.
[Varro, L. L. 6. 81.]

[Cp. Eur. Med. 250 foll. :

    Ὡς τρὶς ἂν παρ' ἀσπίδα
    στῆναι θέλοιμ' ἂν μᾶλλον ἢ τεκεῖν ἅπαξ.]

IV.

(Creon bids Medea depart, granting her a respite of one day.
She sneers at his simplicity : this one day is enough for her
revenge.)

Néquaquam istuc ístac ibit : mágna adest certátio.
nám ut ego illi súpplicarem tánta blandiloquéntia—

[Cp. Eur. Med. 365 foll. :

    Ἀλλ' οὔτι ταύτῃ ταῦτα, μὴ δοκεῖτέ πω.
    ἔτ' εἴσ' ἀγῶνες . . .
    δοκεῖς γὰρ ἄν με τόνδε θωπεῦσαί ποτε,
    εἰ μή τι κερδαίνουσαν ἢ τεχνωμένην ;]

V.

(From the same passage.)

Ílle travérsa ménte mi hódie trádidit repágula,
quíbus ego iram omném recludam atque illi perniciém
    dabo,
míhi maerores, illi luctum, exítium illi, exilium mihi.

[Cic. De Nat. Deor. 3. 25.]

[Cp. Eur. Med. 371 foll. :

'Ο δ' ἐς τοσοῦτον μωρίας ἀφίκετο
ὥστ', ἐξὸν αὐτῷ τἄμ' ἑλεῖν βουλεύματα
γῆς ἐκβαλόντι, τήνδ' ἐφῆκεν ἡμέραν
μεῖναί μ', ἐν ᾗ τρεῖς τῶν ἐμῶν ἐχθρῶν νεκροὺς
θήσω· . . . .
πικροὺς δ' ἐγώ σφιν καὶ λυγροὺς θήσω γάμους,
πικρὸν δὲ κῆδος καὶ φυγὰς ἐμὰς χθονός.]

VI.

(The Chorus appeal to the Sun-god to stay the hand of Medea.)

Iúppiter tuque ádeo summe Sól, qui res omnés spicis
quíque maria térram caelum cóntines tuo lúmine,
ínspice hoc facinús! prius quam fíat, prohibésseis
    scelus.

[Probus in Verg. Ecl. 6. 31.]

[Cp. Eur. Med. 1251 foll. :

'Ιὼ Γᾶ τε καὶ παμφαὴς
ἀκτὶς 'Αελίου, κατίδετ' ἴδετε τὰν
ὀλομέναν γυναῖκα, πρὶν φοινίαν
τέκνοις προσβαλεῖν χέρ' αὐτοκτόνον.]

PHOENIX.

Phoenix was falsely accused of incontinence by Phthia, the concubine of his father Amyntor, who in his anger puts his son's eyes out. Phoenix flies to the court of Peleus, where he recovers his sight through the skill of Chiron, and is made king of the Dolopes. He seems to rebuke the nurse, who tempts him by the revelation of her mistress's passion (I, II); and he confronts his angry father, and proclaims his own innocence (III).

I.

. . . stultust quí cupita cúpiens cupientér cupit.

[Nonius, *s. v.* cupienter.]

II.

Plús miser sim, sí scelestum fáxim quod dicám fore.

[Nonius, *s. v.* faxim.]

III.

Séd virum virtúte vera vívere animatum áddecet
fórtiterque innóxium adstare ádversum adversários.
éa libertas ést qui pectus púrum et firmum géstitat;
áliae res obnóxiosae¹ nócte in obscurá latent.

[Aul. Gell. 6. 17.]

TELAMO.

Telamon receives with fortitude the (false) tidings of the death of both his sons (I); he resents the indifference of the gods, and sneers at the pretensions of priests and seers (II).

I.

Égo cum genui túm morituros scívi et ei re sústuli.
praéterea ad Troiám cum misi ob défendendam Graéciam,
scíbam me in mortíferum bellum nón in epulas míttere.

[Cic. *Tusc. Disp.* 3. 13.]

II.

Égo deum genus ésse semper díxi et dicam caélitum,
séd eos non curáre opinor quíd agat humanúm genus;
nám si curent, béne bonis sit, mále malis; quod núnc
    abest.

. . . . .

Séd superstitiósi vates ínpudentesque árioli,

---

¹ *obnoxiosae*, 'in the thraldom of passion.'

Q. ENNIUS. 63

aút inertes aút insani aut quíbus egestas ímperat.
quí sibi semitám non sapiunt álteri monstránt viam.
quíbus divitias póllicentur áb eis drachumam ipsí petunt.
de hís divitiis síbi deducant dráchumam, reddant cétera.

[Cic. *De Div.* 1. 58 ; 2. 50.]

THYESTES.

THYESTES, in his old age, returns home, trusting to an oracle of Apollo (I) ; and seeking reconciliation with his brother. But Atreus treacherously sets before him the flesh of his own children to eat ; and when Thyestes realises what he has done, he denounces himself as a moral leper (II), and calls down terrible curses on Atreus (III).

I.

Sét me Apollo ipsús delectat átque ductat Délphicus.

[Nonius, *s. v.* delectare.]

II.

Nolíte, hóspités, ád me adíre! ílico ístím,
ne cóntágió méa. bonís úmbrave óbsit!
meó tánta vís scéleris ín córpore haérét.

[Cic. *Tusc. Disp.* 3. 12.]

III.

Ípse summis sáxis fixus ásperis, evísceratus,
látere pendens, sáxa spargens tábo, sanie et sánguine
    atro,
néque sepulchrum quód recipiat hábeat. portum córporis.
úbi remissa humána vita córpus requiescát malis!

[Cic. *Tusc. Disp.* 1. 44.]

SATURAE.

Book I.

1. Nunquám poëtor nísi sim podager.

[PRISC. 29.]

2. Malo hércle magno suó convivat síne modo.

[NONIUS, *s. v.* convivare.]

Book II.

Réstitant, occúrsant, obstant. óbstringillant, óbagitant.

[NONIUS, *s. v.* obstringillare.]

Book III, sive Scipio.

(*The poet sounds his own welcome.*)

Enní poeta sálve qui mortálibus
versús propinas flámmeos medúllitus.

[NONIUS, *s. v.* propinare.]

(*The terror of Scipio's name.*)

Africa terribili tremit horrida terra tumultu.

[CIC. *De Orat.* 3. 42.]

(*Voyage of Scipio to Africa, through calm seas* [Livy 28. 17].)

. . . mundus caéli vastus cónstitit siléntio,
ét Neptunus saévus undis ásperis pausám dedit;
Sól equis itér repressit úngulis volántibus,
cónstitere amnés perennes, árbores ventó vacant.

[MACROB. *Sat.* 6. 2. 26.]

Q. ENNIUS.

(*After the battle of Zama.*)

Testes sunt campi magni . . .
lati campi, quos gerit Africa terra politos.

[Cic. De Orat. 3. 42. 167 : Nonius, s. v. politiones.]

(*Scipio's high services to Rome.*)

Desine Roma tuos hostes *horrere superbos*:
namque tibi monimenta mei peperere labores.

[Cic. De Orat. 3. 42 ; De Fin. 2. 32.]

(*His contempt of the slanders brought against him.*)

Meum nón est, ac si mé canis memórderit.

[Aul. Gell. 6. 9. 1.]

Nam is nón bene volt tibi, qui me falso críminat
apúd te.

[Nonius, s. v. criminat.]

AMBRACIA.

(*Exploits of M. Fulvius Nobilior ; depression of Antiochus.*)

Pér gentes Asiaé cluebat ómnium misérrimus.

[Nonius, s. v. cluet.]

(*After the taking of Ambracia.*)

. . . agros
audaces populant servi domini dominorum.

[Nonius. s. v. populat.]

EPICHARMUS.

Ennius dreams that the philosopher Epicharmus appears to him in the world of shades, and expounds his system of physics.)

I.

Nam videbar sómniare mé *lecto* esse mórtuum.

[Cic. Acad. Pr. 2. 16. 52.]

F

II.

Ánimus cernit, ánimus audit, réliqua caeca et súrda sunt[1].
[TERTULL. *De An.* 18.]

[1] νόος ὁρῇ καὶ νόος ἀκούει· τἄλλα κωφὰ καὶ τυφλά.
Epicharmus ap. Plut. Mor. 98 B.

III.

ágĭlis hic
ést de sole súmptus ignis ísque totus móntis est.
[VARRO, *L. L.* 5. 59.]

IV.

Ístic est is Iúpiter quem díco, quem Graecí vocant
áërem : qui véntus est et núbes, imber póstea
átque ex imbre frígus, tenuis póst fit aër dénuo,
haéce propter Iúpiter sunt ísta, quae dicó tibi,
quándo mortalís atque urbes béluasque omnés iuvant.
[VARRO, *L. L.* 5. 65.]

V.

Sóle Luna lúce lucet álba leni láctea.
[MARTIAN. CAP. p. 170.]

HEDYPHAGETICA (after Archestratus).

(*When the Punic Wars brought wealth and Greek civilisation to Rome, gastronomy became a science, and plain old-fashioned dinners were despised.*)

Omnibus ut Clipeae praestat mustela marina,
mures sunt Aeni, spissa ostrea plurima Abydi;
Mytilenaest pecten charadrusque apud Ambraciai

l. 1. The passage is a free rendering from Archestratus, quoted by Athenaeus, *Deipn.* 3. 92 D.

> Τοὺς μῦς Αἶνος ἔχει μεγάλους, ὄστρεια δ' Ἄβυδος,
> τοὺς ἄρκτους Πάριον, τοὺς δὲ κτένας ἡ Μυτιλήνη,
> πλείστους δ' Ἀμβρακία παρέχει . . .

This fragment suggests a lacuna in the Latin after *Abydi*. The *mus* is a sort of sea-crayfish. l. 3. *pecten* = 'scallop'; *charadrus*?; *elops* or *helops* is, perhaps, the 'sturgeon.'

finis. Brundisio sargust, hunc, magnus erit si,
sume tibi: apriclum scito primum esse Tarenti;
Surrenti fac emas elopem, glaucum prope Cumas.
quid scarus? praeterii cerebrum Iovis paene supremi.
Nestoris ad patriam hic capitur magnusque bonusque.

[APUL. *De Magia*, 39.]

EPIGRAMMATA.

The first of these Epigrammata purports to be written by the poet as his own epitaph. The second and third refer to Scipio Africanus.

I.

Nemo me lacrumis decoret nec funera fletu
    faxit. cur? volito vivus per ora virum.

[CIC. *Tusc. Disp.* 1. 15. 34.]

II.
De Africano.

Hic est ille situs cui nemo civis neque hostis
    quivit pro factis reddere opis pretium.

[CIC. *De Legg.* 2. 22. 57.]

III.

A sole exoriente supra Maeotis paludes
    nemost qui factis aequiperare queat.
si fas endo plagas caelestum ascendere cuiquamst,
    mi soli caeli maxima porta patet.

[CIC. *Tusc. Disp.* 5. 17. 49.]

M. PACUVIUS.

(220-132 A. C.)

TRAGOEDIAE.

ANTIOPA.

ANTIOPA, daughter of the Boeotian King Nycteus, being with child by Jupiter (I), is driven from her home by her father's threats (II). She finds refuge with Epopeus, King of Sicyon, who marries her. Nycteus on his death-bed commits the duty of punishing Antiopa to his brother Lycus, who slays Epopeus and carries Antiopa into captivity. On her way she bare two sons, whom she is forced to leave exposed on Mount Cithaeron. A herdsman finds them, and brings them up, giving them the names of Amphion and Zethus, the former devoting himself to music and philosophy, the latter to the rough life of herdsman and hunter III). Antiopa, being cruelly treated in her captivity by Lycus' wife, Dirce, finds means of escape. She comes to the young men's homestead, and tells them the piteous story of her sufferings (IV, V, VI). Amphion is touched by the sight of her misery (VII, inc. fab. VI, Ribb.); but Zethus, thinking her to be a runaway slave, and hating all womankind (VIII, inc. fab. LIV, Ribb.), would not receive her. Meanwhile, a festival in honour of Bacchus is celebrated, and Dirce, accompanied by her train of Maenads with flying hair (IX), comes to the place where Antiopa is seeking refuge. The young men bid them depart (X), but Dirce claims the surrender of her captive, and is about to slay her (XI, inc. fab. IV, Ribb.). But the herdsman having revealed to the brothers that Antiopa is their mother, she joyfully greets them, and they set her free (XII). Dirce is then tied by her hair to a wild bull and dragged about till she is torn to pieces. Lycus would also have been slain, but Hermes saves his life and bids him hand over his kingdom to Amphion.

The highly-wrought description of Antiopa's sorrows is ridiculed by Persius (1. 77): 'Sunt quos Pacuviusque et verrucosa moretur Antiopa aerumnis cor luctificabile fulta,' which last words may be actually borrowed from Pacuvius. A strong point of interest in the play is the contrast between the blunt, practical Zethus and the artistic, contemplative Amphion. This is alluded to in Horace (*Ep.* 1. 18. 39 foll.), and is worked out elaborately in the Antiope of Euripides. Zethus is characteristic of the old Greek burgher, hating philosophy (XIII, inc. fab. II, Ribb.); Amphion is the Greek 'sophist.' We find him dealing with the necessity of change and alternation in nature (XIV), and propounding a perplexing riddle in involved language about his 'tortoise-lyre,' which Hermes gave him (XV).

I.

Iovis éx Antiopa Nýctei natí [duo].

[Prob. *in Verg. Ecl.* 2. 25.]

II.

Mínitabiliterque íncrepare díctis saevis íncipit.

[Nonius, *s. v.* minitabiliter.]

III.

Tu córnifrontes páscere armentás soles.

[Serv. *in Verg. Aen.* 3. 540.]

IV.

illuvie córporis
ét coma prolíxa impexa cónglomerata atque hórrida.

[Schol. *ad Pers.* 1. 77.]

V.

. . . perdita inluvie atque insomnia.

[Charis. 1. 78 P, insomnia, sing.]

VI.

Frendére noctes mísera quas perpéssa sum.

[Nonius, *s. v.* frendere = gemere.]

VII.

Miserét me, lacrimis língua debilitér stupet.

[Nonius, *s. v.* debiliter.]

VIII.
Haud fácile femina úna invenietúr bona.
[NONIUS, s. v. facul (?).]

IX.
cérvicum
florós dispendite crínes.
[SERV. in Verg. Aen. 12. 605, floros = flavos.]

X.
Nonne hínc vos propere a stábulis amolímini?
[NONIUS, s. v. amolimini = recedite.]

XI.
Agite, rápite, volvite, ferte coma,
tractáte per aspera sáxa et humum,
scindíte vestem ocius.
[MAR. VICTORIN. p. 2522 P.]

XII.
Salvéte gemini, méa propages sánguinis!
[NONIUS, s. v. propages.]

XIII.
Ódi ego homines ígnava opera et phílosopha senténtia.
[AUL. GELL. 13. 8.]

XIV.
Sól si perpetuó siet,
flámmeo vapóre torrens térrae fetum exússerit:
nócti ni intervéniat, fructus pér pruinam obríguerint.
[VARRO, L. L. 6. 6. M.]

XV.
AMPHIO. Quadrupés tardigrada agréstis humilis áspera,
brevi cápite, cervice ánguina, aspectú truci,

evíscerata¹ inánima cum animalí sono.
ASTICI. Ita saéptuosa díctione abs tó datur,
quod cóniectura sápiens aegre contuit :
non íntellegimus, nísi si aperte díxeris.
AMPHIO. Testudo.

[CIC. *De Div.* 2. 64.]

ARMORUM IUDICIUM.

THE play opens with the funeral games at the pyre of Achilles, and the announcement by Agamemnon that the Arms of Achilles will be the prize for the best warrior (I, II). The competition is open to all who desire to contend (III) ; but Ajax, who considers his own claims to be paramount, protests against this method of decision (IV), and refuses to be pitted against Ulysses [cp. Ov. *Metam.* 13. 5 foll. and 16 foll.]. He takes his stand on his signal services to the Greek army (V) ; contemptuously comparing the record of Ulysses with his own (VI). Agamemnon refers the difficulty to Nestor (VII) ; who advises that the question be committed to the Trojan prisoners, who are bound by an oath to confess which of the heroes had inflicted most suffering on the Trojans (VIII). Agamemnon accepts his counsel (IX). In X and XI we find an allusion to the greatness of Ajax before the evil spirit came upon him : but Ulysses sneers at the misplaced wrath of the unhappy man, which is directed against his innocent rival, rather than against the Trojan prisoners who gave the decision. To the monologue of Ajax before his suicide may be referred that bitter complaint of the ingratitude of the Atridae (XII), which was in later times chanted at the funeral games after the assassination of Caesar, 'ad miserationem et invidiam caedis eius' (SUET. *Iul.* 84).

I.

. . . séque ad ludos iam índe abhinc exérceant.

[CHARIS. 2. p. 175 P.]

¹ *eviscerata.* So Hermes, in the process of making a tortoise into a lyre, αἰῶν' ἐξετόρησεν ὀρεσκῴοιο χελώνης, so as to leave only the shell. *Hymn. Merc.* 43.

II.

Quí viget vescátur armis ut pércipiat praémium.

[Nonius, s. v. vesci = uti.]

III.

. . . qui sése adfines ésse ad causandúm volunt,
dé virtute is égo cernundi dó potestatem ómnibus.

[Nonius, s. v. causari = causam dicere : cernere = dimicare.]

IV.

Án quis est qui té esse dignum quícum certetúr putet ?

[Nonius, certetur pro certet.]

V.

. . . si non ést ingratum reápse quod fecí bene.

[Festus, reapse = re ipsa.]

VI.

túque te
désidere [in lécto residem], nós hic esse [in míseriis máluisti.]

[Festus, reses = ignavus.]

VII.

. . . dic quid fáciam : quod me móneris, effectúm dabo.

[Nonius, s. v. moneris = monueris.]

VIII.

Próloqui non paénitebunt líberi ingrato éx loco.

[Nonius, s. v. paenitebunt.]

IX.

. . . et aequum et réctum est quod tu póstulas :
iuráti cernant.

[Nonius, s. v. cernere = iudicare.]

X.

Cúm recordor éius ferocem et tórvam confidéntiam
. . . feróci ingenio, tórvus, praegrandí gradu . . .

[FESTUS, s. v. torvitas. NONIUS, s. v. confidentia.]

XI.

Nám canis, quando ést percussa lápide, non tam illum
ádpetit,
qúi sese icit, quam íllum cumpse lápidem, qui ipsa icta
ést, petit.

[NONIUS, s. v. icit.]

XII.

. . . mén servasse, ut éssent qui me pérderent!

[SUET. Iul. 84.]

CHRYSES.

IN this play the story of Iphigenia in Tauris is produced in a novel form. Orestes, Pylades, and Iphigenia, who had carried off the image of Diana from her temple, encounter a storm on their voyage; and when the calm weather returns (I), they land on a promontory of the island Sminthe (II), and survey the spot (III). To this moment we may refer the reflections introduced on the instability of Fortune (IV [inc. fab. XIV, Ribb.]). Here they find the younger Chryses, son of the unfortunate Chryseis of the Iliad, serving as priest of Apollo. Thoas pursues the fugitives V [inc. fab. LXXIII, Ribb.]), who, on being discovered, implore the protection of Chryses and the inhabitants of the isle (VI; and Orestes reveals to the citizens the terrible deed of bloodguiltiness to which he has been driven by the importunities of his countrymen, and the command of the gods (VII). But Thoas calls on the priest to exact expiation for the theft of the sacred image; yet only the actual perpetrator of the sacrilege is to be put to death, that is to say, Orestes. But which is Orestes? and which is Pylades? Each of the friends generously claims the name (VIII [inc. fab. XIII, Ribb.]), and when Thoas is baffled, they urge him to put them both to death. However, Thoas thinks he has found

the real culprit, and congratulates himself on the discovery (IX).
When Chryses finds that Orestes and Iphigenia are the children of
Agamemnon, all the bitter memories of the past come back upon
him, and a deep desire for revenge (X). Orestes' fate seems sealed,
and Thoas contemptuously laughs at the prayer of his captives
(XI). At this moment of danger, Chryseis intervenes, reveals to
her son the secret of his birth, and turns away his wrath (XII).
Chryses is her son, not by Apollo but by Agamemnon, and so
Orestes is his brother. The priest at once espouses the cause of the
fugitives, and delivers them from the hands of Thoas, who falls in
the fray.

Two famous passages (XIII. XIV), conceived in the spirit of the
Anaxagorean philosophy, have been generally referred to this
play, though it is difficult to harmonise them with the general
plot. If they are put into the mouth of Chryses, the sentiments
seem inconsistent with the position of a priest of the gods. Although the references in Cicero and Nonius seem to be to the
'Chryses,' the striking similarity between these passages and a
fragment (836) from the 'Chrysippos' of Euripides suggests that
the word 'Chryses' is given in error for 'Chrysippos'; and indeed
the variants in the MSS. of Cicero point in the same direction.

I.

interea loci
flúcti flacciscúnt, silescunt vénti, mollitúr mare.

[NONIUS, s. v. flucti.]

II.

Ídae promuntúrium quoius língua in altum próicit.

[AUL. GELL. 4. 17.]

III.

incipio sáxum temptans scándere
vórticem, summúsque in omnes pártes prospectum aúcupo.

[NONIUS, s. v. aucupo.]

IV.

Fórtunam insanam ésse et caecam et brútam perhibent
philosophi,

sáxoque instare in globoso praedicant volubilei.
quia quo id saxum impulerit fors, eo cadere Fortunam
  aútumant,
insanam autem esse aiunt quia atrox incerta instabilís-
  que sit:
caécam, ob eam rem esse iterant quia nil cérnat quo
  sese ádplicet:
brútam, quia dignum átque indignum néqueat internós-
  cere.
súnt autem alii philosophi, qui cóntra Fortunám negant
ésse ullam, sed témeritate res regi omnis aútumant.
id magis veri símile esse usus reápse experiundo édocet:
vélut Orestes módo fuit rex, fáctust mendicús modo
naúfragio: nempe érgo id fluctu, haud fórte fortuna
  óptigit.
[RHET. *Ad Herenn.* 2. 23. 36.]

V.

Téla, famuli, téla tela própere! sequitur mé Thoas.
[CENSORIN. frag. c. 14, p. 95.]

VI.

adiutámini et deféndite!
[NONIUS, *s. v.* adiutamini.]

VII.

Civés, antiqui amíci maiorúm meum,
consilium socii, augúrium atque extum intérpretes,
postquám prodigium horríferum, portentúm pavor . . .
[CIC. *Orat.* 46. 155.]

VIII.

P. Égo sum Orestes. O. ímmo enim vero ego sum,
  ínquam, Orestes.

UTERQUE. . . ámbo ergo igitur símul una enicárier
cómprecamur.
[Cic. De Fin. 5. 22 ; De Amic. 7. 24.]

IX.

Invéni, opino, Oréstes uter essét tamen.
[Nonius, s. v. opino.]

X.

Sed césso inimicitiam íntegrare?
[Nonius, s. v. integrare.]

XI.

pró merenda grátia
simúl cum videam Graíos nil medióeriter
redámptruare opibúsque summis pérsequi . . .
[Festus, Nonius, s. v. redantruare.]

XII.

Di mónerint meliora átque amentiam áverruncassínt
tuam!
[Nonius, s. v. monerint = monuerint. Varro, L. L. 7. 102 M.]

XIII.

. . . nam isti quí linguam avium intóllegunt
plusque éx alieno iécore sapiunt quam éx suo,
magis aúdiendum quam aúscultandum cénseo.
[Cic. De Div. 1. 57. Nonius, s. v. auscultare est obsequi.]

XIV.

Hóc vide circúm supraque quód complexu cóntinet
terram.
sólisque exortú capessit cándorem, occasú nigret,
id quod nostri caélum memorant Grái perhibent aéthera :

quídquid est hoc, ómnia animat fórmat alit augét creat
sépelit recipitque ín seso omnia, ómniumque idem ést
  pater,
índidemque eadem aéque oriuntur de íntegro atque
  eodem óccidunt.

. . . . . .

máter est terra: éa parit corpus, ánimam aether ádiugat.[1]
     [VARRO, *L. L.* 5. 17 M. NONIUS, *s. v.* adiugare.]

DULORESTES.

ORESTES appears on the stage disguised as a slave (δοῦλος), driving his flock from Delphi to Mycenae (I). At the palace a marriage is about to be celebrated (II, III); for the unnatural Clytemnestra has determined to give her daughter Electra to Oeax, one of the sons of Nauplius (IV), who drew the Greek fleet to its destruction on the Euboean coast by false fire-signals (V). Such an alliance with the avowed enemies of her country would prevent the daughter of Agamemnon from succeeding in any scheme of vengeance! Aegisthus, the swaggering tyrant (VI), tries by threats to force her into compliance (VII); but, revolting from the shame which would attend such a union (VIII), she defies her mother's authority. She is strengthened in her resolve by a conviction that

---

[1] Cp. EUR. Nauck, *Frag. Trag.* p. 633 f. ed. 1889:
Γαῖα μεγίστη καὶ Διὸς Αἰθήρ.
ὁ μὲν ἀνθρώπων καὶ θεῶν γενέτωρ,
ἡ δ' ὑγροβόλους σταγόνας νοτίους
παραδεξαμένη τίκτει θνατοῖς,
τίκτει δὲ βορὰν φῦλά τε θηρῶν·
ὅθεν οὐκ ἀδίκως
μήτηρ πάντων νενόμισται.
χωρεῖ δ' ὀπίσω
τὰ μὲν ἐκ γαίας φύντ' ἐς γαῖαν,
τὰ δ' ἀπ' αἰθερίου βλαστόντα γονῆς
εἰς οὐράνιον πάλιν ἦλθε πόλον·
θνῄσκει δ' οὐδὲν τῶν γιγνομένων,
διακρινόμενον δ' ἄλλο πρὸς ἄλλου
μορφὴν ἑτέραν ἀπέδειξεν.

her brother is not far off (IX), and having found him she decides at once upon vengeance (X), and conspires with him against Aegisthus, though the task is a hard one XI), as all the sons of Nauplius rally to his aid. Aegisthus seems, in his perplexity, to have consulted some oracle, and to have received a dubious answer (XII); but Oeax interprets the reply, and announces its meaning to be that Clytemnestra must have no chance of recognising Orestes (XIII). Pylades begins the struggle by slaying some of the defenders of Aegisthus, and, after a long civil strife between the partisans of Clytemnestra and of Agamemnon, the guilty tyrant and his adulterous consort are put to death.

I.

Délphos venum pécus egi, inde ad stábula haec itiner cóntuli.

[Nonius, s. v. itiner.]

II.

. . . hymenaeúm fremunt
aequáles, aula résonit crepitu músico.

[Nonius, s. v. sonit pro sonat.]

III.

Gnatám despondit, núptiis hanc dát diem.

[Nonius, s. v. diem *masc. et fem.*]

IV.

Páter Achivos ín Capharei sáxis pleros pérdidit.

[Priscian, 5, p. 668 P, s. v. pleros.]

V.

nisi me cálvitur suspício
hóc est illud quód fore occulte Oéax praedixít . . .

[Nonius, s. v. calvitur=frustratur.]

VI.

Amplus rubicundó colore et spéctu protervó ferox.

[Festus, s. v. spectu sine praepos.]

VII.

Nam te ín tenebrica sépe lacerabó fame
clausam, ét fatigans ártus torto dístraham.
                                     [Nonius, s. v. torto pro tormento.]

VIII.

Sí quis hac me orátione incilet, quid respóndeam ?
                                       [Nonius, s. v. incilare = increpare.]

IX.

Aut híc est aut hic ádfore actutum aútumo.
                                       [Nonius, s. v. autumare = sperare.]

X.

Utinam nunc matréscam ingenio, ut meúm patrem
ulcisci queam !
                                       [Nonius, s. v. matrescam = matri similis fiam.]

XI.

. . . éxtemplo Aegisthí fidem
núncupantes cónciebunt pópulum . . .
                                       [Nonius, s. v. conciere.]

XII.

Nil cóniectura quívi interpretárier
quorsúm flexidica vóce se conténderet.
                                       [Nonius, s. v. contendit = proripuit.]

XIII.

Respónsa explanat: mándat ne matrí fuat
cognóscendi unquam aut cóntuendi cópia.
                                       [Nonius, s. v. fuat = sit.]

HERMIONA.

A STORY of love and rivalry. Neoptolemus comes to Delphi to consult the god as to the childlessness of his wife Hermione, who, with Menelaus and the old Tyndareus, accompanies him (I). At the same moment arrives Orestes with his friend Pylades to obtain deliverance from the haunting Furies (II). Orestes seeks refuge from them in the temple of Apollo, but they lay wait for him at the entrance, and pounce upon him as he departs. Then he espies Hermione, once his betrothed, but stolen from him by Neoptolemus with the connivance of Menelaus. He cannot believe his eyes, except he may touch her (III)! He determines to claim her. Hermione is torn between love and duty: she recalls the shadow thrown on her life by the guilt of Helen, her mother (IV). In vain she invokes Eloquence, 'the queen that sways all hearts,' to find some convincing plea (V: she dreads to think of the calamity she may be bringing upon her family (VI). Orestes declares that Hermione had been irrevocably given to him (VII). The rivals assert their respective claims: Neoptolemus recounts his own achievements and those of his sire Achilles (VIII, IX): to him alone the Greeks owe their return from Troy (X). He taunts Tyndareus with his old age (XI); and his ill-judged haste in betrothing his grand-daughter in the absence of her father Menelaus (XII). Orestes retorts that Neoptolemus had only married Hermione in the hope of succeeding to the throne of Sparta (XIII). He has powerful advocates in the fanatical priests of Apollo, for Neoptolemus had offended the god; and, at the moment of his expiatory sacrifice, they fling themselves upon him. Orestes espouses the cause of the god; Neoptolemus is slain, and Orestes, in recompense, is purified from his bloodguiltiness. Hermione returns to her old lover, and peace is made between Argos and Delphi (XIV).

I.

quo tandem ipsa órbitas
grandaévitasque Pélei penúriam
stirpis subauxit.
[Nonius, s. v. grandaevitas.]

II.

Tristítia atque animi intóleranda anxitúdine.
[Nonius, s. v. anxitudo.]

III.

. . . át non cernam nísi tagam.

[Festus, s. v. tagam.]

IV.

Cum néque me aspicere aequáles dignarént meae.

[Diomed. 1, p. 395 P, s. v. digno.]

V.

Ó flexanima atque ómnium regína rerum orátio!

[Cic. De Orat. 2. 44.]

VI.

Quántamque ex discórditate cládem importem fámiliae.

[Nonius, s. v. discorditas.]

VII.

Príus data est quam tibi dari dicta, aút quam reditumst Pérgamo.

[Nonius, s. v. dicere = promittere.]

VIII.

Quód ego in acie célebra obiectans vítam bellando áptus sum . . .

[Nonius, s. v. aptus = adeptus.]

IX.

Quíd benefacta meí patris cuius ópera te esse ultum aútumant?

[Nonius, s. v. autumo.]

X.

Nam sólus Danais híc domum itioném dedit.

[Nonius, s. v. domutionem ? .]

XI.

Habet hóc senectus ín se, cum pigra ípsa sit
spisse út videantur ómnia ei confíeri.

[Nonius, s. v. spissum = tarde.]

XII.

Paucís absolvit né moraret diútius.

[Diomed. 1, p. 395 P, s. v. moro.]

XIII.

régni alieni cúpiditas
pelléxit.

[Varro, L. L. 6. 94 M, s. v. pellexit.]

XIV.

Concórditatem hospítio adiunctam pérpetem
probitáte conservétis.

[Nonius, s. v. concorditas.]

ILIONA.

Polydorus, youngest son of Priam and Hecuba, was entrusted to the care of his sister Iliona, wife of Polymestor the king of the treacherous (I) Thracians. She, however, brought him up at her breast (II), as her own child, letting her husband believe that the child which she had born him was really Polydorus. While the two children were still young, Troy fell, and the Achaeans, desiring to destroy the whole house of Priam, bribed Polymestor by a gift of gold and the promise of the possession of Electra (III), to slay Polydorus. Through Iliona's device it was Polymestor's own son that was slain. The bloodstained ghost of the supposed Polydorus rises from the waves, and appears to his sleeping mother, awaking her with the piteous tale of his murder (IV). This is the scene about which Horace (*Sat.* 2. 3. 60 foll.) tells the amusing story of the drunken Fufius, who played the part of Iliona, sleeping through the passionate appeal of Catienus, who represented the murdered boy. Iliona cries to the poor ghost to stay and repeat the story (V), and she sends her servants to search the shore for the corpse (VI, VII, inc. fab. XXXI, Ribb.). Polydorus, who had visited the oracle of Apollo, learns with surprise at the shrine that his ancestral city had been burned, his father slain, and his mother carried away captive. When he returns to Thrace he finds that none of these disasters had occurred (VIII); but Iliona then tells him the secret of his birth (IX, X ex inc. inc. fab. XLII, Ribb.), and the brother and sister conspire against Polymestor, whom they first blind, and then slay (XI, XII). Fuller tidings come of the fall of Troy (XIII); of the fate of Hecuba, and of Cassandra, once beloved by Apollo (XIV). Polydorus remains as the hope of the royal house; but the chance of his restitution to the kingdom is slight indeed (XV)!

I.

Sed hí cluentur hóspitum infidíssimi.

[Nonius, s. v. cluet.]

II.

ab Ilio
depúlsum mamma paédogogandum áccipit
repótialis Líber.[1]

[Festus, s. v. repotia.]

III.

blándam hortatricem ádiugat
voluptátem.

[Nonius. s. v. adiugat.]

IV.

Matér, te appello, tú quae curam sómno suspensám levas
neque té mei miseret, súrge et sepeli nátum [tuum]
  prius quám ferae
volucrósque . . .
neu réliquias quaesó mias sieris dénudatis óssibus
per térram sanie délibutas foéde divexárier.

[Cic. Tusc. Disp. I. 44.]

---

[1] The 'festive draught' seems to mean 'mother's milk.' This is the conjecture of O. Müller. Scaliger would read '*repotiali lacte.*'

V.

Age ásta: mane, audi: íteradum eadem istaéc mihi.

[Cic. Acad. Pr. 2. 27.]

VI.

aut stágnorum umidórum rimarém loca.

[Nonius, s. v. rimari.]

VII.

Omnes latebras, súbluta¹ mole [ómnes] abstrusós sinus.

[Suet. Ap. Isidor. De Nat. Rer. 44.]

VIII.

Quos égo ita ut volui offéndo incolumis . . .

[Nonius, s. v. offendo = invenio.]

IX.

Ne pórro te error quí nunc lactat máceret.

[Nonius, s. v. lactare = decipere.]

X.

Quá tempestate Hélenam Paris innúptis iunxit núptiis,
égo tum gravida explétis iam fere ád pariendum mén-
 sibus,
pér idem tempus Pólydorum Hecuba pártu postremó
 parit.

[Cic. De Orat. 3. 58.]

XI.

Fac út coepisti, hanc óperam mihi des pérpetem:
oculós transaxím.

[Festus, perpetem pro perpetuo.]

XII.

Occidisti, ut múlta paucis vérba unose obnúntiem.

[Nonius, s. v. unose = simul.]

¹ *Subluta mole:* 'where the cliff is washed by the sea.'

XIII.

Profécto aut inibi est aút iam potiuntúr Frugum¹.
[Nonius, s. v. inibi pro sic et mox.]

XIV.

Paélici supérstitiosae cúm vecordi cóniuge.
[Festus, vecors, mali cordis.]

XV.

Úsi honore crédo Achivi hunc scéptrum patientúr poti!
[Nonius, s. v. poti pro potiri.]

NIPTRA.

This play probably follows the lines of the Νίπτρα ἢ Ὀδυσσεὺς ἀκανθοπλήξ of Sophocles. Telegonus, son of Ulysses by Circe, having been wrecked one dark night on the shore of Ithaca, enters unwittingly his father's house, where the old hero was resting after his many years of wandering. As in the Odyssey, the old nurse (I) bathes her master's feet (Νίπτρα = foot-bath), and recognises him by his winning address and his fair, soft skin (II, III). He talks with her as if he had only just returned from Troy, and not from that later wandering to the land of the Thesprotians, whither, after the Slaying of the Suitors, he journeyed in accordance with the command laid on him by Teiresias in the Νέκυια. He speaks of the rude boat he built (IV), and of his visit to the Cyclops of Aetna (V, VI). Warned by an oracle that danger awaited him at the hands of his son, Ulysses repels from his doors this new intruder, who calls him 'father.' Telegonus resists; and in the fray which follows he wounds Ulysses with his spear, tipped with the bone of a poisonous sea-fish. Ulysses is brought to the stage on a litter (VII), tortured with pain from his wound. And now the mystery is cleared up. The stranger is indeed his son, and the fatal weapon has been put in his hand by the jealous Circe (VIII). Ulysses recognises the fulfilment of the warning, and resigns himself to death (IX).

¹ *Frugum* = Phrygum.

I.

Gédo tuum pedém mi, lymphis flávis flavum ut púl-
    verem
mánibus isdem, quíbus Ulixi saépe permulsi, ábluam
lássitudinémque minuam mánuum mollitúdine.
[Aul. Gell. 2. 26.]

II.

Lénitudo orátionis, móllitudo córporis.
[Cic. Tusc. Disp. 5. 16.]

III.

Páriter te esse erga íllum video, ut íllum ted ergá scio.
[Nonius, s. v. pariter.]

IV.

Nec úlla subscus[1] cóhibet compagem álvei,
sed súta limo et spárteis serílibus[2] . . .
[Festus, s. vv. subscudes : serilia.]

V.

Inde Aétnam montem advénio in scruposám specum.
[Nonius, s. v. specus, fem.]

VI.

    aetate íntegra
feróci íngenio, fácie protervá virum . . .
[Aul. Gell. 13. 30 (29). 3.]

VII.

Ulixes. Pedetémptim ac sedató nisu,
    ne súccussu arripiát maior
    dolor.

---

[1] *Subscus* = 'tenon' or 'dovetail.'
[2] *Sĕrilia* (sero-ui) = 'ropes,' made from *spartum*, a sort of broom.

Chorus. Tu quóque, Ulixes, quamquam graviter
cernimus ictum, nimis paéne animo es
mollí, qui consuetús in armis
aevom agere . . .

Ulixes. Retinéte, tenete! opprímit ulcus:
nudáte! heu miserum me, éxcrucior!
operíte; abscedite iám iam!
mittíte: nam attrectatu ét quassu
saevom ámplificatis dolórem.
[Cic. *Tusc. Disp.* 2. 21.]

VIII.

Barbáricam pestem súbinis nostris óptulit[1],
nová figura fáctam, commissam ínfabre.
[Nonius. *s. v.* infabre – foede.]

IX.

Cónquerí fortúnam adversam nón lamentarí decet:
íd viri est offícium, fletus múliebri ingenio ádditus.
[Cic. *l. c. supr.*]

[1] *Subinis*, see *sup.* p. 40. The word, which has various forms '*sybinis*' and '*sibunis*' is described (Fest. 336 M) as 'telum venabuli simile.'

TEUCER.

The opening of the play sets before us the aged Telamon exhausted by fruitless wanderings in search of tidings about Ajax and Teucer (I), and the Salaminian matrons in mourning for their lost sons (II). When Teucer appears on the scene without his brother or the young Eurysaces, he is received by his father with the most furious denunciation (III): the effect of the words being studiously heightened by the frequent recurrence of the sibilant *s* (sigmatismus), and the *homoeoteleuta*. Teucer in his reply describes the despatch of the fleet from Troy by the reluctant Agamemnon (IV, ex inc. inc. frag. XLVI, Ribb.). The ships set sail: Teucer commands the Thessalian contingent, as well as his own vessels (V). The voyage begins in the sunlight, among the sporting dolphins (VI, VII, inc. fab. XLIV, XLV, Ribb.): but at sundown the storm bursts on them (VIII, IX); and in the confusion Eurysaces is lost to sight. Yet Telamon admits no excuse, and refuses to listen to Teucer till his grandson is restored to him. The old man is described as plunged in grief, and brooding on Teucer's guilt (XI), who, however, is not wanting in friends to speak for him (XII), and to be hopeful of a reconciliation (XIII). But all is in vain! How Teucer quits his country to found a new home in the Cyprian Salamis is told by Horace (*Od.* 1. 7. 21 foll.): but the only reference to this among the fragments of Pacuvius is the famous line, the original of which appears in Aristoph. *Plut.* 1151 πατρὶς γάρ ἐστι πᾶσ' ἵν' ἂν πράττῃ τις εὖ (XIV, ex inc. inc. fab. XLIX, Ribb.).

I.

Postquám defessus pérrogitandod ádvenas
[fuit] de gnatis, néque quemquam invenít sciam . . .
[Priscian, 4. 634 P, *s. v.* scius.]

II.

Quae désiderio alúmnum, paenitúdine,
squalé scabreque, incúlta vastitúdine . . .
[Nonius, *s. v.* paenitudinem.]

III.

Ségregare abs te aúsu's aut sine íllo Salaminam íngredi,
néque paternum aspéctum es veritus, quom aétate exacta
indigem
liberum lacerásti orbasti extínxti, neque fratrís necis
néque eius nati párvi qui tibi in tutelam est tráditus—
[Cic. *De Orat.* 2. 46.]

IV.

. . inter se strépere aperteque ártem obterero extíspicum:
sólvere imperát secundo rúmore aversáque avi.
[Cic. *De Div.* 1. 16.]

V.

mihi classem imperat
Théssalam nostrámque in altum ut próperiter dedúcerem.
[Nonius, s. v. properiter = celeriter.]

VI.

Nérei repándirostrum incúrvicervicúm pecus.
[Quintil. Inst. Orat. 1. 5. 67.]

VII.

Síc profectióne laeti píscium lascíviam
íntuentur, néc tuendi cápere satietás potest.
ínterea prope iam óccidente sóle inhorrescít mare,
ténebrae condúplicantur, noctisque ét nimbum obcaecát
    nigror,
flámma inter nubés coruscat, caélum tonitru cóntremit.
grándo mixta imbrí largifico súbita praecípitans cadit,
úndique omnes vénti erumpunt, saévi existunt túrbines,
férvit aestu pélagus.
[Cic. De Div. 1. 14.]

VIII.

Rápide retro citróque percito aéstu praecipitém ratem
réciprocare, undaéque e gremiis súbicetare adílígere...
[Festus, s. v. reciprocare.]

IX.

... ármamentum strídor, flictus navium,
strépitus fremitus clámor tonitruum ét rudentum síbilus...
[Serv. in Verg. Aen. 1. 87.]

X.

Haúd sinam quidquám profari príus quam accepso quód
    peto.
[Nonius, s. v. accepso = accipio.]

XI.

Profúsus gemitu, múrmure 'occisti' ántruat.

[Festus, *s. v.* profusus.]

XII.

Nós illum interea próliciendo própitiaturós facul rémur.

[Nonius, *s. v.* facul = faciliter.]

XIII.

Nam Teúcrum regi sápsa res restíbiliet.

[Festus, *s. v.* sapsa = ipsa.]

XIV.

... pátria est ubicunque ést bene.

[Cic. *Tusc. Disp.* 5. 37.]

FABULA PRAETEXTA.

PAULUS.

The play deals with the exploits of the consul, L. Aemilius Paulus, the conqueror of the Macedonian king Perseus at Pydna, B.C. 168. Another notable character is introduced, the young Scipio Nasica, who fought on the heights of Mount Olympus with Milon, one of the generals of Perseus, and forced his way over the dizzy pass (I). We see Paulus on the morning of the battle sacrificing to Jupiter, from whom, through Ascanius, the gens Aemilia traced its descent (II). We see the Roman and Macedonian armies in the thick of the fight (III). An episode in the battle is the exploit of young Marcus, son of the old Cato, who was Censor in B.C. 184. Marcus lost his sword in the struggle, and fearing the disgrace which would fall on his honoured father if his son was found without a sword, he prays to Jupiter for instant aid (IV), and after strenuous efforts recovers his lost weapon.

I.

Quã víx caprigeno géneri gradilis gréssio est.

[MACROB. *Sat.* 6. 5. 14.]

II.

Patér supreme, nóstra progeníí patris.

[AUL. GELL. 9. 14, progenii a progenies.]

III.

Nivít sagittis, plúmbo et saxis grándinat.

[NONIUS, s. v. nivit pro ninguit.]

IV.

Núnc te obtestor, célere saucto súbveni censório!

[NONIUS, s. v. celere pro celeriter.]

CAECILIUS STATIUS.
(219-166 A.C.)

FABULAE PALLIATAE.

ASOTUS.

A YOUNG profligate tells the story, how he had surreptitiously introduced his mistress into his father's house (I). The father seems to have announced to some friend his intention of cutting off his son's allowance. 'Then he will borrow,' says the friend. 'Let him, for aught I care!' replies the father (II). The familiar character of the parasite is next introduced, as a regular 'barathrum macelli' (Hor. *Ep.* 1. 15. 31) (III). He has been kicked out of the club of boon-companions (IV); and reproaches his patron with his cruel indifference.

I.

                    námque ego
duábus vigiliís transactis dúco desubitó domum.

[NONIUS, *s. v.* desubito.]

II.

'Ad amícos curret mútuatum.' 'Mútuet
mea caúsa!'

[NONIUS, *s. v.* mutuet.]

III.

Iam dúdum depopulát macellum . . .

[NONIUS, *s. v.* populat.]

IV.

Meritíssimo hic me ciécit ex hac décuria.

[NONIUS, s. v. meritissimo.]

V.

Nihílne, nil tibi´ésse quod edim!

[NONIUS, s. v. edim pro edam.]

HYMNIS.

An angry father purchased a Milesian slave-girl, and made her over to one of his own friends, in order to 'block the pass in the way of his son,' who is in love with her (I . The youth evidently tries to stop the bargain that is being made with the *leno*; however, he is plainly told that to succeed in love one *must* be supplied with 'the sinews of war' (II). He seeks the advice of a confidential slave, whose counsel to him is, not to attempt a Quixotic combat, 'with a sword against a brass caldron' (III). But the young man is not convinced: his motto is 'a short life and a merry one.' Leave the old man to drag out his years 'drop by drop' to the very end! (IV, V).

I.

habes
Milétidam: ego illam huic déspondebo, et gnáto saltum
    obsípiam.

[DIOMED. p. 387 P. s. v. obsipio = obsaepio.]

II.

Desíne blanditiae.¹ núgas blateras, níhil agit
in amóre inermus.

[NONIUS, s. v. blaterare.]

III.

Macháera quin licitári adversum ahénum coepistí sciens?

[NONIUS, s. v. licitari = pugnare.]

¹ gen. sing., as 'desine querelarum' Hor. *Od.* 2. 9. 17.

IV.

Míhi sex menses sátis sunt vitae, séptimum Orco spóndeo.
[Cic. *De Fin.* 2. 7.]

V.

Síne suam senectútem ducat úsque ad senium sórbilo.
[Festus, p. 339 M. *s. v.* senium.]

PLOCIUM.

A SPECIAL interest attaches to this comedy, because Aul. Gellius (2. 23) takes occasion, by comparing it with the original play of Menander, to show the great inferiority of the Latin poet. The title is obscure: some have suggested that it is the actual name of the heroine; others, with better reason, render it 'Ringlet,' or 'Necklace'—something, at any rate, which serves as a material piece of evidence in the dénouement of the play. The plot is probably somewhat as follows: Two families live near together on friendly terms. The head of one of these is an elderly husband, smarting under the tyranny and jealous suspicion of his ugly but richly-dowered wife, Crobyle, who has compelled him to part with his dangerously attractive waiting-maid, and coarsely boasts of her success. In the bitterness of his soul he tells the story to his crony; and they pass very uncomplimentary remarks on the haughty and repulsive dame (I–III). Crobyle's son was betrothed to a daughter of the other family; and the marriage was about to take place, when the startling news is brought that the girl has given birth to a child. The marriage is hastily postponed (IV); and we gather from the corresponding play of Menander that Crobyle urges her son to forget his old love, and to marry a rich relation. But the unfortunate girl, who has been repudiated, has a faithful friend in her slave Parmeno. He gains the confidence of the young man, and they discuss various views of life— how it is money which covers 'the multitude of sins' (V); how old age brings with it many things one would rather not see (VI); how one must make the best of bad bargains (VII, VIII). Then Parmeno begins to calculate back the months before the birth of this child; and he reminds the young man of a certain night, when he had been in the company of a fair young stranger, whom

he had not recognised (IX XI). And we may suppose that the
'Necklace' somehow turns out to be the proof of his own father-
hood of the child, whose birth seemed to have ruined his hopes.
Evidently all difficulties were surmounted, and Parmeno gained
his freedom for his success (XII).

I.

. . . Is démum miser est quí suam aerumnám nequit
óccultare fóris: ita uxor meá forma et factís facit,
étsi taceam, támen indicium meaé quae, nisi dotem,
    omnia
quae nólis habét. qui sapít de me díscet,
quí quasi ad hostis cáptus liber sérvio salva úrbe atque
    arce.
dum éius mortem inhio, égomet inter vívos vivo mórtuus.
quaé mihi quidquid plácet eo privatum ít me ser-
    vatám velim?
éa me clam se cúm mea ancilla aít consuetum. id me
    árguit:
íta plorando orándo instando atque óbiurgando me óp-
    tudit,
eam utí venderém. nunc credo ínter suás
aequális, cognátas, sermónem serít:
'quís vostrarúm fuit íntegra aetátula
quae hóc idem a viro
ímpetrarít suo, quod ego anus modo
efféci, paelice út meum privarém virum?'
haéc erunt concília hocedie: dífferor sermóne misere.
                           [AUL. GELL. *l. c.*]

II.

'Sed túa morosane úxor quaeso est?' 'Quám, rogas?'
'Qui tándem?' 'Taedet méntionis, quaé mihi

ubi domum adveni ac sédi. extemplo sávium
dat iéiuna anima.' 'Níl peccat de sávio:
ut dévomas volt quód foris potáveris.'

[Aul. Gell. *l. c.*]

III.

Placére occepit gráviter postquam emórtuast!

[Nonius, *s. v.* graviter = multum.]

IV.

Abi íntro atque istaec aúfer, si tamen hódie extollat
núptias.

[Nonius, *s. v.* extollere = differre.]

V.

. . . is demum ínfortunatúst homo,
paupér qui educit ín egestatem líberos:
cui fórtuna et res núda est, continuó patet.
nam opulénto famam fácile occultat fáctio.

[Aul. Gell. *l. c.*]

VI.

Edepól, senectus, sí nil quicquam alíud viti
adpórtes tecum, cúm advenis, unum íd sat est,
quod diú vivendo múlta quae non vólt videt.

[Cic. *Cat. Mai.* 8. 25.]

VII.

Potíre quod dant, quándo optata nón danunt.

[Nonius, *s. v.* danunt = dant.]

VIII.

Vivás ut possis, quándo non quis út velis.

[Donat. *in Ter. Andr.* 4. 5. 10.]

IX.

'Sóletne mulier décimo mense párere?' 'pol nonó
quoque.
étiam septimo átque octavo.'

[AUL. GELL. 3. 16.]

X.

Pudébat credo cómmemoramentúm stupri.

[NONIUS, s. v. commemoramentum.]

XI.

Properátim in tenebris ístuc confectum ést opus.

[NONIUS, s. v. properatim.]

XII.

'Libérne es?' 'non súm, verum inibi est . . .'

[NONIUS, s. v. inibi = mox.]

The comments made by Gellius (2. 23) are as follows: '*Caecili
Plocium legebamus; handquaquam mihi et qui aderant displicebat.
Libitumst Menandri quoque Plocium legere, a quo istam comoediam
verterat. Sed enim postquam in manus Menander venit, a principio
statim, di boni, quantum stupere atque frigere quantumque mutare a
Menandro visus est! Diomedis hercle arma et Glauci non dispari
magis pretio existimata sunt. Accesserat dehinc lectio ad eum locum
in quo maritus senex super uxore dicite atque deformi querebatur,
quod ancillam suam, non inscito puellam ministerio et facie haut
inliberali, coactus erat venundare, suspectam uxori quasi pelicem.
Nihil dicam ego quantum differat: versus utrimque eximi iussi et aliis
ad iudicium faciundum exponi. Menander sic:*

ἐπ' ἀμφότερα νῦν ἡ 'πίκληρος ἡ καλὴ
μέλλει καθευδήσειν. κατείργασται μέγα
καὶ περιβόητον ἔργον· ἐκ τῆς οἰκίας
ἐξέβαλε τὴν λυποῦσαν ἣν ἐβούλετο,
ἵν' ἀποβλέπωσι πάντες εἰς τὸ Κρωβύλης
πρόσωπον, ᾗ τ' εὔγνωστος οὖσ' ἐμὴ γυνὴ
δέσποινα, καὶ τὴν ὄψιν ἣν ἐκτήσατο·

ὄνος ἐν πιθήκοις ἐστὶ δὴ τὸ λεγόμενον.
τοῦτο δὲ σιωπᾶν βούλομαι τὴν νύκτα τὴν
πολλῶν κακῶν ἀρχηγόν. οἴμοι Κρωβύλην
λαβεῖν ἔμ' ἑκκαιδεκατάλαντον, ὦ θεοί,
γύναιον οὖσαν πήχεως· εἶτ' ἐστὶ τὸ
φρύαγμά πως ὑπόστατον; μὰ τὸν Δία
τὸν Ὀλύμπιον καὶ τὴν Ἀθηνᾶν, οὐδαμῶς,
παιδισκάριον θεραπευτικὸν δὲ καὶ λόγου
τάχιον.

[Then follows the quotation from Caecilius I) 'is demum miser ... misere': after which Gellius proceeds] '*Praeter venustatem autem rerum atque verborum, in duobus libris nequaquam parem, in hoc equidem soleo animum attendere, quod quae Menander praeclare et opposite et facete scripsit, ea Caecilius ne qua potuit quidem conatus est enarrare, sed quasi minime probanda praetermisit et alia nescio quae inimica inculcavit; et illud Menandri de vita hominum media sumptum, simplex et verum et delectabile, nescio quo pacto omisit. Idem enim ille maritus senex cum altero sene vicino colloquens et uxoris locupletis superbiam deprecans haec ait,*

ἔχω δ' ἐπίκληρον Λάμιαν· οὐκ εἴρηκά σοι
τοῦτ'; εἶτ' ἄρ' οὐχί; κυρίαν τῆς οἰκίας
καὶ τῶν ἀγρῶν καὶ τῶν πατρῴων ἀντικρὺς
ἔχομεν, Ἄπολλον, ὡς χαλεπῶν χαλεπώτατον.
ἅπασι δ' ἀργαλέα 'στίν, οὐκ ἐμοὶ μόνῳ,
υἱῷ, πολὺ μᾶλλον θυγατρί.
πρᾶγμ' ἄμαχον λέγεις.

Caecilius vero hoc in loco ridiculus magis quam personae isti quam tractabat aptus atque conveniens videri maluit. Sic enim haec corrupit': [Then follows frag. II 'Sed tua morosane ... potaveris'] '*Quid de illo quoque loco in utraque comoedia posito existimari debeat manifestum est, cuius loci haec ferme sententia: filia hominis pauperis in pervigilio vitiata est. Ea res clam patrem fuit, et habebatur pro virgine. Ex eo vitio gravida mensibus exactis parturit. Servus bonae frugi cum pro foribus domus staret et propinquare partum erili filiae atque omnino vitium esse oblatum ignoraret, gemitum et ploratum audit puellae in puerperio enitentis: timet, irascitur, suspicatur, miseretur, dolet. Hi omnes motus eius affectionisque animi in Graeca quidem comoedia mirabiliter acres et illustres, apud Caecilium autem pigra istaec omnia et a rerum dignitate atque gratia vacua sunt. Post ubi idem servus percontando quod acciderat repperit, has aput Menandrum versus facit:*

> ὦ τρισκακοδαίμων, ὅστις ὢν πένης γαμεῖ
> καὶ παιδοποιεῖθ'. ὡς ἀλόγιστός ἐστ' ἀνήρ.
> ὃς μήτε φυλακὴν τῶν ἀναγκαίων ἔχει,
> μήτ' ἂν ἀτυχήσας εἰς τὰ κοινὰ τοῦ βίου
> ἐπαμφιέσθαι τοῦτο δύναται χρήμασιν,
> ἀλλ' ἐν ἀκαλύπτῳ καὶ ταλαιπώρῳ βίῳ
> χειμαζόμενος ζῇ, τῶν μὲν ἀνιαρῶν ἔχων
> τὸ μέρος ἁπάντων, τῶν δ' ἀγαθῶν οὐ δυνάμενος.
> ὑπὲρ γὰρ ἑνὸς ἀλγῶν, ἅπαντας νουθετῶ.

Ad horum autem sinceritatem veritatemque verborum an adspiraverit Caecilius consideremus. Versus sunt hi Caecili, trunca quaedam ex Menandro dicentis et consarcientis verba tragici tumoris: [Then follows frag. V 'is demum ... factio.'] *Itaque, ut supra dixi, cum haec Caecili seorsum lego neutiquam videntur ingrata ignavaque, cum autem Graeca comparo et contendo, non puto Caecilium sequi debuisse quod assequi nequiret.*

SYNEPHEBI.

In place of the ordinary lover, complaining of the severity or stinginess of his father, we have, as an amusing surprise, a young man sorely vexed at the embarrassing indulgence and generosity of his parent, and envying the lot of those happy sons who can enjoy to the full the delight of over-reaching a father's niggardliness (I. His comrade has an equally strange story to tell, for he announces as a prodigy demanding instant expiation, the discovery of a courtesan who refused to take money from her lover II). Another touch of unselfishness is given in Frag. III.

I.

In amóre suave est súmmo summáque ínopia
paréntem habere avárum, inlepidum, in líberos
diffícilem, qui te néc amet nec studeát tui.
aut tu íllum furto fállas aut per lítteras
avértas aliquod nómen aut per sérvolum

percútias pavidum, póstremo a parcó patre
quod súmas quanto díssipes libéntius!

. . . . . .

Quem néque quo pacto fállam nec quid inde aúferam
nec quém dolum ad eum aut máchinam commóliar
scio qúicquam : ita omnis meós dolos fallácias
praestígias praestrínxit commoditás patris.

[Cic. De Nat. Deor. 3. 29.]

II.

Pró deum, populárium omnium, ómnium adulescéntium
clámo, postulo, óbsecro, oro, plóro, atque imploró fidem!

. . . . . .

. . . in civitáte fiunt fácinora capitália;
nám ab amíco amánte argentum accípere meretrix nócnu
    volt.

[Cic. De Nat. Deor. 1. 6.]

III.

Serít arborés quae alterí saeclo prósint.

[Cic. Cat. Mai. 7. 24.]

EX INCERTIS FABULIS.

I.

' Trust me not at all, or all in all.'

Si cónfidentiam ádhibes, confide ómnia.

[Isidor. Orig. 10. 40. s. v. confidens.]

II.

' Love is still the Lord of all.'

    deúm qui non summúm putet,
aut stúltum aut rerum esse ímperitum exístumem:

cui ín manu sit, quém esse dementém velit,
quem sápere, quem sanári, quem in morbum ínici,
. . . . . .
quem cóntra amari, quem éxpeti, quem arcéssier.

[Cic. *Tusc. Disp.* 4. 32.]

III.
' The path of duty was the way to glory.'

Homo hómini deus est sí suum officiúm sciat.

[Symmachus, *Ep.* 9. 114.]

IV.
Wisdom under a ragged coat.

Saépe est etiam súb palliolo sórdido sapiéntia.

[Cic. *Tusc. Disp.* 3. 23.]

AQUILIUS.

(Fl. 174-154 A.C.)

BOEOTIA.

(AULUS GELLIUS (3. 3. 4) informs us that Varro assigned the 'Boeotia' to Plautus, basing his judgment on the passage here quoted as unmistakably in the Plautine style. But the allusion to the introduction of sun-dials (Pliny, *N. H.* 7. 60) seems to make the date between B. C. 174 and 154. It is evident from the passage in Pliny that Varro himself knew the date of their introduction, although he ascribes the passage to Plautus. The parasite found his own belly the best time-keeper!)

Ut illúm di perdant prímus qui horas répperit,
quique ádeo primus státuit hic solárium:
qui míhi comminuit mísero articulatím diem.
Nam unúm me puero vénter erat solárium
multo ómnium istorum óptimum et veríssimum:
ubi is nón monebat ésse, nisi cum níl erat?
nunc étiam cum est, non éstur, nisi solí lubet.
itaque ádeo iam oppletum óppidumst soláriis,
maiór pars populi ut áridi reptént fame.

[AUL. GELL. *l. c.*]

LICINIUS IMBREX.

(Fl. 200 A C.)

NEAERA.

(The identity in meaning of Imbrex and Tegula suggests that the author of the 'Neaera' is the P. Licinius Tegula, the writer of a sacred hymn ordered by the decemvirs, B.C. 200, to be sung in the streets of Rome by a chorus of nine maidens, so as to expiate certain prodigies [Livy 31. 12]. The fragment quoted of the 'Neaera' is the complaint of some dashing officer that his wife is not sufficiently distinguished by her name Neaera, which he proposes should be altered to Neriene, or Nerio, the spouse of the War-god.)

Nolo égo Neaeram té vocent, sed Nérienem,
cum quídem Mavorti es ín conubiúm data.
[AUL. GELL. 13. 23.]

TITINIUS.

(circ. 190-150 A.C.)

TOGATAE.

BARBATUS.

This title is said to have been a colloquial name for a sort of dumpy bucket; but the fragments throw no light on the title. An embroiderer [*Phrygio*] has done well for himself, and is leaving his employers (I. A cowardly bully is introduced, who runs up to his foe like a skirmisher (*veles*), and then—runs back (II). A joke is made upon the mincing pronunciation of young men of fashion, who are not strong enough to say the simplest word in full. 'Edepol,' 'medius fidius,' or even 'medi,' entail too much exertion. 'Edi' is the utmost they can do.

I.

. . frygió fui primó beneque id opus scívi ;
relíqui acus aciásque ero atque eraé nostrae . . .

[NONIUS, *s. v.* frygio.]

II.

ita spúrcus
animátur ira in proélium : velés eques recipít se
. . . . . . neque ferit quemquam hostem.

[NONIUS, *s. v.* veles.]

III.

id necessest?

Edi!

[Charis. 2. p. 178 P.]

FULLONIA.

Fullonia : sc. fabula, i. e. 'The play about the Fullers'; a set of men whose occupation afforded endless amusement to the Latin comic poets. Here the merriment seems to turn partly on the quarrelling between the Fullers and the Weaving-women, and partly on the bickering between a husband and wife. Probably a Fuller had married a Weaver with a bit of money of her own, and she chafes at his extravagance I). Her husband taunts her with the days of his courtship, and the change since then (II); to which she retorts with much self-satisfaction (III). Then there is quarrelling between the employer and his workmen (IV); and between the Fullers, 'who never get a holiday' (V), and the lazy women 'who take ten years over one gown' (VI). But the Weavers think themselves indispensable (VII, and laugh at the Fullers for their amphibious life (VIII). But both sides agree in despising the work of the delving rustic IX).

I.

Ego mé mandatam meó viro male árbitror,
qui rém disperdit ét meam dotém comest.

[Nonius, s. v. comest = comedit.]

II.

víderam ego te vírginem
fórmosam, formá ferocem, míhi esse sponso tuó superbam.

[Nonius, s. v. ferox.]

III.

Aspécta formam atque ós contempló meum.

[Nonius, s. v. contempla.]

IV.

Da pénsam lanam, quí non reddit témperi
putátam recte, fácito ut multetúr malo.

[Nonius, s. v. putare.]

V.

Nec nóctu nec diú licet fullónibus quiéscant.

[Nonius, s. v. diu=die.]

VI.

quae intrá decem
annós nequisti tógulam unam detéxere.

[Nonius, s. v. toga.]

VII.

Ni nós texamus, níl siet, fullónes, vobis quaésti.

[Nonius, s. v. quaesti.]

VIII.

Térra istaec est, nón aqua, ubi tu sólitu's argutarier
pédibus, cretam dúm compescis, véstimenta qui lavas.

[Nonius, s. v. argutari - subsilire.]

IX.

Homó formicae pól persimil est rústicus.

[Nonius, s. v. simile (?).]

SETINA.

'The lady of Setia'—a dull, secluded town overlooking the Pomptine Marshes. The good citizen, who does not like this swamp, would gladly have the water led from the Tiber to his town (I). It may be the same provincial wit who sees how far a little wisdom goes (II). But he is so cautious that he is afraid to marry (III); and his friend Caeso has to try and raise his pluck (IV). The young lady is so grand! (V) and such a paragon of perfection, that, in praising her, one must add 'without offence!' to avert the 'fascinatio' which waits on boasting (VI). For frag. VII see sup Barbatus III.

I.

Vidístin Tiberim? Vídi : qui illam dérivet, beáverit agrúm Setinum.

[SERV. *in Verg. Aen.* 11. 457.]

II.

Sapiéntia gubernátor navem tórquet, haut valéntia;
cocus mágnum ahenum, quándo fervit, paúla confutát
 trua.

[NONIUS, *s. v.* trua, &c.]

III.

Ipsús quidem hércle ducere eam sané nevult.

[NONIUS, *s. v.* nevult.

IV.

Accédo ad sponsam audácter, virgo núlla est talis Sétiae.

[NONIUS, *s. v.* tale (?).

V.

sed iam metuo hércle, Caeso, né nimis stulte fécerim,
qui ex tánta factióne atque opibus puéllam sum ausus
 ádgredi.

[NONIUS, *s. v.* factio = nobilitas.]

VI.

Paulá mea, amabo, pól tuam ad laudem áddito
'praefiscini.'

[CHARIS. 2. p. 189 P.]

VII.

An quía 'pol edepol' fábulare, 'edí' 'medi' meminísti?

[CHARIS. 2. p. 178 P.]

SEXTUS TURPILIUS.

(180-103 A.C.)

PALLIATAE.

EPICLEROS.

The Epicleros (Heiress) of Menander opened with a monologue. Turpilius has changed this to a dialogue between the slave Stephanio, and his uneasy young master, who rouses him from his bed to roam about with him at night (I). Stephanio protests against this caprice (II). The young man is pressed by his parents to marry the heiress: they assure him she is the best of wives for him (III); and the father hopes that their advice will not make a breach between them and their son (IV). It is difficult to fit in the remaining fragments. Perhaps the young man, wishing to wash his hands of the affair, appeals to the 'cognatus,' who by rights ought to marry the orphan heiress himself (V). The man is touched by the youth's sorrow (VI), and he acknowledges that the father's importunity has made his son 'rich in excuses' (VII). Finally, the relative seems to accept his duty (VIII), and the young man is relieved.

I.

St. Quaeso édepol quo ante lúcem te subitó rapis,
Ere, cum úno puero? Ph. Néqueo esse intus, Stéphanio,
St. Quid ita? Ph. ut solent, me cúrae somno ségregant
forásque noctis éxcitant siléntio.

[Priscian, *De Metris Com.* p. 1326 P.]

II.

Curréndum sic est, síc datur, nimium úbi sopóri sérvias
potiús quam domino.

[PRISCIAN, *l. c.*]

III.

Cum légere te optimum ésset atque aequíssimum
qua cum aetas degenda ét vivendum essét tibi.

[NONIUS, *s. v.* legere.]

IV.

. . . sperabám consilia nóstra dividiaé tibi,
cum aetás accesset, nón fore.

[NONIUS, *s. v.* dividia.]

V.

Ni Cállifonis núnc te miseret líberum.

[NONIUS, *s. v.* liberum, *gen. plur.*]

VI.

Sed néqueo ferre hunc diútius sic lámentari et cónqueri,
nec ésse suae parum óbsequellae . . .

[NONIUS, *s. v.* obsequela.]

VII.

Té quidem omniúm pater iam cópem causarúm facit.

[NONIUS, *s. v.* copem = copiosum.]

VIII.

Séd volo ut familia nostra officia fungatúr sua.

[NONIUS, *s. v.* fungi *cum accus.*]

LEUCADIA.

'THE Lady of Leucas' is a parody on the story of Sappho. The Phaon of the play is a hideous Lesbian boatman, who once ferried over the water Venus, disguised as an old woman, so evidently poor that Phaon excused her the fare. In recompense, she made him, in spite of his ugliness, the idol of all the women. One of the Lesbian damsels is so smitten that she turns from her old lover, and gives all her heart to Phaon. Her lover is amazed at her choice and at Phaon's grand airs I-IV). He attempts his former familiarities; but the girl repulses him (V), and makes desperate love to Phaon (VI), confessing her jealousy of some other woman (VII). Phaon being obdurate, the girl wanders to the desolate cliff (VIII), and, calling the gods and the winds to her aid, takes the Lovers' Leap (IX). Phaon orders out a boat (X), and the poor girl is rescued, very wet and cold (XI). But the charm is broken. Dorcium is reconciled to her old lover (XII). and holiday clothes are donned for the marriage (XIII).

I.

Quem olim óderat, sectátur ultro et détinet:
ille insólens autem út fastidit cárnifex!

[Nonius, s. v. insolens.]

II.

Víden tu Frygis incéssum? quam est confídens! di
istunc pérduint.

[Nonius, s. v. confidentia.]

III.

... víden ut fastidít mei?

[Nonius, 496. 18, genit. pro accus.]

IV.

Ei périi! víden ut ósculatur cáriem? num hilum illa
haec pudet?

[Nonius, s. v. caries.]

V

... 'ne me áttigas, atque aúfer
manum!' 'Heía, quem ferócula est!'

VI.

Intercapedine interficior, desiderio differor:
tu es mihi cupiditas, suavitudo et mei animi expectatio.

[Nonius, s. v. suavitudo.]

VII.

Verita sum, ne amoris causa cum illa limassis caput.

[Nonius, s. v. limare = coniungere.]

VIII.

me miseram terrent omnia,
maris scopuli, sonitus, solitudo, sanctitudo Apollinis.

[Nonius, s. v. sanctitudo.]

IX.

Te, Apollo sancte, fer opem, teque, omnipotens Neptune, invoco
vosque adeo venti! . . . nam quid ego te appellem, Venus?

[Cic. Tusc. Disp. 4. 34.]

X.

hortari coepi nostros ilico
ut celerent lembum.

[Nonius, s. v. lembus.]

XI.

ó utinam nunc apud ignem aliquem magnum adsidam!

[Nonius, s. v. apud = iuxta.]

XII.

Ante facta ignosco: mitto tristitatem, Dorcium.

[Nonius, s. v. tristitas.]

XIII.

Etiam amplius illam apparare condecet,
quandoquidem voti condemnata est . . .

[Nonius, s. v. damnare (voti).]

L. ACCIUS.

(170-86 A.C.)

TRAGOEDIAE.

ANDROMEDA.

The first fragment (I) of the Andromeda suggests that the sea-monster, to whom the princess was to be surrendered, came up from the depths month after month to devour his prey (I). Perhaps the Prologue introduced Cepheus or Cassiopea lamenting over the terrible floods and snow-storms which the angry Neptune had sent upon the land (II). The wrath of the gods can only be appeased by the sacrifice of Andromeda to the monster; and already Perseus has promised to be her champion (III); but he is baffled by the hopelessness of the task and ashamed at his own weakness (IV). Andromeda is chained in a narrow, circumscribed spot [*templum*], heaped up with dead men's bones (V), as she herself describes it (VI, VII). When Cepheus promises the hand of Andromeda to her rescuer, Perseus assures him this gracious act will not be wasted (VIII). By-and-by, Cepheus repents his promise (IX, ex inc. inc. fab. CIII, Ribb.): he professes that he cannot bear to part with the darling of his old age (X). But Perseus will not give up his love; and if her father seeks to part them, he may as well slay them both (XI).

I.

Qua Lúna circlos ánnuo in cursu ínstitit.

[Nonius. *s. v.* circulus.]

II.

Cum nínxerit caelóstium molém mihi.

[Priscian, 10. p. 882 P. ninguo.]

III.

Nísi quid tua facúltas nobis túlat opem, pereám!

[Macrob. De Diff. Gr. et Lat. verbi.]

IV.

Nec quí te adiutem invénio : hortari píget, non pro desse id pudet.

[Nonius, s. v. piget, pudet.]

V.

Immáne te habet témplum obvallatum óssibus.

[Nonius, s. v. immane.]

VI.

Mísera obvalla sáxo sento, paédore alguque ét fame.

[Nonius, s. v. algu = algore.]

VII.

Quí neque terraest dátus, nec cineris caúsa unquam evasít vapos.

[Nonius, s. v. vapor et vapos.]

VIII.

Quód beneficium haut stérili in segete, réx, te obsesse intélleges.

[Nonius, s. v. seges = terra.]

IX.

Meminístin te spondére mihi gnatám tuam?

[Varro, L. L. 6. 72.]

X.

Alui éducavi : id fácite gratum ut sít seni.

[Nonius, s. v. alere et educare.]

I

XI.

Nosque út sevorsum divídos leto ófferes.

[NONIUS, *s. v.* dividos = separatos.]

ARMORUM IUDICIUM.

IN this drama Accius omits the motive which Pacuvius introduces from the Cyclics: that the decision is referred to the Trojan captives. But in their main outlines the two plays are similar. Though the heroes are eager, one and all, to succeed to the inheritance of the Arms of Achilles (I), Ajax will not take part in the tournament, nor be pitted against Ulysses II. III. The decision is to turn, he says, on the ruling (*dictio*), which had been laid down by Thetis (or, perhaps, by Calchas), that the Arms may be given only to a man like Achilles. And Ajax puts his claim on two grounds: 1, relationship—for Ajax and Achilles had both the same grandsire; and, 2, his own deeds of valour (IV, ex inc. inc. fab. XXX Ribb.). He recounts the feigned madness of Ulysses at the beginning of the war; the consequences of which were averted only by the sagacity of Palamedes (V, ex inc. inc. fab. XXXI Ribb.). Ironically, he pretends to credit Ulysses with his own great achievements (VI, ex inc. inc. fab. XXXII Ribb.). After his fit of frenzy has passed, Ajax thinks with grief of the sorrow which will fall upon Telamon (VII): he demands a sight of Eurysaces, whom Tecmessa had removed, with a caution which was at least excusable (VIII); and he questions his wife as to all that took place during his fit of madness; though she can scarcely dare to answer freely (IX). Then comes the famous prayer of Ajax for his son (X, Soph. *Aj.* 550). The Chorus is in great anxiety about the fate of the mighty champion of Greece (XI), whose loss of Minerva's friendship is deplored (XII). The play ends with the reconciliation between Teucer and the Atridae, by the intervention of Ulysses (XIII). 'Let all old feuds be buried in a general amnesty!' (XIV).

I.

Sed íta Achílli armis ínclutis vescí studet
ut cúncta opima lévia iam prae illís putet.

[NONIUS, *s. v.* vesci.]

II.

... quid est cúr componere aúsis mihi te aut mé tibi?
[Nonius, s. v. componere.]

III.

... nám tropaeum férre me a fortí viro
púlchrum est: si autem víncar, vinci a táli nullum mi
ést probrum.
[Macrob. Sat. 6. 1. 56.]

IV.

Apérte fatur díctio, si intéllegas;
talí dari arma, quális qui gessít fuit.
iubét, potiri sí studeamus Pérgamum.
quem ego mé profiteor ésse, mest aequúm frui
fratérnis armis míhique adiudicárier,
vel quód propinquus, vél quod virtuti aémulus.
[Rhet. Ad Herenn. 2. 26.]

V.

Cuius ípse princeps iúris iurandí fuit.
quod ómnes scitis, sólus neglexit fidem:
furere ádsimulare, né coiret, ínstitit.
quod ní Palamedi pérspicax prudéntia
istíus perspexit málitiosam audáciam,
fidé sacratae íus perpetuo fálleret.
[Cic. De Off. 3. 26.]

VI.

Vidí te, Ulixes, sáxo sternentem Héctora,
vidi tegentem clípeo classem Dóricam:
ego túnc pudendam trépidus hortabár fugam.
[Charis. 4. p. 252 P.]

VII.

Maiór erit luctus, cúm me damnatum aúdiet.
[Nonius, s. v. damnare.]

VIII.

Úbi cura est, ibi ánxitudo acérbast, ibi cunctátio,
cónsiliorum errátio et fortúnaest.

[Nonius, s. v. anxitudo.]

IX.

Hem, véreor plus quam fás est captivam híscere.

[Nonius, s. v. hiscere = loqui.]

X.

Virtúti sis par, díspar fortunís patris.

[Macrob. Sat. 6. 1. 58.]

XI.

In quó salutis spés supremas síbi habet summa exérciti.

[Nonius, s. v. exerciti.]

XII.

Nám non facile síne deum opera humána propria súnt
bona.

[Nonius, s. v. proprium = perpetuum.]

XIII.

Cur vétera tam ex alto áppetissis díscidia, Agamemno?

[Nonius, s. v. altum = vetus.]

XIV.

nóxitudo . . .
oblítteretur Pélopidarum, ac pér nos sanctescát genus.

[Nonius, s. v. noxitudo.]

ATREUS.

It is probable that the prologue to this play recounted the victory of Pelops over Oenomaus, the marriage of Hippodamia, and the birth of Atreus (I). Atreus, who is the true type of a despot (II), is bitterly incensed at the return of his brother Thyestes from exile, uninvited. Some signal punishment he must devise (III) for the man who had seduced his wife Aërope (IV, V, and had stolen the Golden Lamb, on which depended the prosperity of the kingdom (VI). Perhaps Atreus welcomed his brother with a suspicious cordiality, which would account for the warning against treachery, which Thyestes conveys to his sons who had accompanied him (VII, VIII). Thyestes is bidden, as a special honour, to a royal banquet at which no other guest might be present (IX). Some eye-witness describes the preparation of the horrid meal (X) by the hands of the inhuman Atreus, whose crime had thrown all his brother's misdeeds in the shade (XI). The Sun turns back his car, and the thunder rolls angrily, and terrifies the Chorus of Mycenean citizens (XII). After the meal, Thyestes enquires of his sons' welfare ; and, when Atreus shows him their hands and feet, he prays that he may be allowed to bury them. 'The sons are entombed in the sire' is the awful enigma that is hurled at him by Atreus (XIII). The unhappy father denounces his brother's broken faith, which Atreus denies he ever plighted (XIV) ; and aghast at the horrors in which he had taken an unconscious part (XV), Thyestes feels that all his hopes of advancement are ruined, and it only remains to him to hide himself in exile (XVI).

I.

Simul ét Pisaea praémìa arrepta á socru possedit suo.
[PRISCIAN, 6. p. 698 P. socrus *masc.*]

II.

óderint
dum métuant.
[SENECA, *De Ira* 1. 20. 4 ; CIC. *De Off.* 1. 28.]

III.

Iterúm Thyestes Átreum adtrectatum ádvenit,
iterúm iam adgreditur me ét quietum exsúscitat :
majór mihi moles, maíus miscendúmst malum!
qui illíus acerbum cór contundam et cómprimam.
[CIC. *De Orat.* 3. 58.]

IV.

Qui nón sat habuit cóniugem illexe ín stuprum.
[Cic. De Nat. Deor. 3. 26.]

V.

. . . quod re in súmma summum esse árbitror
períclum, matres cónquinari régias.
contáminari stírpem ac miscerí genus.
[Cic. l. c.]

VI.

Adde húc quod mihi porténto caelestúm pater
prodígium misit régni stabilimén mei,
agnum ínter pecudes aúrea clarúm coma
quondám Thyestem clépere ausum esse e régia.
qua in re ádiutricem cóniugem cepít sibi.
[Cic. l. c.]

VII.

. . . vigilándumst semper: múltae insidiae súnt bonis.

VIII.

Íd quod multi invídeant multique éxpetant inscítiast
póstulare, nísi laborem súmma cum cura écferas.
[Cic. Pro Sest. 48; Pro Planc. 24.]

IX.

ne cúm tyranno quísquam epulandi grátia
accúmbat mensam aut eándem vescatúr dapem.
[Nonius, s. v. vesci.]

X.

cóncoquit
partém vapore flámmae. veribus ín foco
lacérta tribuit.
[Nonius, s. v. lacerta neutr. gen.]

XI.

Epulárum fictor, scélerum fratris délitor.

[PRISCIAN, 9. p. 873 P. delitor a delinere.]

XII.

Sed quid tonitru turbída torvo
concússa repente aequóra caeli
sensímus sonere?

[NONIUS, s. v. sonere.]

XIII.

ATREUS. natís sepulchro ipse ést parens.

[CIC. De Off. 1. 28.]

XIV.

THYEST. fregistí fidem.
ATREUS. Néque dedi neque do infideli cuíquam ...

[CIC. De Off. 3. 28.]

XV.

Ípsus hortatúr me frater út meos malís miser
mánderem natós.

[CIC. Tusc. Disp. 4 36.]

XVI.

Égone Argivum impérium attingam aut Pélopia dignér
  domo?
quó me ostendam? quód templum adeam? quem óre
  funesto alloquar?

[NONIUS, s. v. dignatus.]

EPIGONI—ERIPHYLA.

WHEN Eriphyle, bribed by the gift of a necklace, had sent her husband Amphiaraus forth to certain death, in the war of the Seven against Thebes, the duty of punishing the treacherous wife devolved upon her sons Alcmaeon and Amphilochus. When, ten years later, the Epigoni gathered their avenging army again at Thebes, the oracle promised them victory if Alcmaeon should be chosen leader. His stern duty bade him remain at home, but Eriphyle, bribed by Thersander and Polynices, sends her son to the battle. Thebes is taken, and the heroes return. In obedience to his father's mandate, and in compliance with the oracle, Alcmaeon slays his mother; and, like Orestes, he becomes at once the victim of the avenging Furies. The play opens with an altercation between Alcmaeon and Thersander, who urges the young hero, on whom so many eyes are fixed, to undertake the command (I): his own Argives are impatient for the fray (II). Alcmaeon commends coolness and deliberation (III): Thersander appears to philosophise upon the temperament of the brave man (IV). Amphilochus is now seen on the stage (V). He seems to have inherited something of his father's gift of divination. Alcmaeon, who burns to avenge his father, speaks, apparently, of some importunate apparition, which urges him on (VI): he cannot understand his brother's plea of delay (VII). The ghost of Amphiaraus recounts the treachery of his wife (VIII, ex inc. inc. fab. LXXVII Ribb.); at whose bidding he went forth, with death full in view (IX, ex inc. inc. fab. LXXVIII). Before the final catastrophe, Demonassa, Eriphyle's daughter, has a foreboding of her mother's danger, and Eriphyle seeks to understand her anxiety (X, XI). Alcmaeon braces himself to the terrible deed. There is his mother, still wearing the fatal necklace (XII ! He approaches her: she denounces his impiety (XIII, XIV); but the deed is done. Alcmaeon must seek expiation by burnt-offerings (XV), or by cleansing flood (XVI). But the curse of bloodguiltiness is upon him, and he must fly from the land.

I.

quibus oculis quísquam nostrum póterit illorum óptui vúltus. quos iam ab ármis anni pórcent . . . ?

[Nonius, s. v. porcet = prohibet.]

II.

Et nónne Argivos frémere bellum et vélle vim vulgúm vides?

[Nonius, s. v. vulgus. *masc. gen.*]

III.

Ita ínperitus stúpiditate erúmpit se, inpos cónsili.

[Nonius, s. v. stupiditas.]

IV.

Sápimus animo, frúimur anima: síne animo anima est débilis.

[Nonius, s. v. animus et anima.]

V.

Sed iam Ámfilocum huc vadére cerno, et
nobis datur bona pausá loquendi
tempúsque in castra revórti.

[Charis. De Vers. Saturn.]

VI.

Quí, nisi genitorem úlso, nullum meís dat fínem míseriis.

[Nonius, s. v. ulso = ultus fuero.]

VII.

Fáteor; sed cur própter te haec pigrem aút huius dubitem párcere . . .

[Nonius, s. v. pigrare = retinere.]

VIII.

. . . avárum est mulierúm genus
. . . auro véndidit vitám viri.

[Cic. De Inv. 1. 50.]

IX.

prudens ét sciens
ad péstem ante oculos pósitam . . .

[Cic. Ad Fam. 6. 6. 6.]

X.

Quid istúc, gnata unica, ést, Demonassa, óbsecro,
quod mé tanto expetens timidam e tecto excies?

[Charis. De Vers. Saturn.]

XI.

Elóquere propere ac meúm hunc pavorem expéctora.

[Nonius, s. v. expectorare.]

XII.

Séd quid cesso ire ád eam? em praesto est: cámo vide collúm gravem!

[Nonius, s. v. collus, masc. gen.]

XIII.

Viden út te inpietas stímulat nec moderát metus?

[Nonius, s. v. modero, active.]

XIV.

Age age ámolire, amítte, cave vestem áttigas!

[Nonius, s. v. attigas = contigas.]

XV.

Núnc pergam ut suppliciis placans caélitum aras éxpleam.

[Nonius, s. v. supplicium = supplicatio.]

XVI.

Ápud abundantem ántiquam amnem et rápidas undas Ínachi.

[Nonius, s. v. amnis, femin. gen.]

EPINAUSIMACHE.

THIS title represents the μάχη ἐπὶ ταῖς ναῦσι of Hom. *Il.* 13; but, in the drama of Accius, the death of Patroclus seems to precede the fighting at the ships. Patroclus has fallen, and Achilles burns for revenge. He is reminded that he has no armour in which to fight; to which he replies that his courageous spirit is armour enough for him (I). His friends seek to dissuade him from his rash venture (II): he has to remember that his very reputation is at stake (III .

But Achilles cares only, he says, for the approval of the good (IV): he will shake off this paralysing sorrow, which is no better than the helpless grief of (say) Patroclus' horse over his master V. When Thetis comes with her Nereids and warns her son of his approaching doom, his mind can take in no other thought except that of vengeance (VI): his friend's corpse is more in his eyes than whole heaps of slain (VII). When he is armed for the fray, the battle that begins at the ships spreads to the Scamander, and from thence to the town; and none can resist this terrible warrior VIII, IX), who is like a devouring flame in the pine forest (X, cp. *Il.* 20. 490 foll.). He returns from the field proud of his achievement (XI). His meeting with Hector was like that of two war-gods contending (XII): nor can Achilles conceal his satisfaction in thinking that, though he has restored to Priam his son's corpse, there is no more a Hector in the Trojan host (XIII, inc. fab. XIII Ribb.).

I.

Ut núnc cum animatus íero satis armátus sum.

[Nonius, *s. v.* anima = ira.]

II.

At cóntra, quantum obfúeris si victús sies
consídera, et quo révoces summam exérciti.

[Nonius, *s. v.* exerciti, *gen. sing.*]

III.

Quod sí procedit néque te neque quemquam árbitror
tuae paéniturum laúdis, quam ut servés vide.

[Nonius, *s. v.* paeniturum.]

IV.

Probís probatum pótius quam multis fore.

[Nonius, *s. v.* pauci boni.]

V.

Item ác maestitiam mútam infantum quádrupedum...

[Nonius, *s. v.* mutus.]

VI.

Mórs amici súbigit, quod mi est sénium multo acérrimum.

[Nonius, s. v. senium = mala aetas.]

VII.

Nec pérdoliscit flígi socios, mórte campos cóntegi.

[Nonius, s. v. fligi = adfligi.]

VIII.

Ab clásse ad urbem téndunt, nec quisquám potest fulgéntium armum armátus ardorem óptui.

[Nonius, s. v. armum, gen. plur.]

IX.

Incursio ita erat acris.

[Charis. 1. p. 93 P.]

X.

Lucifera lampade ábietem exurát Iovis . . .

[Priscian, 6. p. 695 P. Iovis, casu nominativo.]

XI.

Nam Scamandriam úndam salso sánctam obtexi sánguine, átque acervos álta in amni córpore explevi hóstico.

[Nonius, s. v. amnis, gen. fem.]

XII.

Mavórtes armis duó congressos créderes.

[Charis. 1. p. 101 P. s. v. duo.]

XIII.

Immo enim vero córpus Priamo réddidi, Hectorem ábstuli.

[Cic. Tusc. Disp. 1. 44.]

MEDEA SIVE ARGONAUTAE.

Jason has carried off Medea and the golden fleece from Colchis, and Aeetes is in hot pursuit of the fugitives. When the herdsmen on the banks of the Hister see the large bulk of the Argo—the first ship that has ever appeared there—they take it to be a huge sea monster (I). As the vessel comes nearer they espy the young sailors aboard, and hear their melodious songs (II); and absorbed in wonder they leave their herds untended (III).

Jason and Medea explain to this simple folk how ships came to be built: how, as men gradually left their savage ways (IV), they felt the desire to see the world, and ships must be made to brave the perils of the deep (V). The Scythian king looks with awe on the famous sorceress (VI). Medea begins to be suspicious of Jason, and there is a tone of bitterness in her allusion to all she has done for him—taming the fire-breathing bulls (VII); and quelling the dragon, and the warriors that rose from the furrow (VIII, ex inc. inc. fab. XCIV)—without her aid Jason would have been a lost man (IX). Aeetes then appears upon the stage, lamenting the death of his sons (X); his sorrows being echoed by the Chorus in a Canticum (XI). The terrible murder by Medea of one of her brothers, to gain time when she and Jason were being pursued, may belong to this drama (XII, ex inc. inc. fab. XCIII).

I.

tánta moles lábitur
fremibúnda ex alto ingénti sonitu et spíritu,
prae se úndas volvit. vórtices vi súscitat.
ruít prolapsa, pélagus respargít redlat.
ita dum ínterruptum crédas nimbum vólvier,
dum quód sublime véntis expulsúm rapi . . .
saxum aút procellis vél globosos túrbines
exístere ictos úndis concursántibus :
nisi qúas terrestris póntus strages cónciet,
aut fórte Triton fúscina everténs specus
suptér radices pénitus undante ín freto
molem éx profundo sáxeam ad caelum erigit.
[Cic. *De Nat. Deor.* 2. 35.]

II.

Sicút inciti atque álacres rostris pérfremunt
delphíni, item alto múlcta Silvaní melo
consímilem ad auris cántum atque audítúm refert.

[Cic. *l. c.*]

III.

Vagánt, pavore pécuda in tumulis déserunt.
A! qui nos pascet póstea?

[Nonius, *s. v.* pecuda.]

IV.

Primum éx immani víctum ad mansuetum ápplicans...

[Nonius, *s. v.* immane.]

V.

ut tristis túrbinum
toleráret hiemes, máre cum horreret flúctibus.

[Nonius, *s. v.* horridum.]

VI.

Tun día Medes. cúius aditum exspéctans pervixi úsque
adhuc?

[Nonius, *s. v.* aditus.]

VII.

Perite in stabulo frénos immitténs feris.

[Nonius, *s. v.* ferus.]

VIII.

Nón commemoro quod draconis saévi sopivi ímpetum,
nón quod domui vím taurorum et ségetis armataé manus.

[Charis. 5. p. 252 P.]

IX.

Exul inter hóstis, exspes éxpers desertús vagus.

[Nonius, *s. v.* exspes.]

X.

Perníci orbificor líberorum léto et tabificábili.

[Nonius, *s. v.* tabificabile.]

XI.

Fors dóminatur, neque quícquam ulli
proprium ín vitast.

[Nonius, s. v. proprium = perpetuum.]

XII.

postquam pater
ádpropinquat iámque paene ut cómprehendatúr parat,
púerum interea optrúncat membraque árticulatim dívidit,
pérque agros passím dispergit córpus : id ea grátia,
út, dum nati díssipatos ártus captarét parens,
ípsa interea effúgeret, illum ut maéror tardarét sequi,
síbi salutem ut fámiliari páreret parricídio.

[Cic. De Nat. Deor. 3. 26.]

MELEAGER.

Oeneus, father of Meleager, having neglected the due sacrifice to Diana, the goddess sent a huge wild-boar to ravage the harvest-fields of Calydon (I). Meleager had married Cleopatra, the type of the quiet housewife, the complete contrast to Atalanta, a daring huntress, who claims for women a full right to join in the chase (II). Far better that, than to be a husband's drudge! (III) Spartan maidens know how to use their womanhood! (IV. ex inc. inc. fab. CXI Ribb.) So when Meleager sallies forth to attack the boar, Atalanta joins him and boldly confronts the savage beast (V); her spear being the first to touch it. When Meleager has slain the monster, the country folk joyfully greet him (VI); and he gives the crown of victory and the skin of the boar to Atalanta (VII). But the sons of Thestius, the brother of Althaea, Meleager's mother, rob the maiden of her prize : and when she appeals to Meleager, he slays some of the robbers, and declares that the prize is hers alone (VIII), and that the men are but cowards (IX, ex inc. inc. fab. CXIII Ribb.). This bloodshed wakes the Erinnys of the family, and Althaea, half in terror for herself, and half in indignation at the death of the Thestiadae (X, XI), brings from its concealment the brand, with the preservation of which the life of Meleager was mysteriously bound up, and commits it to the flames (XII). Meleager, as the brand consumes, feels the curse working in him XIII, and Althaea, aghast at her doing, bids her servant use his best speed (XIV, XV) to go and quench the brand. But it is too late! The mother feels the indelible shame she has brought on herself XVI ; and Meleager resigns himself to death (XVII).

I.

. . . frugis próhibet pergrandéscere.

[Nonius, s. v. grandire.]

II.

Vagént ruspantes sílvas. sectantés feras.

[Nonius, s. v. ruspari = scrutari.]

III.

Quam invíta ancillans, dicto obediéns viri.

[Nonius, s. v. ancillari.]

IV.

Nihil hórum similest ápud Lacaenas vírgines,
quibus mágis palaestra Euróta sol pulvís labor
milítia studio est quám fertilitas bárbara.

[Cic. Tusc. Disp. 2 15.]

V.

Frígit *aper saetás* rubore ex óculis fulgens flámmeo.

[Nonius, s. v. frigit.]

VI.

Gaúdent currunt célebrant. herbam cónferunt donánt, tenent,
pró se quisque cúm corona clárum connectít caput.

[Nonius, s. v. herbam = palmam.]

VII.

Cuíus exuvias ét coronam huic múneravit vírgini.

[Nonius, s. v. munerare, *cum dat.*

VIII.

Rémanet gloria ápud me; exuvias dígnavi Atalantaé dare.

[Nonius, s. v. dignavi = dignum duxi.]

IX.

Vós enim, iuvenes, ánimum geritis múliebrem, illa virgó viri.

[Cic. De Off. 1. 18.]

X.

timida elíminor,
É clamore simul ac nota vóx ad auris áccidit.

[Nonius, s. v. eliminare.]

XI.

Heú! cor ira férvit caecum, améntia rapiór ferorque.

[Nonius, s. v. fervit.]

XII.

Eúm suae vitae finem ac fatis íternecioném fore
Méleagro, ubi tórris esset ínterfectus flámmeus.

[Nonius, s. v. torris.]

XIII.

Quae vástitudo haec aút unde invasít mihi?

[Nonius, s. v. vastitudo = horror.]

XIV.

Cave lássitudo póplitum cursúm levet.

[Nonius, s. v. levare = minuere.]

K

XV.

Labórem aut minuat ítiner ingressúm viae.

[NONIUS, *s. v.* itiner.]

XVI.

Qui erít qui non me spérnens, incílans probris,
sermóne indecorans túrpi fama dífferet?

[NONIUS, *s. v.* incilare.]

XVII.

Érat istuc viríle, ferre advórsam fortunám facul.

[NONIUS, *s. v.* facul.]

MYRMIDONES.

THE play opens with the despatch of the embassy sent to attempt a reconciliation between Achilles and Agamemnon (Hom. *Il.* 9). It also includes the going forth of Patroclus to battle. Antilochus, Nestor's son, the young friend of Achilles, seeks, even before the arrival of the embassy, to turn him from his obstinate purpose. But Achilles answers that his fixed resolve is not obstinacy but firmness (I). The ancient Phoenix admonishes his pupil (II); but Achilles defends himself (III), and expresses his readiness to leave Troy and return home (IV, cp. *Il.* 9. 356 foll.); and he upbraids Ajax for no longer espousing his cause or standing at his side (V). Antilochus and Patroclus seem to be pleading on behalf of some one—possibly Phoenix—whose freedom had given Achilles offence (VI): and the words of his rebuke are certainly severe (VII). As the news from the field grows more alarming, and the Myrmidons are impatient to take part in the fight, Patroclus tells Achilles the plain truth, that he will be looked upon as responsible for any disaster that may befall the Achaean host (VIII). It is doubtful whether this last fragment is to be referred to the 'Myrmidones' or to the 'Achilles'; if they are two distinct plays.

I.

Tu pértinaciam ésse, Antiloche, hanc praédicas,
ego pérvicaciam aío et ea me utí volo:

haec fórtis sequitur, íllam indocti póssident.
tu addís quod vitio est, démis quod laudí datur:
nam pérvicacem díci me esse et víncere
perfácile patior, pértinacem níl moror.

[Nonius, s. v. pervicacia, pertinacia.]

II.

Íram infrenes, óbstes animis, réprimas confidéntiam.

[Nonius, s. v. confidentia = temeritas.]

III.

Égo me non peccásse plane osténdam aut poenas súf-
feram.

[Nonius, s. v. sufferre.

IV.

Clássis trahere in sálum me et vela véntorum animae
immíttere . . .

[Nonius, s. v. anima = ventus.]

V.

Quódsi, ut decuit, stáres mecum aut meús te maestarét
dolor,
iám diu inflammári Atridae návis vidissént suas.

[Nonius, s. v. maestare.]

VI.

. Nolo équidem: sed tu huic quém scis quali in té siet
fidélitate, ob fídam naturám viri
ignósce.

[Nonius, s. v. fidelitas.]

VII.

Tua honéstitudo Dánaos decepít diu.

[Nonius, s. v. honestitudo.]

VIII.

Qua re ália ex crimine inimicorum effúgere possis. délica.

[NONIUS, s. v. delicare = explanare.]

OENOMAUS.

OENOMAUS, King of Pisa, father of the beautiful Hippodamia, having been warned that death would come to him from his son-in-law, kept at bay all his daughter's suitors by the condition that they should race against his famous team, and, if conquered, be beheaded. Pelops came to the ordeal, and at once won the heart of Hippodamia by his kingly beauty. The lovers bribe Myrtilus, the royal charioteer, to draw the linch-pin from the wheel, so that the car of Oenomaus was overthrown. Pelops wins Hippodamia, and puts his accomplice Myrtilus to death. Pelops, in the play, announces his intention of entering the lists (I); though he sees with horror the heads of the unsuccessful suitors at the palace gates (II). He assures Oenomaus that he need have no fear from the warning of the oracle (III), which seems to have been revealed to the king in the early hours of the morning, 'when dreams are true' (IV). But Oenomaus felt that some malign influence was sapping his power, like the undermining waters that fret the base of the cliff (V). Great preparations are made for the contest, and a solemn sacrifice to the gods performed (VI). Then the race begins, and as Oenomaus gallops forward, we may imagine that Pelops sends after him the warning cry that his hours are numbered (VII).

I.

Coniúgium Pisis pétere, ad te itiner téndere . . .

[NONIUS, s. v. itiner.]

II.

Hórrida honestitúdo Europae príncipum prima éx loco . . .

[NONIUS, s. v. honestitudo.]

III.

Ego ut éssem adfinis tibi, non ut te extínguerem.
tuam pétii gnatam : número te expugnát timor.

[Festus, etc., numero = nimium.]

IV.

Forte ánte auroram, rádiorum ardentum índicem,
cum e sómno in segetem agréstes cornutós cient,
ut rórulentas térras ferro fúmidas
proscíndant glebasque árvo ex molli exsúscitent . . .

[Nonius, s. v. segetem.]

V.

Sáxum id facit angústitatem, et súb eo saxo exúberans
scátebra fluviae rádit rupem.

[Nonius, s. v. angustitatem.]

VI.

Vos íte actutum atque ópere magno edícite
per úrbem, ut omnes qui árcem Alfeumque áccolunt
civés ominibus faústis augustam ádhibeant
favéntiam, ore obscéna dictu ségregent.

[Nonius, s. v. faventia : obscenum.]

VII.

Atque hánc postremam sólis usurám cape!

[Nonius, s. v. usura.]

PHILOCTETES.

In this play Accius seems to have borrowed freely from Aeschylus, while he follows the general outline of the Sophoclean drama, and introduces details from Euripides: as, for example, in the opening scene, where the *canticum* is sung by a chorus of sailors who have accompanied Ulysses and Diomede to Lemnos (I). Ulysses replies by describing, in similar verse, the island scenery, as he knew it long ago (II). A Lemnian comes on the stage, and Ulysses questions him about the abode of Philoctetes (III), and learns how he clothes and feeds himself (IV), and how wild and dangerous is his temper (V, VI). Philoctetes describes, either in monologue or to some friend, his painful sufferings (VII), his lonely home that rings with his cries (VIII), and his trust to his arrows for his daily food (IX); a use of weapons which, as a warrior, he despises (X). He espies and accosts Ulysses, whom he does not recognise, and whose arrival surprises him (XI); and, though he is ashamed to be found in his condition of savagery and squalor (XII), he conducts him to his cavern (XIII), and is drawn on to tell him the adventures of his companions in arms. He enquires about the Arms of Achilles, and bitterly regrets the award (XIV). The wily Ulysses seeks to win his confidence, and to gain possession of the coveted arrows. The arrival at this crisis of a Trojan embassy with tempting proposals, intending to conciliate Philoctetes and to rob him of his arrows, has half persuaded the hero (XV); but he remembers that it is a Phrygian Trojan who has been the source of all his woes (XVI). After a long struggle with conflicting feelings, the patriotism and self-respect of Philoctetes carry the day; and he turns aside from the temptations offered by the Trojans, and, in spite of his suffering (XVII) he accompanies the Greeks on board their ship.

I.

Inclúte, parva prodíte patria,
nomíne celebri claróque potens
pectóre, Achivis classíbus ductor,
gravis Dárdaniis gentíbus ultor.
Laértiade!

[APULEIUS, *De Deo Socr.* 24 : CIC. *Tusc. Disp.* 2. 10.]

II.

Lemnía praesto
litóra rara, et celsá Cabirum
delúbra tenes, mistéria quae

pristína castis concépta sacris . . .
Volcánia iam templá sub ipsis
collíbus in quos delátus locos
dicítur alto ab limíne caeli . . .
nemus éxpirante vapóre vides,
unde ígnis cluet mortálibus clam
divísus : cum dictús Prometheus
clepsísse dolo poenásque Iovi
fato éxpendisse suprémo.
[Varro, *L. L.* 7. 11 M. : Cic. *Tusc. Disp.* 2. 10.]

III.

. . . ubi habet? úrbe agrone?
[Nonius. *s. v.* habere = habitare.]

IV.

Confígit tardus céleris stans volátilis.
pro véste pinnis mémbra textis cóntegit.
[Cic. *De Fin.* 5. 11.]

V.

Quem néque tueri cóntra neque farí queas.
[Macrob. *Sat.* 6. 1. 55.]

VI.

. . . cui potéstas si detúr, tua
cupiénter malis mémbra discerpát suis.
[Nonius, *s. v.* cupienter.]

VII.

E víperino mórsu venae víscerum
venéno inbutae taétros cruciatús cient.
[Cic. *Tusc. Disp.* 2. 14.]

VIII.

. . . iaceo in tecto úmido

quod ćiulatu quéstu gemitu frémitibus
resonándo mutum flébilis vocés refert.

[Cic. *l. c.*]

IX.

Recíproca tendens nérvo equino cóncita
tela.

[Varro, *L. L.* 7. 80 M.]

X.

. . . pinnigero, nón armigero in córpore
tela éxercentur haéc abiecta glória.

[Cic. *Ad Fam.* 7. 33.]

XI.

Quis tu és mortalis, qui ín deserta et tésqua te adportás
loca?

[Varro, *L. L.* 7. 11.]

XII.

quod te óbsecro aspernábilem
ne haec taétritudo meá me inculta fáxsit . . .

[Nonius, *s. v.* taetritudo.]

XIII.

Contémpla hanc sedem, in qua égo novem hiemes sáxo
stratus pértuli.

[Nonius, *s. v.* contempla.]

XIV.

heu Múlciber!
arma érgo ignavo invícta es fabricatús manu.

[Macrob. *Sat.* 6. 5. 2.]

XV.

Ipsam Frygiam mítiorem esse áio immani Graécia.

[Nonius, *s. v.* immanis.]

XVI.

Pári dyspari, si impár esses tibi, égo nunc non essém miser.

[QUINTIL. 5. 10. 84.]

XVII.

Ágite, ac vulnus né succusset gréssus caute ingrédimini.

[NONIUS, s. v. succussare.]

PHOENISSAE.

THE prologue opens like that in the Phoenissae of Euripides (I). Accius adopts the form of the story which represents Oedipus as making over the sovereignty to his sons, to be enjoyed by each in alternate years (II). He has pronounced no curse upon them; the arrangement he proposes is to secure concord (III), and to give each son a share of his father's power (IV). After his year on the throne, Eteocles refuses to make way for Polynices. Polynices protests; he has not enjoyed the privileges which his father designed for him (V). Eteocles replies by a brutal dismissal of his brother (VI); who, in quitting the city, bids farewell to all its holy places (VII). Thebes must be saved (so the seers say) by the sacrifice of one of Creon's sons—not Haemon the elder (VIII), who is betrothed to Antigone, but Menoeceus. Thebes is besieged, and we see some one of the royal house, perhaps Haemon, superintending the defences, and looking to the wounded (IX). The drama ends with Creon's command to Oedipus to quit the city (X); and the bitter complaint of the old man at this crowning hardship, which robs him of all he has (XI).

I.

Sol qui micantem cándido curru átque equis
flámmám citatis férvido ardore éxplicas,
quianám tam adverso augúrio et inimico ómine
Thebís radiatum lúmen ostentás tuum?

[PRISCIAN, De Metr. Terent. p. 1325 P.]

II.

Vicíssitatemque ímperitandi trádidit.

[Nonius, s. v. vicissitas.]

III.

ne horum dívidiae discórdiae
díssipent distúrbent tantas ét tam opímas cívium
dívitias.

[Nonius, s. v. dividiae = dissensiones.]

IV.

Natús uti tute scéptrum poteretúr patris
[uterque].

[Nonius, s. v. potiri *cum accus.*]

V.

Num páriter videor pátriis vesci praémiis?

[Nonius, s. v. vesci.]

VI.

Égredere, exi, ecfér te, elimina úrbe . . .

[Nonius, s. v. eliminare = exire.]

VII.

delubra[1] caelitum, árae, sanctitúdines!

[Nonius, s. v. sanctitudo.]

VIII.

Áb dracontis stírpe armata exórtus genere antíquior.

[Nonius, s. v. antiquior.]

IX.

Obít nunc vestra moénia, omnis saúcios
convísit, ut curéntur diligéntius.

[Nonius, s. v. saucii.]

---

[1] Cp. Eur. *Phoen.* 631.

X.

Iussit proficisci exilium quovis géntium,
ne scélere tuo Thebáni vastescánt agri.

[Nonius, s. v. vastescant.

XI.

. . . quae ego cuncta ésse fluxa in meá re crepera
cómperi.

[Nonius, s. v. crepera = dubia.]

PRAETEXTAE.

BRUTUS.

The scene opens in the camp at Ardea, changing to the house of Lucretia. The last scene is the Roman Forum. King Tarquin, while besieging Ardea, has a dream, which he recounts to his Seer (I). Tarquin had put to death the elder brother of L. Junius Brutus, and the younger brother only saved his own life by playing the part of a fool, and so diverting the king's suspicion. The Seer interprets the dream (II). Then must follow in order the drinking-bout in the tent of Sextus; the challenge about the best wife; the visit to Collatia; the proof of Lucretia's modest worth; the guilty passion of Sextus; the outrage on Lucretia; the terrible confession of the innocent wife (III), and her suicide; the oath of Brutus, and his speech in the Forum, in which he recalls the loyalty of Servius Tullius IV). [This line Cicero (*Pro Sest.* 58) declares to have been applied to him, amid thunders of applause in the theatre, where the play was being acted: 'nominatim sum appellatus in Bruto.'] The last fragment gives the establishment of consuls, and the intention of the office (V).

I.

Quom iám quiéti córpus nocturno ímpetu
dedí sopore plácans artus lánguidos,
visum ést in somnis pástorem ad me adpéllere
pecús lanigerum exímia pulchritúdine,
duos cónsanguineos árietes inde éligi
praecláriorémque álterum immoláre me.
deinde eius germanum córnibus conítier
in me árietare, eoque ictu me ad casúm dari:
exím prostratum térra, gráviter saúcium,
resupínum in caelo cóntueri máximum
mirificum facinus: déxtrorsum orbem flámmeum
radiátum solis liquier cursú novo.
[Cic. De Div. 1. 22.]

II.

Réx, quae in vita usúrpant homines, cógitant curánt
    vident,
quáeque agunt vigilántes agitantque, ea si cui in somno
    áccidunt,
minus mirum est, sed dí rem tantam haut témere im-
    províso ófferunt.
proín vide, ne quém tu esse hebetem députes aeque ac
    pecus,
ís sapientiá munitum péctus egregié gerat
téque regno expéllat: nam id quod dé sole ostensum
    ést tibi
pópulo commutátionem rérum portendít fore
pérpropinquam. haec béne verruncent pópulo! nam
    quod déxterum
cépit cursum a laéva signum praépotens, pulchérrime
auguratum est rém Romanam públicam summám fore.
[Cic. l. c.]

III.

Nocte íntempesta nóstram devenít domum.

[VARRO, *L. L.* 6. 7.]

IV.

Túllius qui líbertatem cívibus stabilíverat.

[CIC. *Pro Sest.* 58.

V.

. . . qui recte cónsulat, consúl cluat.

[VARRO, *L. L.* 5. 80 M.

DECIUS.

THIS play records the victory of the two consuls, Q. Fabius Maximus Rullianus and P. Decius Mus over the joint armies of the Samnites and Gauls, at Sentinum, B. C. 295. It contrasts the cool, deliberate temper of Fabius with the impetuosity of Decius, 'ferocior et aetate et vigore animi' (Liv. 10. 28); and describes the solemn act by which Decius, following the example of his father in the Latin War (B. C. 340), devotes himself for the salvation of the Roman army. The scene opens with the camp at night: 'All well' is reported (I). A scout comes in from Clusium, and Fabius questions him as to the disposition of the hostile troops (II). In forming the line of battle, Decius is posted opposite the Gauls (III). A hind pursued by a wolf runs between the lines; the hind approaches the Gauls and is slain; the wolf comes to the Romans. The pontiff Livius offers sacrifice, and prays for a happy fulfilment of the portent (IV). But the offerings seem less propitious for Decius (V). Fabius seeks to calm the ardour of Decius (VI; but he answers impatiently (VII). The Gauls march forward with their wild war-cries (VIII); and with their scythe-armed chariots throw the Roman squadrons into confusion. Decius takes his stern resolve (IX): he bids the pontiff dictate to him the formula of devotion, as his father used it (X); and dashing into the hosts of the enemy, he falls. But the day is won for Rome; and Fabius makes over the Gallic camp to the troops of Decius, who had done such signal service (XI).

I.

Nil néque pericli néque tumulti est, quód sciam.

[Nonius, s. v. tumulti.]

II.

Díce, summa ubi pérduellum est? quórsum aut quibus
    a pártibus
gliscunt?

[Nonius, s. v. gliscere.]

III.

Vim Gállicam obduc cóntra in acie exércitum:
lue pátrium hostili fúsum sanguen sánguine.

[Nonius, s. v. sanguen.]

IV.

Te sáncte venerans précibus, invicte, ínvoco
porténta ut populo pátriae verruncént bene.

[Nonius, s. v. verruncent = vertant.]

V.

Et núnc quo deorum ségnitas? ardét focus.

[Nonius, s. v. segnitas.]

VI.

Quód periti súmus in vita atque úsu callemús magis.

[Nonius, s. v. callet = scit.]

VII.

Fáteor: sed saepe ígnavavit fórtem in spe expectátio.

[Nonius, s. v. ignavavit = ignavum fecit.]

VIII.

. . . Caleti vocé canora
fremitú peragrant minitábiliter.

[Nonius, s. v. minitabiliter.]

IX.

Pátrio exemplo et mé dicabo atque ánimam devoro hóstibus.

[Nonius, s. v. devoro (?) = devovero.]

X.

Quíbus rem summam et pátriam nostram quóndam adauctavít pater.

[Nonius, s. v. adauctavit.]

XI.

Cástra haec vestrum est: óptime essis méritus a nobis...

[Nonius, s. v. castra *femin. gen.*]

FRAGMENTA.

DIDASCALICA.

(A History of Greek and Roman poetry, with special attention to dramatic art, and treating also of the poet's own times. The majority of the fragments seem to be in Sotadean metro.)

Book I.

The honour paid by Achilles to Nestor (I); a rationalistic interpretation of the vulture of Prometheus (II).

I.

sapiéntiaeque invíctae
grátia atque honóris patera Néstorem mactávit
aúrea.

[Nonius. s. v. mactare = honorare.]

II.

Num érgo aquila, ita ut híce praedicant, sciciderat péctus ?
[Aul. Gell. 6. 9. 16.]

Book II.

Certain faults common in dramatic performances (I); objections to the Euripidean chorus (II).

I.

Ut dum brevitátem velint cónsequi verbórum,
áliter ac sit réllatum redhóstiant respónsum.
[Nonius, *s. v.* redhostit = reddit.]

II.

       sed Eúripidis quí choros temérius
in fabulis . . .
[Nonius, *s. v.* temerius.]

Book VIII.

A description of the equipment of actors in tragedy.

Áctoribus mánuleos et báltea et machaéras.
[Nonius, *s. v.* balteum, *neut.*]

Book IX.

A fragment from some general sketch of poetry.

Nám quae varia haéc genera poématorum, Baébi,
quámque longe dístincta alia áb aliis sint, nósce.
[Charis. *s. v.* poematorum.]

EX LIBRIS INCERTIS.

Accius was the first to examine into the question of the authenticity of the plays currently assigned to Plautus. He rejects several that were commonly received :

Nám nec 'Gemini lenones,' nec 'Condalium,' nec
'Plauti anus,' nec 'Bís compressa,' nec 'Boeotia'[1] únquam
fúit, neque adeo 'Agroecus' néque 'Commorientes'
Mácci Titi.
[AUL. GELL. 3. 3. 9.

[1] *Boeotia.* Vid. sup. sub Aquilio, p. 102.

C. LUCILIUS.

(Circ. 180-103 A.C.).

SATURAE.

BOOK I.

I.

(Atheism and immorality.)

Tubulus si Lucius unquam,
si Lupus aut Carbo, Neptuni filius (?) putasset
esse deos, tam periurus, tam impurus fuisset?

[CIC. *De Nat. Deor.* 1. 23.]

Lucius Hostilius Tubulus, praetor B.C. 142, 'cum quaestionem inter sicarios exercuisset, ita aperte cepit pecunias ob rem iudicandam ut anno proximo P. Scaevola, tribunus plebis, ferret ad plebem, vellentne de ea re quaeri,' Cic. *De Fin.* 2. 16. Tubulus went into exile, and, being brought back to trial, poisoned himself. Cp. 'Cui Tubuli nomen non odio est?' Cic. *De Fin.* 5. 22.

Lupus, perhaps L. Cornelius Lentulus Lupus, consul B.C. 157, afterwards convicted, 'repetundarum reus.' Cf. Hor. *Sat.* 2. 1. 68 'famosisque Lupo cooperto versibus': Pers. *Sat.* 1. 115.

Carbo. There were three bad brothers, C., Cn., and M. Carbo. The allusion here seems to be to C. Papirius Carbo, the friend of Tib. Gracchus, suspected of being concerned in the murder of Scipio Africanus. Carbo tribune B.C. 131, consul 120, was charged with some crime by the young orator L. Licinius Crassus, and without awaiting a trial, poisoned himself.

Neptuni filius. Cp. Aul. Gell. 15. 21 'ferocissimos et immanes et alienos ab omni humanitate, tamquam e mari genitos, Neptuni filios dixerunt.' If the reading *filius putasset* is right, *filius* must be scanned as a disyllable.

II.

(*A day in Rome in the time of Lucilius.*)

Nunc vero a mani ad noctem festo atque profesto,
toto ibidem pariterque die populusque patresque
iactare indu foro se omnes, decedere nusquam ;
uni se atque eidem studio omnes dedere et arti,
verba dare ut caute possint, pugnare doloso ;
blanditia certare, bonum simulare virum se ;
insidias facere, ut si hostes sint omnibus omnes.

[LACTANT. *Inst.* 5. 9. 20.]

Book II.

I.

(*Scaevola's ridicule of the affectation of Greek manners and speech by Albucius.*)

Graecum te Albuci quam Romanum atque Sabinum,
municipem Ponti, Tritani, centurionum,
praeclarorum hominum ac primorum signiferumque,
maluisti dici. graece ergo praetor Athenis,
id quod maluisti te, cum ad me accedis, saluto ;
'χαῖρε,' inquam, 'Tite!' ; lictores turma omnis cohorsque
'χαῖρε Tite!'—hinc hostis mi Albucius, hinc inimicus.

[CIC. *De Fin.* 1. 3.]

Titus Albucius is described by Cicero (*Brut* 35) as 'doctus Graecis vel potius paene Graecus ... fuit autem Athenis adulescens, perfectus Epicureus evaserat.' Q. Mucius Scaevola, on his way to his province as propraetor in Asia, B.C. 121, meets Albucius at Athens, and in recognition of his Greek tastes salutes him 'Graeco more'; his whole retinue taking up and carrying on the joke.

L. 2

Ponti. Cp. Cic. *De Senect.* 10, 'ne vos quidem T. Pontii centurionis vires habetis.' *Tritani,* unknown.

II.

(A further caricature of the style of Albucius.)

Quam lepide λέξεις compostae ut tesserulae omnes
arte pavimento atque emblemate vermiculato!

[Cic. *Or.* 44. 149.]

Cicero, in this passage, deprecates over-nicety in the combination of words: 'nam esset cum infinitus tum puerilis labor, quod apud Lucilium scite exagitat in Albucio Scaevola.' *tesserulae,* the small cubes forming a 'tessellated pavement.' *arte,* 'skilfully.' *emblemate vermiculato,* 'intertwined mosaic work.' ἔμβλημα is anything 'inlaid.' *vermiculatus* is that which runs in twining, 'wriggling,' patterns, as distinct from geometrical lines.

III.

(Scaevola refers to his son-in-law, L. Licinius Crassus, the most famous Roman orator before Cicero's time.)

Crassum habeo generum, ne rhetoricoteros tu scis!

[Cic. *De Orat.* 3. 43.]

rhetoricoteros, i.e. ῥητορικώτερος.

Book III.

See Porphyr. ad Hor. *Sat.* 1. 5. 1: 'Lucilio hac satura aemulatur Horatius iter suum a Roma Brundisium usque describens, quod et ille in tertio libro fecit, primo a Roma Capuam usque et inde fretum Siciliense.'

I.

(Orders are given to measure off the road exactly.)

viamque
degrumabis uti castris mensor facit olim.

[Nonius, *s. v.* grumae.]

degrumabis, from 'gruma' or 'groma,' a surveyor's pole.

II.

(Distance to Capua, and from Capua to the Straits.)

Millia porro bis quina octogena videbis
commoda, de Capua quinquaginta atque ducenta.

[NONIUS, s. v. commodum.]

commoda is interpreted by Nonius as 'integra' = 'full,' 'complete.' The readings have been variously altered to harmonise the numbers with actual geography.

III.

(The rough work begins near Setia, on a mountain ridge rising from the Pomptine marshes.)

Verum haec ludus ibi susque omnia deque fuerunt,
susque ea deque fuere, inquam, omnia, ludus iocusque :
illud opus durum, ut Setinum accessimus finem ;
αἰγίλιποι montes, Aetnae omnes, asperi Athones.

[AUL. GELL. 16. 9.]

Susque deque, lit. 'both up and down'; i.e. as much up as down, 'about on a level.' So Gellius, l. c. 'significat autem "susque deque ferre" animo aequo esse, et quod accidit non magni pendere,' etc. Cp. Cic. *Att.* 14. 6. 1 'de Octavio susque deque.' αἰγίλιποι. The genuine Greek form is αἰγίλιψ, Hom. *Il.* 9. 15. The word may be connected with αἰγίς, 'storm.'

IV.

(The roads are bad.)

Praeterea omne iter est hoc labosum atque lutosum.

[NONIUS, s. v. labosum.]

Labosum may be connected with *labes. Lamosus* from *lama* (cp. Hor. *Ep.* 1. 13. 10) is a likely emendation.

V.

(The donkeys are overloaded.)

Mantica cantheri costas gravitate premebat.

[PORPHYR. ad Hor. *Sat.* 1. 6. 106.]

VI.

(They take ship and coast along Lucania.)

Hinc media remis Palinurum pervenio nox.

[SERV. *ad Verg. Aen.* 10. 244.]

nox, pro 'nocte,' Serv. *l. c.*

VII.

(Thick weather comes on, and soundings are taken.)

Hinc catapeiratera puer deorsum dedit, unctum
plumbi pauxillum raudus liniquo mataxam.

[ISID. *Etym.* 19. 4.]

Catapeiratera, cp. καταπειρητηρίη, Hdt. 2. 5 = 'sounding-line'. The *raudus* (lump of metal) is greased, in order that it may bring up, when it is raised, shells, sand, or the like, to show the nature of the bottom. *Mataxa* (metaxa) is properly 'raw silk'; here used generally for a cord.

BOOK IV.

I.

(It is uncertain to what book the next fragment is to be referred; but it forms a good prelude to the general scope of the fourth as a protest against luxury and crime.)

Virtus, Albine, est pretium persolvere verum
quis in versamur, quis vivimus rebus, potesse ;
virtus est homini scire id quod quaeque valet res ;
virtus scire homini rectum utile quid sit honestum,
quae bona quae mala item, quid inutile, turpe, inhon-
      estum ;
virtus, quaerendae finem rei scire modumque ;
virtus, divitiis pretium persolvere posse ;
virtus, id dare quod re ipsa debetur honori ;
hostem esse atque inimicum hominum morumque
      malorum.

contra defensorem hominum morumque bonorum,
magnificare hos, his bene velle, his vivere amicum ;
commoda praeterea patriai prima putare,
deinde parentum, tertia iam postremaque nostra.
[LACTANT. Inst. 6. 5. 2.

II.

(The protest of 'Laelius the Wise' against gluttony.)

O lapathe, ut iactare, nec es satis cognitus qui sis!
in quo Laelius clamores σοφὸς ille solebat
edere, compellans gumias ex ordine nostros.
[Cic. De Fin. 2. 8.]

Lapathe, 'sorrel,' how thou art lauded to the skies, and yet enough is not known of what you really are!' It is easy to talk finely about a light, vegetable diet, but who strictly keeps to it? *in quo,* perhaps 'over which,' i.e. on the occasion of his own meal of sorrel. *Laelius,* surnamed Sapiens, the intimate friend of the younger Scipio Africanus. In his honour, Cicero wrote his treatise 'Laelius sive de Amicitia.' From the teaching of Diogenes and Panaetius he had learned to accept the doctrines of the Stoic school. *compellans* = 'rebuking.' *gumias* = 'gluttons.'

III.

(Publius Gallonius is familiar to us from Horace, Sat. 2. 2. 47.)

'O Publi, o gurges, Galloni, es homo miser' inquit ;
cenasti in vita numquam bene, cum omnia in ista
consumis squilla atque acupensere cum decumano.
[Cic. ibid.

Cum—cum, both are to be taken as conjunctions, as in Lucilius, 'cum pacem peto cum placo cum adeo et cum adpello meam.' *decumano,* 'huge'; as fluctus decumanus.

IV.

(The gladiators Aeserninus and Pacidianus.)

Aeserninus fuit Flaccorum munere quidam
Samnis, spurcus homo, vita illa dignus locoque ;

cum Pacideiano componitur, optimus multo
post homines natos gladiator qui fuit unus.

[Nonius, *s. v.* spurcum.]

Cicero, *Ad Quint. Fr.* 3. 4, says: 'cum Aesernino Samnite Pacidianus comparatus viderer, auriculam fortasse mordicus abstulisset.' Aeserninus is armed as a 'Samnite' with the 'winged helmet, scutum, ocreae, and manica.' The pair is matched (*componitur*) at some show (*munere*); and we may suppose that Aeserninus bit off his opponent's ear. *unus* = 'beyond all others,' as 'rem unam omnium difficillimam,' Cic. *Brut.* 6. 25.

V.

(Pacidianus expresses his hatred of Aeserninus.)

'Occidam illum equidem et vincam, si id quaeritis,'
    inquit;
'verum illud credo fore: in os prius accipiam ipse
quam gladium in stomacho furiae ac pulmonibus sisto.
odi hominem, iratus pugno; nec longius quicquam
nobis, quam dextrae gladium dum accommodet alter:
usque adeo studio atque odio illius ecferor ira.

[Cic. *Tusc. Disp.* 3. 21.]

füriae = 'madman' (al. *fari*). Cp. Cic. *Pro Sest.* 14. 33 of Clodius, 'illa furia ac pestis patriae.' *longius*, i. e. 'more wearisome': he can hardly wait.

Book V.

I.

(Lucilius complains of the neglect of a friend, who failed to visit him when he was sick.)

Quo me habeam pacto, tametsi non quaeris, docebo;
quando in eo numero mansti, quo in maxima nunc est
pars hominum.
ut periisse velis, quem visere nolueris cum

debueris. hoc 'nolueris' et 'debueris' te
si minus delectat quod τεχνίον Isocratium est
ληρῶδεςque simul totum et συμμειρακιῶδες,
non operam perdo.   [Aul. Gell. 18. 8.]

Gellius, l. c. adds this comment: 'ὁμοιοτέλευτα et ἰσοκατάληκτα et πάρισα et ὁμοιόπτωτα, ceteraque huiusmodi scitamenta quae isti ἀπειρόκαλοι, qui se Isocraticos videri volunt, in conlocandis verbis immodice faciunt et rancide, quam sint insubida et inertia et puerilia, facetissime hercle significat in quinto saturarum Lucilius.'

mansti: if this correction be right, the meaning is, 'you *continue* to be like the rest of the world': if *mansi*, 'I *continue* to be, in spite of my illness, of no more interest to you than the rest of the world.' τεχνίον, so Scaliger: al. ἄτεχνον et I. συμμειρακιῶδες, 'altogether childish.' The general sense is, 'if you think the jingle of "nolueris" and "debueris" a mark of bad taste, I take no further trouble.'

Book VI.

I.

(A miser's passion for his money-bag.)

Cui neque iumentum est nec servus nec comes ullus,
bulgam et quicquid habet nummorum secum habet ipse:
cum bulga cenat, dormit, lavat; omnis in unast
spes homini bulga: bulga haec devincta lacertost.

[Nonius, s. v. bulga.]

bulga, a Gallic word; French, *bougette*; our *budget*.

II.

(A word not to be got into an hexameter line.)

servorum ast festus dies hic,
quem plane hexametro versu non dicere possis.

[Porphyr. ad Hor. Sat. 1. 5. 87.]

The last days of the Saturnalia were called the Sigillaria, when friends made presents of little images (*sigilla, signa*) to one another. Ausonius, *Ecl. fer. Rom.* 52. calls the festival 'festa Sigillorum.'

Book IX.

I.

(*The difference between* poëma *and* poësis.)

Nunc haec quid valeant, quidque huic intersiet illud
cognosces. primum hoc quod dicimus esse poëma
pars est parva poësis; id est, *epigrammata, porro
disticha,* epistula item quaevis non magna poëmast.
illa poësis opus totum, ut tota Ilias summast
una poësis, ut Annales Enni. Atque si hoc unumst,
est maius multo quam quod dixi ante poëma.
quapropter dico: nemo, si culpat Homerum,
perpetuum culpat. neque. quod dixi ante, poësin:
versum unum culpat, verbum, enthymema, locumve.

[Nonius, *s. v.* poësis, poëma.]

The general sense is plain, that a poëma is a short composition, and only the fragment of a poësis. But the readings are most uncertain. I have filled up a lacuna, as suggested by Bährens, and followed, generally, Wordsworth's ed. for the rest. '*enthymema, locumve,* 'a (single) reflection or one passage.'

II.

(*On the needlessness of writing a vowel double, in order to show that
it is long.*)

A primast: hinc incipiam, et quae nomina ab hoc sunt.
'ΑΑ geminum longa, Α brevis syllaba.' nos tamen
           unum
hoc faciemus, et uno eodemque, ut dicimus, pacto
scribemus pācem, plācide, Iānum, āridum, ācetum:
Ἄπες Ἄπες Graeci ut faciunt.

[Scaurus, *De Orthograph.*]

Scaurus explains the passage: 'Accius' (L., the tragic poet
'geminatis vocalibus scribi natura longas syllabas voluit.' Ἄπες Ἄπες.
Hom. *Il.* 5. 31: see also Martial 9. 12 'Et Graeci quibus est nihil

negatum, et quos ꞌApes ꞌApes decet sonare.' Lucilius denies the use of this duplication of the vowel, and would write *ā* and *a* identical, depending only on the pronunciation to distinguish them, *ut dicimus*.

III.

'*In the plural we may write* EI, *in the gen. of the O declension; in such datives as* ILLI *only the single* I.'

Iam 'puerei venere' E postremum facito atque I,
ut pueri plures fiant. I si facis solum.
'pupilli, pueri, Lucili,' hoc unius fiet.
'hoc illi factum est uni', tenue hoc facies I ;
'haec illei fecere.' addes E, ut pinguius fiat.

[VELL. LONG. 56 K. et L.]

BOOK XV.

I.

(*The Homeric Cyclops.*)

Multa homines portenta in Homeri versibus ficta
monstra putant : quorum in primis Polyphemus ducentos
Cyclops longus pedes, et porro huic maius bacillum
quam malus navi in corbita maximus ulla.

[NONIUS, s. v. corbita.]

See Hom. *Odys.* 9. 167 foll. His club (*ib.* 319 foll.) is described as ὅσσον θ' ἱστὸν νηὸς ἐεικοσόροιο μελαίνης, φορτίδος εὐρείης, which last words are the equivalent of *corbita*.

II.

(*Only children are frightened at goblins.*)

Terriculas Lamias, Fauni quas Pompiliique
instituere Numae, tremit, has insomnia ponit :
ut pueri infantes credunt signa omnia ahena
vivere et esse homines, sic isti somnia ficta

vera putant, credunt signis cor inesse in alienis.
pergula pictorum, veri nihil, omnia ficta!

[LACTANT. I. 22. 13.]

insomnia (Bährens conj. for hic omnia) = visions of the night.
pergula, 'studio.'

BOOK XXVI.

I.

(*The metres in this book, probably the earliest of the saturae, are mostly trochaic tetrameter catalectic. Lucilius writes for 'the general public,' not up to the level of the most cultivated, nor down to the requirements of the ignorant.*)

. . . nec doctíssimis: nam Gáium
Pérsium haec légere nólo, Iúnium Congúm volo.

[CIC. *De Orat.* 2. § 25 with Wilkins' note : PLIN. *Praef. N. H.* § 7.]

Pérsium non cúro legere, Laélium Decumúm volo.

[*Ibid.*]

The reading *Manium* of Pliny for *Gaium* is wrong; if, that is, *Persium* be right. C. Persius is spoken of by Cic., *Brut.* 26. 99, as 'litteratus homo.' The other names must represent the average citizen.

II.

(*The strength of Rome comes out in a long campaign.*)

Ut Romanus pópulus victus vi ét superatus proéliis
saepe est multis, béllo vero númquam, in quo sunt
ómnia.

[NONIUS, *s. v.* bellum et proelium.]

BOOK XXVII.

I.

(*Lucilius does his best for his readers.*)

Rém populi salútem fictis vérsibus Lucílius,

quíbus potest, inpértit totúmque hóc studióse et sédulo.
> [Nonius, s. v. fingere, componere.]

II.

(He feels that life is short, and he must use it to the full.)

Cúm sciam nihil ésse in vita próprium mortalí datum,
iám qua tempestáte vivo χρῆσιν ad me récipio.
> [Nonius, s. v. proprium, i. e. perpetuum.]

χρῆσιν or *chresin* is Lachmann's emendation for the reading *arte sine* of MSS.

III.

(He never looks askance at other men's treasures.)

Núlli me invidére, non strabónem fíeri saépius
déliciis me istórum.
> [Nonius, s. v. strabones.]

IV.

(The simulated grief of hired mourners.)

Út mercedé quaé conductae flént alieno in fúnere
praéficae multum ét capillos scíndunt et clamánt magis.
> [Nonius, s. v. praeficae.]

Book XXVIII.

I.

(He plays with the Empedoclean doctrine (Lucret. 1. 714 foll.) of the four elements, by making an absurd application of it.)

'Quaprópter certum est fácere contra ac pérsequi
et nómen deferre hóminis'—'hoc cum féceris,
cum céteris reus úna tradetúr Lupo.'
'non adérit'—'ἀρχαῖς hóminem et στοιχείοις simul
privábit: igni cúm et aqua interdíxerit
duo habét στοιχεῖα'—'at frúitur anima et córpore

γῆ córpus, anima est πνεῦμα'—'posterióribus στοιχείοις, si id malúerit, privabít tamen.'

[Nonius, s. v. deferre.]

A man is summoned for trial before the praetor Lupus. He won't turn up. Then Lupus will proceed, by 'interdictio,' to deprive him of two elements, fire and water. But he has the two other elements in his own body—earth and air. Well, the praetor will next deprive him of these; and that will complete the affair.

T. QUINCTIUS ATTA.

(Ob. 77 A.C.).

TOGATAE.

The fragments of Atta are too scanty to enable us to judge of that skill in representing character—and especially female character—with which he is credited.

AEDILICIA.

AEDILICIA : sc. fabula. We may suppose that at an entertainment given by the Aediles a money-present is made to some popular actor (I); and that, later in the day, there is a little trouble between a noisy citizen and the police (II).

I.

Datúrin estis aúrum? exultat plánipes.

[Diomed. 3. p. 487 P.]

II.

Sed si pepugero, métuet . . .

[Aul. Gell. 6 (7). 9. 10.]

AQUAE CALDAE.

The scene is laid in some popular watering-place, where the company is both gay and mixed. The respectable ladies complain that the courtesans are not obliged to wear their distinguishing dress, as in Rome (I). Then there seems to have been some quarrelling between the bathers and the manager of the baths about the water-supply. They complain that the water only comes trickling in; and he tells them if they are not content he shall close the spring altogether (II).

I.

Cum nóstro ornatu pér vias meretrície lupántur.

[Nonius, *s. r.* lupari.]

II.

Aquae ita muginántur hodie—Átqui ego fontem occlúsero.

[Nonius, *s. r.* muginari = murmurare (?).]

SATURA.

The only fragment referred to this title has a curious history. Isidore of Seville (*Origin.* 6. 9) asserts that the Romans were forbidden to use, like the Greeks or Etrurians, an iron stylus for writing on their waxen tablets: 'ceram ferro ne caedito.' They were obliged to use a bone-point (I).

I.

vertamus vómerem,
in céra mucrone aéque aremus ósseo.

[Isidor. *l. c.*]

L. AFRANIUS.
(Nat. circ. 144 A.C.).

TOGATAE.

COMPITALIA.

The *Compitalia* was a feast held in the winter in honour of the Lares, and was celebrated at the spots where cross-roads met. This play is interesting, because, in the Prologue, Afranius acknowledges, with unblushing frankness, that he took his plays not only from Menander, but from any author, Latin as well as Greek, who happened to serve his purpose (I). He expresses his marked preference for Terence (II, III).

I.

... fateor, súmpsi non ab illó modo,
sed út quisque habuit cónveniret quód mihi,
quod mé non posse mélius facere crédidi,
etiam á Latino.
[Macrob. *Sat.* 6. 1. 4.]

II.

Terénti numne símilem dicent quémpiam?
[Suet. *Vit. Terent.* c. 5, p. 33.]

III.

... ut quícquid loquitur, sál merum est!
[Priscian, 5. 8, p. 659 P.]

DIVORTIUM.

Two sisters, very happily married, seem to have had their comfort disturbed by the stupid interference of their father, who tries to make a breach between them and their husbands (I) ; accusing one of the husbands of an intrigue, which he was keeping secret, in order that his wife might not be able to claim her dowry and leave him (II). The father seems to have been put up to this by the influence of a second wife, whom one of the sisters or the accused husband addresses in uncomplimentary language (III ; reminding her how pleasant she seemed, when she first came into the family IV). The *meretrix*, about whom all this disturbance arose, appears on the stage, and gives herself a high character (V).

I.

O dígnum facinus! ádulescentis óptimas
béne cónvenientes, béne concordes cúm viris
repénte viduas fáctas spurcitiá patris!
[Nonius, *s. v.* spurcus = saevus.]

II.

. . . qúi concre clanculum
rus ire, dotem ne repromittas, vafer,
honéste ut latites ét nos ludas diútius.
[Nonius, *s. v.* vafer.]

III.

Muliér, novercae nómen huc addę ímpium,
spurcá gingivast, gánnit hau dici potest . . .
[Nonius, *s. v.* spurcus.]

IV.

Quam pérspicace, quám benigne, quám cito,
quam blánde, quam materno visa's pectore — !
[Nonius, *s. v.* perspicace = perspicaciter.]

V.

Vigiláns ac sollers, sícca sana sóbria:
virósa non sum, et sí sum non desúnt mihi
qui ultró dent: aetas íntegra est, formaé satis.

[Nonius, s. v. virosa = virorum appetens.]

EPISTULA.

A young man is found prowling about in the cold by his ladylove's house, and is asked to explain his business (I). He is dressed in a petticoat to look like a girl and so gain admission (II); in which he succeeds, though he is not used to such disguises (III. The mother comes on the scene, and asks the daughter to explain the intruder's presence; she states that he is taking refuge from a footpad (IV), and she defends her own modesty—she is not a girl who wants a host of lovers! (V). When the quarrel is over, the daughter tells the story to some friend—about her own suppressed laughter, and her mother's fury (VI, and their ultimate reconciliation (VII).

I.

quis tu ventoso ín loco
soleátus, intempésta noctu súb Iove
apérto capite, sílices cum findát gelus?

[Nonius, s. v. gelus, masc.]

II.

tace!
puélla non sum, súpparo si indúta sum?

[Nonius, s. v. supparum.]

III.

Quamquam ístaec malitiósa non tam cálleo
tamén fefelli.

[Nonius, s. v. callere, cum accus.]

IV.

Huc vénit fugiens ténebrionem Tírrium.

[Nonius, s. v. tenebrio.]

V.

Nám proba et pudíca quod sum, cónsulo et parcó mihi,
quóniam comparátum est uno ut símus contentaé viro.

[Nonius, s. v. comparare = constituere.]

VI.

Ego mísera risu clándestino rúmpier,
turgére mater, ámens ira férvere.

[Nonius, s. v. rumpere, fervere.]

VII.

Me auctóre, mater, ábstinebis—.   Quíd nisi?

[Festus, s. v. quid nisi?]

EXCEPTUS.

A young man has an intrigue with a Neapolitan girl, Moschis (I). His father meets him walking with her, dressed as a respectable lady; for which the son finds a sort of excuse (II). Rudely separated from Moschis, the young man attempts to drown himself, but he is rescued (*exceptus*) by a fishing-boat (III V). How is Moschis to win him back again? She is advised to let him overhear her weeping for his supposed loss (VI-VIII).

I.

Ubi hícc Moschis, quaéso, habet, meretrix Neapolítis?

[Nonius, s. v. habere = habitare.]

II.

Meretrix cum veste longa?—Peregrino ín loco
solént tutandi caúsa sese súmere.

[Nonius, s. v. meretrices.]

III.

Ábi tu: appellant húc ad molem nóstram naviculam.

[Nonius, s. v. appellare (?.]

IV.

Túm conscendo cúmbam interibi lúci piscatóriam,
. . . vénio, iacitur ánchora, inhibent léniter.

[Nonius, s. v. cumba.]

V.

iubeo hominem tólli
et cónlocari et cónfoveri : solvo operam Diánae.

[Nonius, s. v. operari = sacrificare.]

VI.

De víta ac morte dómini fabulábere
advórsum fratrem illíus ac dominúm suum.

[Nonius, s. v. advorsum = apud.]

VII.

. . . si ille haec nunc séntit, facere illí satis
vis, quánta illius mórs sit maceriés tibi?

[Nonius, s. v. maceries = maceratio.]

VIII.

Quod vítae studium aut quód praesidium in pósterum
mihi súpponebas, mé cum privarés tui?

[Nonius, tui, *gen. pro ablat.*]

FRATRIAE.

A NIGGARDLY father wishes to get his pretty daughter off his hands, without having to settle a dowry on her (I); and so he betroths her to a baker! (II). 'Why not to a pastry-cook?' cries the mother, 'and she might have kept the family in tarts' (III . The girl moves heaven and earth to get off the marriage (IV) ; and when her own lover brings her in, smartly dressed, to plead her case (V), she seems to have been successful, as we find her afterwards living in style (VI).

I.

Formósa virgo est: dótis dimidiúm vocant
istí, qui dotis néglegunt uxórias:
praetérea fortis.

[Nonius, s. v. fortis.]

II.

Dat rústico nesció cui vicinó suo
perpaúperi, cui dícat dotis paúlulum.

[Nonius, s. v. dicere = promittere.]

III.

Pistóri nubat? cúr non scriblitário,
ut míttat fratris fílio lucúnculos?

[Nonius, s. v. lucuns.]

IV.

. . . nullám profecto accéssi ad aram, quín deos
supplíciis sumptu vótis donis précibus plorans óbsecrans
nequíquam defetígarem.

[Nonius, s. v. supplicium = supplicatio.]

V.

curre, núntia
venire et mecum meám speratam addúcere;
inde út puellam cúrent, conformént iube.

[Nonius, s. v. sperata = sponsa.]

VI.

Mea nútrix, surge sí vis, profer púrpuram:
praeclávium contéxtumst.

[Nonius, s. v. praeclavium.]

SIMULANS.

THE reclamation of a drunken and quarrelsome husband. After one stormy scene between the husband and wife, peace is restored through the pleading of their little child (I . The wife's father overhears the bickering with a secret joy (II , for he has taken the advice of a friend (III), and determined on a heroic remedy. Pretending *Simulans*) extreme indignation, he announces his intention of dissolving this unhappy marriage. He bitterly reproaches the husband with his misconduct (IV). [These words were once the occasion of a political demonstration. The *Simulans* was acted in B.C. 57. The consul, Lentulus Spinther, who presided at the representation, was, in co-operation with the *Optimates*, working hard for Cicero's return from exile. It was so arranged that, when these words of reproach were uttered, the Chorus and actors, to a man, fixed their gaze on Clodius, and raised such a storm that he was glad to quit the theatre. Cic. *Pro Sest*. 55.] Now, all the money belonged to the wife, so when the dissolution of the marriage was announced, the husband had to turn out of doors amid the jeers of all the household (V). So he puts his pride in his pocket, and avails himself of the services of his amiable child, to make terms with his wife's father (VI).

I.

Nolí, mea mater, mé praesente cúm patre
coícere!—Non, si noénu vis, o mél meum.

[NONIUS, *s. v.* coicere = certare.]

II.

Ne ego illos velitántes auscultó lubens.

[NONIUS, *s. v.* ausculto.]

III.

Saéviter ferre haéc te simula, et gnátam ab illo abdúcere.

[NONIUS, *s. v.* saeviter.]

IV.

haec, taetérrime,
sunt póstprincipia atque éxitus malaé vitiosae vítae.

[CIC. *Pro Sest*. 55.]

V.

Utí servorum cáptus est, facíllime
domo átque nostra família protrúditur.

[DONAT. *In Ter. Adelph.* 3. 4. 34 *captus* est condicio.]

VI.

tui
verétur, me ad te mísit oratúm pater.

[NONIUS, *s. v.* vereor, *cum genit.*]

VOPISCUS.

THIS is the technical term for the survivor of twin children, when one has died before its birth. In this case, the father, in his unreasonable anger, refuses to acknowledge the living child (I). He seems to have repudiated his wife, and afterwards to have repented; but as he has contracted a new marriage he is barred from return to his first love, as his new wife emphatically reminds him II IV). The rest of the fragments are of a very mixed character: a serious defence of the old practice of exposing children (V): honourable marriage commended to young men (VI): various characters introduced, such as the lady who gets power by capricious alternations of warmth and coolness (VII); the old woman on the look-out for a young lover (VIII); the lady's maid IX); the trusty comrade (X); and the slaves who are spoiled by their masters (XI).

I.

Nón dolorum pártionis veniet in mentém tibi,
quós tu misera pértulisti, ut pártum proicerét pater?

[NONIUS, *s. v.* partio.]

II.

Quo cásu cecidit spés reducendí domum
quam cúpio, cuius ego ín dies impéndio
ex désiderio mágis magisque máceror.

[CHARIS. *s. v.* impendio.]

III.

Voluptátem capio máximam, cruciári tua te cúlpa,
qui de te et de illa péssime, quam déamas, promerére.
[Nonius, s. v. deamare.]

IV.

Igitúr quiesce, et quóniam inter nos núptiae
sunt díctae, parcas ístis verbis, sí placet.
[Nonius, s. v. dicere = promittere.]

V.

Antíquitas peténda in princípió mihi.
maióres vestri incúpidiores líberum
fuére.
[Nonius, s. v. liberum, gen. plur.]

VI.

   eius te súscitat
imágo, cuius effígia, quo gnatu's patre.
[Nonius, s. v. effigia = effigies.]

VII.

Dum mé morigeram, dúm morosam praébeo.
deinde áliquid dedita ópera controvérsiae
concínno, laedo intérdum contuméliis.
[Nonius, s. v. morigera, morosa.]

VIII.

Si póssent homines délenimentís capi
omnés haberent núnc amatorés anus.
aetás et corpus ténerum et morigerátio,
haec súnt venena fórmosarum múlierum:
mala aétas nulla délenimenta ínvenit.
[Nonius, s. v. mala aetas = senectus.]

IX.

novi non inscítulam
ancíllulam, vestrae híc erae vestíspicam.

[Nonius, s. v. vestispici.]

X.

équidem te nunquám mihi
parasítum, verum amícum aequalem atque hóspitem
cotídianum et laútum convivám domi.

[Nonius, s. v. aequales, lautus.]

XI.

male meréntur de nobís eri,
qui nós tanto opere indúlgent in puéritia.

[Nonius, s. v. indulgere, *cum accus.*]

POMPILIUS.

EPIGRAMMA.

(An Epigram, modelled on the Alexandrine style by Pompilius (al. Papinus) in the first half of the seventh century u. c.)

**Pacvi discipulus dicor, porro is fuit *Enni*
  Ennius Musarum ; Pompilius cluco.**

[Nonius, s. v. cluet.]

Pacvi, i. e. Pacuvii ; MSS.

VALERIUS AEDITUUS.

(Fl. circ. 100 A.C.).

EPIGRAMMATA.

Aulus Gellius, 19. 9. 10: 'versus cecinit Valeri Aeditui, veteris poetae, item Porcii Licini et Q. Catuli, quibus mundius, venustius, limatius, tersius graecum latinumve nihil quidquam reperiri puto. Aeditui versus:

I.

Dicere cum conor curam tibi, Pamphila, cordis,
    quid mi abs te quaeram, verba labris abeunt,
per pectus manat subito multus mihi sudor:
    sic tacitus, stupidus, duplo ideo pereo[1].

Atque item alios versus eiusdem addidit, nec hercle minus dulces quam priores:

II.

Quid faculam praefers, Phileros, qua nil opus nobis?
    ibimus sic: lucet pectore flamma satis.
istam nam potis est vis saeva exstinguere venti,
    aut imber caelo candidus praecipitans:
at contra hunc ignem Veneris, nisi si Venus ipsa,
    nullast quae possit vis alia opprimere.'

[1] The reading of the last line is very uncertain. He seems to mean that his sufferings are twofold; first, his passion; secondly, his inability to express it. Bährens reads 'Sic tacitus, subidus dum studeo, pereo.'

Q. LUTATIUS CATULUS.

(Consul, 102 : ob. 87 A.C.).

EPIGRAMMATA.

Q. Lutatius Catulus, consul 102 B. C., was colleague of Marius.

I.

Aufugit mi animus. Credo, ut solet, ad Theotimum
   devenit. sic est: perfugium illud habet.
quid? quasi non interdixem, ne illunc fugitivum
   mitteret ad se intro, sed magis eiceret!
ibimus quaesitum. verum ne ipsi teneamur
   formido. quid ago? da Venus consilium.
                                     [AUL. GELL. *l. c.*]

Wordsworth quotes the original which suggested it, from Callimachus, *Ep.* 42 :—

> ἥμισύ μευ ψυχῆς ἔτι τὸ πνέον, ἥμισυ δ' οὐκ οἶδ'
>   εἴτ' Ἔρος εἴτ' Ἀίδης ἥρπασε, πλὴν ἀφανές.
> ἦ ῥά τιν' ἐς παίδων πάλιν ᾤχετο· καὶ μὲν ἀπεῖπον
>   πολλάκι, 'τὴν δρῆστιν μὴ ὑπόδεχθε, νέοι.'
> Εὐξίθεον δίφησον, ἐκεῖσε γὰρ ἡ λιθόλευστος
>   κείνη, καὶ δυσέρως οἶδ' ὅτι που στρέφεται.

II.

Constiteram exorientem Auroram forte salutans,
   cum subito a laeva Roscius exoritur.
pace mihi liceat, caelestes, dicere vestra;
   mortalis visust pulchrior esse deo.
                                [CIC. *De Nat. Deor.* 1. 28.]

PORCIUS LICINUS.
(Fl. circ. 90 A.C.).

I.

(Aulus Gellius, 17. 21, quotes the opinion of Porcius Licinus about the late rise of poetry in Rome: 'serius poeticam Romae coepisse dicit, in his versibus.')

Poénico belló secundo Músa pinnató gradu
íntulit se béllicosam in Rómuli gentém feram.

[AUL. GELL. *l. c.*]

II.

(Porcius speaks bitterly about Terence and his intimacy with the great men of Rome, which profited him so little.)

Dúm lasciviám nobílium et laúdes fucosás petit,
dum Africani vócem divínam haúrit avidis aúribus,
dum ád Philum se cénitare et Laélium pulchrúm putat,
dúm se amari ab his *cum* credat, crébro in Albanúm *renit*.

. . . . . .

suís postlatis rébus ad summam ínopiam redáctus est.
ítaque ex conspectu ómnium abit ut Graéciae in terram
        últimam,
mórtuost Stympháli, Arcadiae *in* óppido, nil Públius
Scípio profuít, nihil illi Laélius, nil Fúrius,
tres per id tempús qui agitabant fácile nobilíssimi:
córum ille opera né domum quidem hábuit conductítiam,
sáltem ut esset quó referret óbitum domini sérvulus.

[SUETON. *Vita Terent.*]

Philum, so Roth. for reading of MSS. *fixum* or *furium*. The allusion probably is to L. Furius Philus, consul B. C. 136, a contemporary and fellow-student of the younger Scipio and Laelius.

Stymphali for †infalo of MSS., cp. Auson. *Ep.* 18. 15: 'Protulit in scenam quot dramata fabellarum | Arcadiae medio qui iacet in gremio.'

III.

Custodes ovium teneraeque propaginis agnum,
    quaeritis ignem? ite huc. quaeritis? ignis homost.
si digito attigero, incendam silvam simul omnem,
    omne pecus flammast, omnia quae video.
                              [AUL. GELL. 19. 9.

The last words make no sense. We might write: 'omne pecus: flammast omnia quae video'; or with Bährens, 'omnia ab igne meo.'

VOLCATIUS SEDIGITUS.

(Fl. circ. 90 A.C.).

LIBER DE POETIS.

I.

(Cp. Aul. Gell. 15. 24 : 'Sedigitus in libro quem scripsit de poetis, quid de his sentiat qui comoedias fecerunt, et quem ex omnibus praestare ceteris putet, ac deinceps quo quemque in loco et honore ponat, his versibus suis demonstrat) :

Multós incertos cértare hanc rem vídimus,
palmám poetae cómico cui déferant.
eum meó iudicio errórem dissolvám tibi,
ut. cóntra si quis séntiat, nil séntiat.
Caecílio palmam Státio do mímico ;
Plautús secundus fácile exsuperat céteros ;
dein Naévius qui férvet pretio in tértiost ;
si erít quod quarto détur dabitur Licínio.
post ínsequi Licínium facio Atílium ;
in séxto consequétur hos Teréntius ;
Turpílius septimúm, Trabea octavum óptinet ;
nonó loco esse fácile facio Lúscium ;
decimum áddo causa antíquitatis Ennium.'

II.

In Sueton. *Vita Terentii*, the following account of the poet's death is assigned to Sedigitus) :

Sed ut Áfer populo sóx dedit comoédias,
iter hínc in Asiam fécit. at navem út semel
conscéndit, visus núnquam est ; sic vitá vacat.

[SUETON. *l. c.*]

III.

(Donat., *in auctario Suet. vit. Terent.*, quotes Volcatius (?) as accrediting Scipio with the authorship of the Terentian plays. The text is given as in Bährens, *Fragm.*)

Publí Terenti hae quaé vocantur fábulae
cuiaé sunt? non qui iúra gentibús dabat
has súmmo honore afféctas fecit fábulas?

[DONAT. *l. c.*]

HOSTIUS.

BELLUM HISTRICUM.

PROBABLY the war described in this epic is of the date of 125 B.C., in which Sempronius Tuditanus earned his triumph. The earlier Histrian war had been dealt with by Ennius. The few fragments only reach to the second book.

I.

per gentes altivolantum
aetherias atque ardua tesca intraque volabis
templa antiqua deum.

[FESTUS, 356, s. v. (?) tesca.]

II.

non si mihi linguae
centum atque ora sient totidem vocesque liquatae.

[MACROB. Sat. 6. 3. 6.]

III.

Dia Minerva simul. simul autem invictus Apollo,
arquitenens Latonius.

[MACROB. Sat. 6. 5. 8.]

A. FURIUS ANTIAS.

(Fl. circ. 84 A.C.).

(Aulus Gellius, 18. 11, quotes the following 'Furiana,' and defends them against the harsh censure of the grammarian Caesellius Vindex.)

I.

Sanguine diluitur tellus, cava terra lutescit.

II.

Omnia noctescunt tenebris caliginis atrae.

III.

Increscunt animi, virescit vulnere virtus.

IV.

Sicut fulca[1] levis volitat super aequora classis.

V.

Spiritus Eurorum virides cum purpurat undas.

VI.

Quo magis in patriis possint opulescere campis.

---

[1] *fulca* = fulica, 'coot.'

CN. MATIUS.

(Fl. 100-84 A.C.).

ILIAD.

MATIUS is referred to by Aul. Gell. as 'doctus' and 'eruditus.' The few hexameters which remain from his translation of the *Iliad* show a decided advance in point of metre.

I.

Corpora Graiorum maerebat mandier igni.   (Λ. 56.)

[VARRO. *L. L.* 7. 95.]

II.

Obsceni interpres funestique ominis auctor.   (Λ. 62.)

[VARRO, *L. L.* 7. 96.]

III.

Dum dat vincendi praepes Victoria palmam.   (H. 291.)

[AUL. GELL. 7. 6. 5.]

IV.

An maneat specii simulacrum in nocte silentum.

(Φ. 3 ; Ψ. 103.)
[AUL. GELL. 9. 14. 14.]

MIMIAMBI.

HERO(N)DAS, a contemporary of Theocritus, introduced the use of Scazons into light poetry, calling them Mimiambi. Matius brought the verse into Roman literature. 'Hoc mimiambos Matius

dedit metro; | nam vatem eundem Hipponax' est Attico thymo
tinctum | pari lepore consecutus et metro.' Terent. Maur. 6. 397.
2416.

I.

Iam iam albicascit Phoebus et recentatur,
commune hominibus lumen et voluptatis[1].

[Aul. Gell. 15. 25.]

II.

Quapropter edulcare convenit vitam
curasque acerbas sensibus gubernare.

[Aul. Gell. l. c.]

III.

Nuper die quarto[2], ut recordor, et certe
aquarium urceum unicum domi fregit.

[Aul. Gell. 10. 24.]

IV.

Sinuque amicam refice frigidam caldo
columbulatim labra conserens labris.

[Aul. Gell. 20. 9.

V.

Iam tonsiles tapetes ebrii fuco
quos concha purpura imbuens venenavit.

[Aul. Gell. ib.]

---

[1] Probably nom. plur.
[2] *die quarto*: 'quod "nudius quartus" nos dicimus.' Aul. Gell.
l. c.

LAEVIUS.

(Fl. circ. 90 A.C.?).

The *Erotopaegnia* of Laevius, of which not less than six books were composed, may be supposed to have been love-songs and amatory scenes, suited to the freedom of drinking bouts. There are very scanty remains. The peculiarity of the poems of Laevius was the great variety of the metres in which he wrote, as though to test to the utmost the capabilities of the Latin language. The *Alcestis, Ino, Protesilaodamia, Sirenocirca,* &c., are specimens of these attempts. Laevius also borrowed from the Rhodian poets Simmias, Dosiades, and others, the foolish trick of attempting to represent the outlines of various things, such as an altar, a pan-pipe, an egg, by arranging lines of different length in such order that a stroke traced through the first and last letter of each would produce a particular shape. As Simmias had sketched out the 'Wing of Eros,' so Laevius in his 'Phoenix' has attempted by the graduation of his lines to suggest a wing.

EROTOPAEGNIA.

Numquod meum admissum nocens
hostit voluntatem tuam?
[Nonius, *s. v.* hostire = offendere.]

ALCESTIS.

Corpore tenuato pectoreque
undique obeso ac mente exsensa
tardigeniclo senio obpressum.
Aul Gell. 19. 7.]

To this it may be well to add the remainder of the chapter in Gellius, who gives various examples of the *bizarre* language of Laevius : 'item notavimus quod *oblitteram* gentem pro "oblitterata" dixit ; item quod hostes qui foedera frangerent *foedifragos*, non "foederifragos" dixit ; item quod rubentem Auroram *pudoricolorem* appellavit, et Memnona *nocticolorem* ; item quod *forte*, "dubitanter," et ab eo quod est "sileo" *silenta* loca dixit et *pulverulenta* et *pestilenta*, et quod *carendum tui est* pro "te," quodque *magno impete* pro "impetu" ; item quod *fortescere* posuit pro "fortem fieri," quodque *dolentium* pro "dolore," et *arens* pro "libens" ; item *curis intolerantibus* pro "intolerandis," quodque *manciolis*, inquit, *tenellis* pro "manibus" ; et *quis tam siliceo?* ... Item *fieri*, inquit, *impendio infit*, id est "fieri inpense incipit" ; quodque *accipitret* posuit pro "laceret" .... Cetera, quae videbantur nimis poetica ... praetermisimus ; veluti fuit quod de Nestore ait *trisaeclisenex* et *dulciorelocus* : item quod de tumidis fluctibus inquit *multigrumis*, et flumina gelu concreta *tegmine esse onychino* dixit : et quae multiplicia ludens composuit ; quale istud est quod vituperones suos *subductisupercilii carptores appellavit.*'

INO.

Et iam purpureo suras include cothurno,
balteus et revocet volucres in pectore sinus,
pressaque iam gravida crepitent tibi terga pharetra,
derige odorisequos ad certa cubilia canes.

[It will be noticed that the second and fourth hexameter ends in an iambus : this particular form of verse being called *miurus* (μείων .. οὐρά). The lines are quoted by Terent. Maurus, 1931, with the following introduction : ' Livius ille vetus Graio cognomine siuae | inserit Inoni versus, puto, tale docimen : praemisso heroo subiungit namque miuron, | hymnum quando chorus festo canit ore Triviae. | Et iam o. q. s.' There seems to be no doubt that Terent. Maur. is in error in ascribing the Ino to Livius rather than to Laevius, with whose style the language and versification agree. The scene probably represents the wild vision of the hunt which Athamas saw in his delirium, and in which he seemed to be taking part. See Ovid, *Metam.* 4. 512 foll.']

PHOENIX.

| Venus amoris altrix genetrix cuppiditatis, mihi |
| quae diem serenum hilarula praepandere cresti |
| obseculae tuae ac ministrae, |
| etsi ne utiquam, quid foret expavida gravis du- |
| -ra fera asperaque famultas, potui domnio in ac- |
| -cipere superbo. |

[Charis. 288 K.

PROTESILAODAMIA.

It would seem that Laodamia, anxious about her husband in his absence, describes (perhaps in a letter) the charms of some fair Asiatic women, whose attractions have been a danger to Protesilaus.

I.

Gracilentis color est,
dum ex hoc gracilans fit.

[Nonius, *s. v.* gracilens.]

II.

Nunc quaepiam alia de Ilio
Asiatico ornatu affluens
aut Sardiano ac Lydio,
fulgens decore et gratia
pellicuit.

[Priscian, I. 497 H.]

INCERTAE SEDIS.

I.

Lex Licinia introducitur,
lux liquida haedo redditur.

Aul. Gell. 2. 24.]

[See Aul. Gell. *l. c.*: 'Verba Laevii significant haedum qui ad epulas fuerat adlatus dimissum, cenamque ita, ut lex Licinia sanxisset, pomis oleribusque instructam.' This sumptuary law of Licinius was passed before B.C. 103, and was repealed in B.C. 97.]

II.

Antipathes[1] illud quaerito,
philtra omnia undique irruunt:
trochilisci[2], iunges, taeniae,
radiculae, herbae, surculi,
sauri, illices[3] bicodulae,
hinnientium dulcedines[4].

[1] *antipathes*, an antidote against spells; Plin. *N. H.* 37.

[2] *trochilisci*, probably 'little wheels,' on which the ἴυγγες (wrynecks) were tied. Cp. Pindar, *Pyth.* 4. 215 = 382.

[3] *illices*. The 'two-tailed lures' are probably doubled ribbons or threads (licia).

[4] *dulcedines*. See the description of the 'hippomanes,' Verg. *Aen.* 4. 516.

SUEIUS (?).

MORETUM.

I.

The making of some kind of *compôte*, into which the 'peach' (Persica) enters.

Admiscet bacas nucis: haec nunc regia partim,
partim Persica (quod nomen fit denique) fertur
propterea, quod qui quondam cum rege potenti,
nomine Alexandro Magno, fera proelia belli
in Persas tetulere, suo post inde reventu
hoc genus arboris in praelatis finibus Grais
dissevere, novos fructus mortalibus dantes.
mollusca haec nux est, ne quis forte inscius erret.
[Macrob. *Sat.* 3. 18. 10.]

PULLI.

II.

Sueius seems to have had a poultry farm at Ostia; and gives remedies for the diseases of fowls.

Escam hic absinthi e iúre in os pullí dato,
simul ássulatim víscus assumít cibum.
[Nonius, *s. v.* assulatim = minutatim.]

FABULAE ATELLANAE.

The old Oscan farce—fabula Atellana—took a new lease of life and a distinct literary development, in the hands of Pomponius of Bologna and Novius. There are titles preserved of 70 of the plays of Pomponius, and fragments amounting to 200 lines : of the plays of Novius 40 titles and 100 lines. But the remains are so scattered that it is impossible to sketch the entire plot of a single play. The original peculiarity of the Atellanes is preserved to a considerable extent in their new form : that is to say, the retention of certain stereotyped characters—*Maccus*, the prototype of the clown or harlequin of the pantomime—a compound of folly and shrewdness, who was, however, a favourite with the audience ; *Pappus*, the old fool, like the pantaloon, always doing the wrong thing in the wrong way ; *Bucco*, the glutton and swaggerer, like the ἀλάζων of the Attic comic stage ; and *Dossennus*, the hunchback, a man of low cunning and endless resource. M. Patin, describing the resuscitation of the Atellane and the mime, speaks of them as ' ces antiques parades devenues le cadre d'une nouvelle *fabula palliata*, d'une nouvelle *fabula togata*, ou plutôt *tabernaria*. ... La constitution de l'*atellane* changea avec le temps. Elle passa des amateurs aux comédiens, de l'improvisation à une rédaction préliminaire, de l'osque au latin, de la prose aux vers. ... L'*atellane* ainsi renouvelée était particulièrement une sorte de *fabula tabernaria*, qui, sous les masques d'Atella, se moquait des basses classes de la société, surtout de la société *extra muros*, des ridicules de la campagne et de la petite ville [1].'

A few lines must suffice to suggest the subjects with which these farces dealt.

[1] *Études sur la poésie latine*, vol. 2. p. 333.

NOVIUS.
(Fl. 90 A.C.).

I.
DAPATICI.
Instance of rustic Latinity.

prímum quod dicébo
recté, secundum quód dicebo est mélius . . .

[Nonius, *s. v.* dicebo *pro* dicam.]

II.
FULLONES FERIATI.
A hobgoblin with an ogre's appetite.

Vortít se in omnes béstias, comest quídquid tetigit
tántum.

[Nonius, *s. v.* comest.]

III.
GALLINARIA.
'Fierce volubility.'

Ó pestifera pórtentifera trúx tolutiloquéntia!

[Nonius, *s. v.* tolutim.]

IV.
MACCUS EXUL.
Limen means both lintel and sill.

Límen superum, quód mei misero saépe confregít caput,
ínferum autem, dígitos omnes úbi ego defregí meos.

[Nonius, *s. v.* limen. Cp. Plaut. *Merc.* 5. 1. 1.]

V.

MILITES POMETINENSES.

A glutton reminds one of a baby!

Tú púeri pausílli símil es, quía enim ad os fers quidquid nanctu's.

[Nonius, *s. v.* simil(e).]

VI.

PACILIUS.

The author rushes 'like a shot' to his writing.

Ut sól auréscit, cérae castra crébro catapúlta ímpulit.

[Nonius, *s. v.* catapulta.]

VII.

PAPPUS PRAETERITUS.

The old man, rejected as a candidate, will sooner find a seat in his coffin than in the 'curule chair.'

dum istos invitabis súffragatorés, pater,
príus in capulo quam in curuli sélla suspendés natis.

[Nonius, *s. v.* capulum.]

VIII.

TABELLARIA.

A dowerless wife is like a patch on a purple cloak.

Qui habet uxorem síne dote, ei pánnum positum in púrpura est.

[Nonius, *s. v.* pannum, *neut.*]

IX.

EX INCERTIS FABULIS.

A debtor is 'going,' for 1000 sesterces. A bystander asks the amount. Then, as if he were at an auction, and as if the poor man was a 'lot put up' at so much, he says, 'I go no higher: take him off.'

'Quánti addíctus?' 'Mílle nummum.' 'Níhil addo: ducás licet.'

[Cic. *De Orat.* 2. 63.]

X.

A joke in the shape of a truism.

. . . sápiens si algebís tremes.

[Cic. *De Orat.* 2. 70.]

POMPONIUS.

(Fl. circ. 90 A.C.).

XI.

AEDITUMUS.

The sacristan who hates his service.

Quí postquam tibi adpáreo atque aedítumor in templó tuo
nec mortalis nec mortalium úllum in terra míseriust.

[Nonius, *s. v.* aedituor ?).]

XII.

ARMORUM IUDICIUM.

A portable step-ladder is brought on the stage: perhaps for Ajax to get nearer to Athena.

Tum prae se portant áscendibilem sémitam,
quem scálam vocitant.

[Lactant. *in Stat. Theb.* 10. 841.]

XIII.

ARUSPEX VEL PEXOR RUSTICUS.

The village barber is also a soothsayer; but he misunderstands the word *puriter*.

bucco, púriter,
fac ut rem tráctes—Lávi iamdudum manus.

[Nonius, s. v. puriter.]

XIV.

AUCTORATUS.

The gladiator wins the lady's love by his prowess as a *toreador*.

Occídit taurum tórviter, me amóre sauciávit.

[Nonius, s. v. torviter.]

XV.

CAMPANI.

Proclamation of a public σίτησις for Dossennus and the Fullers.

Dantór publicitus Dóssenno et fullónibus
cibária.

[Nonius, s. v. publicitus.]

XVI.

CITHARISTA.

Everyone would be glad if his wife were to die!

nóli, quaeso, iráscere:
móre fit, moríre suam vir quísque ut uxorém velit.

[Nonius, s. v. irascere.]

XVII.
CONDICIONES.

What will hardly keep one will not keep two.

Víx nunc quod edim invénio : quid nam fíet, si quam
dúxero ?

[Nonius, s. v. edim.]

XVIII.
DOTATA.

' Do withdraw for "a little!"' 'How long is "a little"?'

' Possum éxorare te út recedas á me paulispér modo ? '
' Quantíspér sat habes ? '

[Nonius, s. v. quantisper.]

XIX.
ERGASTULUM.

To be bailiff to an absentee is very like being master.

Lónge ab urbe vílicari, quó erus rarentér venit,
id non vilicári sed dominári est mea senténtia.

[Nonius, s. v. rarenter.]

XX.
FULLONES.

A joke on the standing quarrel between the Fullers and the
weaving-women.

Quin érgo, quando cónvenit, complóctite !
' mi fráter, salveto.' ' ó soror, salvé, mea.'

[Nonius, s. v. complectite.]

XXI.
KALENDAE MARTIAE.

Rehearsing for a female character.

'Vócem deducás oportet, út videantur múlieris
vérba.' 'Iube, modo ádferatur múnus, vocem réddam ego
ténuem et tinnulam . . .
étiam nunc vocém deducam?'

[Macrob. *Sat.* 6. 4. 13.]

XXII.
MAIALIS.

After a good dinner, a punster makes a joke on empty bellies.

Míserit me eorum qui sine frustis véntrem frustrarúnt
suum.

[Nonius, *s. v.* frustro.]

XXIII.
PANNUCEATI.

'*Nubere*' used of a man who marries an overpowering wife.

séd meus
fráter maior, póstquam vidit mé vi deiectúm domo,
núpsit posteriús dotatae vétulae varicosaé vafrae.

[Nonius, *s. v.* nubere.]

XXIV.
PAPPUS AGRICOLA.

A young wife's anger at her goodman's unexpected return.

Vólo scire ex te cúr urbanas rés desubito déseris.

[Nonius, *s. v.* desubito.]

o

XXV.
PAPPUS PRAETERITUS.

The philosophy of a rejected candidate: 'better luck next time!'

Populís voluntas haéc enim et vulgó datast:
refrágant primo, súffragabunt póst, scio.

[Nonius, *s. v.* suffragare.]

XXVI.
PHILOSOPHIA.

A professional opinion not to be had gratis

'Ergo, mi Dossénne, cum istaec mémore meministi, indica,
qui illud aurum abstúlerit.' 'non didici áriolari. grátiis.'

[Nonius, *s. v.* memore = memoriter.]

XXVII.
PISTOR.

The cheating miller eats the corn given him to grind.

Décipit vicínos: quod moléndum conduxit, comest.

[Nonius, *s. v.* comest.]

XXVIII.
PRAECO POSTERIOR.

The son takes the father aside to drub him quietly.

Ego dédita opera té, pater, solúm foras
sedúxi, ut ne quis ésset testis tértius
praetér nos, tibi cum túnderem labeás lubens.

[Nonius, *s. v.* labeae.]

XXIX.

PROSTIBULUM.

Pudding is better than praise!

Égo rumorem párvi facio, dúm sit rumen qui ímpleam.
[NONIUS, s. v. rumen, 'the crop.']

XXX.

SATURA.

Wine is the crown of gaiety.

Cuiusvís leporis Liber diademám dedit.
[PRISCIAN, 6. 2, p. 679 P. s. v. diademam.]

XXXI.

SYRI.

The glutton's gross diet; all bacon and no salad!

Lápatium nullum útebatur, lárdum lurchabát lubens.
[NONIUS, s. v. lurchare = cum aviditate cibum sumere.]

M. TERENTIUS VARRO.
(116–26 A.C.)

SATURAE MENIPPEAE.

ABORIGINES (περὶ ἀνθρώπων φύσεως).

This Satura seems to deal with the beginnings of the human race. It opens with a procession of animals, uttering their distinctive cries (I, II); so there is a contrast suggested between the brutes and Man, who is a being urged on by soaring hopes, which disappoint him in the moment of fruition (III). His best companion is Virtue, the only companion suitable alike to the greybeard and the boy—indeed, the old require it even more, for an ass, after a certain age, is no better than one too young (IV). Mankind, according to Varro, makes slow progress, like the growth of a child; and the first beginnings of artistic taste are seen in the desire to fashion and possess dolls and little images (V).

I.
Múgit bovis, ovís balat, equi hínniunt, gallína pípat.
[Nonius, s. v. pipare.]

II.
Grúndit tepidó lacte satúr mola mactátus pórcus.
[Nonius, s. v. grunnire.]

III.
Ita sublimis spéribus
iáctato homines át volitantes áltos nitens trúdito.
[Nonius, s. v. sperem = spem.]

IV.

Sed neque vetulus cantherius quam novellus melior nec canitudini comes virtus.

[Nonius, s. v. canitudo = canities.]

V.

Itaque brevi tempore magna pars in desiderium puparum et sigillorum veniebat.

[Nonius, s. v. pupa.]

ANDABATAE.

ANDABATAE (Cic. *Fam.* 7. 10) were gladiators who wore visored helmets without any aperture for the eyes; and so, to the amusement of the spectators, fought blindfold. There is probably an allusion in this title to the imprisonment of the soul in the bonds of flesh, and its subjection to the slavery of lusts (I, II, III). The tone is distinctly anti-materialistic—'man is anything rather than a mere lump of flesh' (IV): the soul is pent within him, like air in a bladder (V).

I.

Non mirum si caecuttis, aurum enim non minus praestringit oculos quam ὁ πολὺς ἄκρατος.[1]

[Nonius, s. v. praestringere.]

II.

'Edepol' idem 'cáecus non luscitiósus est.'

[Nonius, s. v. lusciosi = qui ad lucernam non vident. Cp. Plaut. *Mil. Glor.* 2. 3. 51.]

III.

Néc manus viscó tenaci tínxerat virí castas.

[Nonius, s. v. castum = a furtis abstinens.]

---

[1] Cp. Menander, *Monostich.* 420 ὁ πολὺς ἄκρατος ὀλίγ' ἀναγκάζει φρονεῖν.

IV.

Sed quidvis potius homo quam caruncula nostra.

[PRISC. 6. p. 209, s. v. caruncula.]

V.

Anima ut conclusa in vésica quandó est arte religáta,
si pertuderis, aëra reddet.

[NONIUS, s. v. aër = sonus.]

ἈΝΘΡΩΠΟΠΟΛΙΣ (περὶ γενεθλιακῆς).

The subject of this Satura seems, generally, to deal with the Family—its foundation, growth, and maintenance. Varro evidently protests against extravagance in the marriage-festivals and marriage settlements. To live up to this excessive rate the head of the family has to borrow, and the usurer takes his bond (*scriptio*) for double the amount actually lent (I); but the possession of wealth will not ensure peace of mind; not even those Mountains of the Persians, which were said (Plaut. *Pers.* 1. 1. 24) to be of solid gold (II). Dowries must be reckoned by so many kingdoms, rather than by so many pounds (III); and the god of Wedlock is a purge that washes out the purse (IV).

I.

Vulgóque avarus fénerator spé lucri
rem scríptione dúplicarat.

[NONIUS, scriptio = syngrapha.]

II.

Non fit thesauris non auro pectus solutum;
non demunt animis curas ac religiones
Persarum montes, non atria divitis Crassi.

[NONIUS, s. v. religio.]

III.

Dotís dato insulám Chrysam, agrum Caécubum, seplásia [1]
Capuaé, macellum Rómuli.

[NONIUS, s. v. seplasium neut. = perfume.]

IV.

Et Hymenaeus qui primo lavere alvum marsuppio solet.

[NONIUS, s. v. lavere.]

BIMARCUS.

THIS Satura turns on a special application of the language of philosophy to practical life. The Sceptics had summed up their objections against any objective certitude in ten points—as we may call them, 'turning-points,' τρόποι. Varro plays upon the ambiguity of this word; introducing himself in a double personality—one 'Marcus' representing the Roman of the past, the other of the present. The honest, old-fashioned 'Marcus,' like the heroes of ancient days (except πολύτροπος 'Οδυσσεύς), is innocent of any 'choppings and changings': the nearest approach to such a word that he can realise is τροπαῖα, 'the trophies raised after the rout (τροπή) of the foe' (I III). A good 'turning-point' for the degenerate sons of Rome would be the descent of the crashing thunderbolt upon their orgies! (IV, V). No Hercules could cleanse such Augean stables! (VI).

I.

Τρόπων τρόπους qui nón modo ignorásse me
clamát, sed omnino ómnis heroás negat
nescísse.

[NONIUS, s. v. negativae duae negativam significantiam non habentes.]

---

[1] *Seplasia (um)*, a street in Capua where perfumes were sold: then, the perfumes themselves.

II.

Ebrius es, Marce; Odyssian enim Homeri ruminari incipis, cum περὶ τρόπων scripturum te Seio receperis.

[Nonius, s. v. recipere = polliceri.]

III.

Ideo fuga hostium graece vocatur τροπή. Hinc spolia capta fixa in stipitibus appellantur τροπαῖα.

[Nonius, s. v. tropaeum.]

IV.

Túnc repente caélitum altum tónitribus templúm tonescat, et pater divúm trisulcum fúlmen igni férvido actum míttat in tholúm macelli.

[Nonius, s. v. tonescit : sulcus.]

V.

Mágna uti treméscat Roma et mágnae mandonúm gulae.

[Nonius, s. v. mandones = edaces.]

VI.

Non Hercules potest qui Augeae egessit κόπρον.

[Nonius, s. v. agere, fortasse pro 'egerere'.]

DOLIUM AUT SERIA.

This mysterious title is really quite unintelligible. As the tub in which Diogenes lived is called 'dolium' in Juv. Sat. 14. 308, it has been conjectured that we have here the excuse given by the philosopher for living in a roofless dwelling, because he had an uninterrupted view of all the glories of the midnight skies.

Mundús domus est maxíma homulli,
quam quínque altitonae flámmigerae

zonaé cingunt, per quám limbus
bis séx signis stellímicantibus
aptús in obliquo aethére Lunae
bigás acceptat.

[PROBUS *in Verg. Ecl.* **6.** 31 caelum : mundus.]

EST MODUS MATULAE (περὶ μέθης.).

'PROVERBIUM monet compotationi finem faciendum esse, quum plenae sunt matulae factae,' Oehler ad l. There seems to be a dispute between a man who enjoys his wine, and a 'temperance advocate,' who complains of the bad example set by the gods.

I.

Vinó nihil iucúndius quisquám bibit:
hoc aegritudinem ád medendam invénerunt,
hoc hílaritatis dúlce semínárium,
hoc cóntinet coágulum convívia.

[NONIUS, *s. v.* coagulum.]

II.

Non vides ipsos deos, si quando volunt gustare vinum,
derepere ad hominum fana, et tamen tum ipsi illi Libero
simpuvio vinum dari?

[NONIUS, *s. v.* simpuvium.]

EUMENIDES.

IN this Satura the Stoics and Cynics seem to be played off against each other. A certain Cynic finds that it is his day for entertaining a party of philosophers, mainly of his own sect: the inscription *Cave Canem*, at the house where they meet, is sufficiently suggestive of the Cynics (I). At table a Stoic proposes the well-known thesis that all men are mad. This sweeping judgment is illustrated by various portraits from life, scenes from the poets, &c. There is Ajax slaughtering beasts in mistake for Ulysses, there is the hard-headed, half-brutalised man, the youth who drinks too much for the good of his health, the effeminate debauchee, the gourmand, the man of fashion, the miser—all these are clear cases of madness (II-VI). The Cynic extends this sentence to all philosophers, with their wild dreams (VII). Then the guests rise and walk about the town to inspect the various instances of madness they may encounter (VIII). They visit the temple of Serapis, and find that all the machinery of oracles, healing, &c. are so many ways of getting at the money of the credulous (IX, X). They move on to the temple of Cybele, and there they hear the sound of the Phrygian flutes, the clashing cymbals, and the song of the eunuch-priests (given in Galliambics) (XI-XIII). The Cynic cannot control his outspoken indignation; so he is pursued by the fanatical crowd, and has to take refuge at an altar (XIV). The guests, continuing their walk, mount an eminence, from which they see the people pursued by three Furies, the third of whom is Infamia—her foot planted on her victims' chest and her wild hair streaming in the wind XV, XVI). The narrator of the story runs down and proffers aid, but he is badly received by the crowd, who scorn his help and proclaim him a madman (XVII). Brought before the bar of public opinion Existimatio) he is registered on the list of the 'insani' (XVIII). But Truth, the pupil of the Attic Academy, saves him by remarking that 'to the jaundiced eye everything looks yellow' (XIX, XX).

I.

Quod ea die mea erat praebitio, in ianuam 'cave canem' inscribi iubeo.

[Nonius, *s. v.* praebitio.]

II.

Aiax tum credit ferro se caedere Ulixem
cum bacchans silvam caedit porcosque trucidat.

[Nonius, *s. v.* caedere.]

III.

Quin mihi caperratám tuam frontém, Strobile, omíttis?

[Nonius, *s. v.* caperrare est rugis frontem asperare.]

IV.

Tu nón insanis quóm tibi vino córpus corrumpís mero?
[Nonius, s. v. merum est solum.]

V.

Aurórat ostrinum híc indutus súpparum.
corónam ex auro et gémmis fulgentém gerit
lúce locum áfficiéns.
[Nonius, s. v. ostrinam.]

VI.

Denique qui sit avarus
sanus? cui si stet terrai traditus orbis,
furando tamen ac morbo stimulatus eodem
ex sese ipse aliquid quaerat cogatque peculi.
[Nonius, s. v. stat : cogere.]

VII.

Postrémo nemo aegrótus quicquam sómniat
tam infándum, quod non áliquis dicat phílosophus.
[Nonius, s. v. infans, i. e. infandum.]

VIII.

Et ceteri scholastici, saturis auribus scholica dape atque
ebriis sophistica ἀπεραντολογίᾳ, consurgimus ieiunis oculis.
[Nonius, s. v. ebrios = expletos.]

IX.

Hospes quid miras nummo curare Serapim?
Quid? quasi non curet tanti item Aristoteles?
[Nonius, s. v. miras = miraris.]

X.

'Ego medicina, Serapi, utor,' cotidie precantur. Intellego recte scriptum esse Delphis '$\theta\epsilon\hat{\omega}\ \tilde{\eta}\rho a$'. [? = $\phi\acute{\epsilon}\rho\epsilon$].

[Nonius, *s. v.* precantur.]

XI.

Commodum praeter Matris Deum aedem exaudio cymbalorum sonitum.

[Nonius, *s. v.* praeter = ante.]

XII.

Phrygius per ossa cornus liquida canit anima.

[Nonius, *s. v.* liquidum.]

XIII.

Tibi typana non inanis sonitus Matris deum
tonimus chorus tibinos tibi nunc semiviri;
teretem comam volantem iactant tibi famuli.

[Nonius, *s. v.* tonimus : tibinos = a tibiis modos (?).]

XIV.

Ubi vident se cantando ex ara excantare non posse, deripere incipiunt.

[Nonius, *s. v.* excantare = excludere.]

XV.

Sed nós simul atque in súmmam speculam vénimus,
vidémus populum Fúriis instinctúm tribus
divérsim ferri extérritum formídine.

[Nonius, *s. v.* specula : exterritum.]

XVI.

Tertia Poénarum,
    Infámia, stans nixa ín vulgi

pectóre, fluctanti intónsa coma,
sordída vestitu, oré severo.

[Nonius, s. v. severum.]

XVII.

'Vix vulgus confluit' non Furiarum sed puerorum atque ancillarum, quae omnes me bilem atram agitare clamitantes opinionem mihi insaniae meae confirmant.

[Nonius, s. v. pueros pro servis.]

XVIII.

Forenses decernunt, ut Existimatio nomen meum in insanorum numerum referat.

[Nonius, s. v. decernere.]

XIX.

Et ecce de improvíso ad nos accédit cana Véritas, Átticos philosóphiae alumna.

[Nonius, s. v. canum = vetus.]

XX.

Nam ut arquatis lutea quae non sunt et quae sunt, lutea videntur, sic insanis sani et furiosi videntur esse insani.

[Nonius, s. v. arquatus.]

ΓΕΡΟΝΤΟΔΙΔΑΣΚΑΛΟΣ.

Two persons may be supposed to be brought together in this Satura—a man of mature years, and a young representative of the luxury of modern Rome. The splendours and the progress of later years are contrasted with the coarseness of old-fashioned times. The elderly man laments the loss of reverence and chastity I , and the simplicity of family life, and the thrift of the housewife II : recommending the manly severity of the consul Curius towards the malingerer (III . With these memories the young Roman contrasts the grandeur of the new country-houses with their cellars and barns and wine-presses—laughing contemptuously at the rough, plain life of his ancestors (IV-VII).

I.

Ergo tum sacra religio castaeque fuerunt
res omnes.
[Nonius, s. v. castum = religiosum.]

II.

Sed simul manibus trahere lanam, nec non simul oculis observare ollam pultis, ne aduratur.
[Nonius, s. v. olla = capacissimum vas.]

III.

Manius Curius consul *in* Capitolio cum dilectum haberet nec citatus in tribu civis respondisset vendidit tenebrionem.
[Nonius, s. v. tenebriones.]

IV.

In quibus Libýssa citrus fásciis cingit fores.
[Nonius, s. v. citras.]

V.

Úbi graves pascántur atque alántur pavonúm greges.
[Nonius, s. v. grave = multum.]

VI.

Vél decem messís ubi una saépiant granária.
[Nonius, s. v. granaria.]

VII.

Víneis ubi ámpla colla tórculum respóndeat.
[Nonius, s. v. torculum, i. e. prelum.]

ΚΟΣΜΟΤΟΡΥΝΗ (περὶ φθορᾶς κόσμου).

ANAXIMANDER, Heracleitus and Empedocles had already speculated on the destruction of the material universe, and the Stoics held that it would be consumed by fire. Others maintained that it would come to an end, not by a violent catastrophe but by a gradual wearing away. This seems to be the underlying idea in ΚΟΣΜΟΤΟΡΥΝΗ, if τορύνη is to be taken as a 'wimble' or 'drill', rather than a 'stirrer' or 'squeezer' (as *tudicula*). Death waits upon the first beginnings of life (I); and war is another fruitful cause of this destruction, whether we think of the soldier going on his campaign and returning in safety (II, III), or of the horrors of civil war (IV). It seems that Varro plays upon the word κόσμος, and extends its meaning to all manner of decorative things, which are liable to the corruption of 'moth and rust' (V).

I.

Propter cunam capulum positum
nutrix tradit pollictori.
    [Nonius, *s. v.* capulum : pollinctores.]

II.

Toga detracta est, et abolla data est,
ad turbam abii, fera militia
 munera belli ut praestarem.
    [Nonius, *s. v.* abolla = vestis militaris.]

III.

Detis habenas animae leni,
dum nos ventus flamine sudo
 suavem ad patriam perducit.
    [Nonius, *s. v.* anima = ventus.]

IV.

Africa terribilis : contra concurrere civis
civi, atque Aeneae misceri sanguine sanguen.
    [Nonius, *s. v.* sanguen.]

V.

Singulos lectos stratos ubi habuimus, amisimus propter cariem et tineam.

[NONIUS, *s. v.* caries est vetustas.]

MANIUS.

I MAY venture here to reproduce the sketch given of this Satura in Mommsen's Roman History, B. v. Chap. xii: 'The Satire of "Manius" (Early Up!) describes the management of a rural household. Manius summons his people to rise with the sun, and in person conducts them to the scene of their labours (I). The youths make their own bed, which labour renders soft to them, and supply themselves with waterpot and lamp (II). Their drink is the clear fresh spring, their fare bread, and onions as a relish (III). Everything prospers in house and field. The house is no work of art, but an architect might learn symmetry from it (IV). Care is taken of the field, that it shall not be left disorderly and waste, or go to ruin through slovenliness and neglect (V); in return, the grateful Ceres wards off damage from the produce, that the high-piled sheaves may gladden the heart of the husbandman (VI). Here hospitality still holds good; everyone who has but imbibed his mother's milk is welcome (VII). The bread-pantry, and wine-vat, and the store of sausages on the rafters, lock and key are at the service of the traveller, and piles of food are set before him (VIII; contented sits the sated guest, looking neither before nor behind, dozing by the hearth in the kitchen (IX). The warmest double-wool sheepskin is spread as a couch for him (X). Here people still, as good burghers, obey the righteous law, which neither out of envy injures the innocent, nor out of favour pardons the guilty. Here they speak no evil against their neighbours (XI). Here they trespass not with their feet on the sacred hearth, but honour the gods with devotion and sacrifices, throw to the familiar spirit his little bit of flesh into the appointed little dish (XII), and when the master of the household dies accompany the bier with the same prayer with which those of his father and of his grandfather were borne forth' (XIII).

I.

Manius mane suscitat, rostrum sub rostra adfert, populum in forum conducit.

[Nonius, s. v. conducere.]

II.

Lecto strato matellam, lucernam, ceteras res esui usuique prae se portant.

[Nonius, s. v. matella = aquarium vas.]

III.

Dúlcem aquam bibát salubrem et flébile esitét cepe.

[Nonius, s. v. cepe, neutr.]

IV.

harum aédium
symmétria confutábat architéctones.

[Nonius, s. v. confutare.]

V.

Ager út relinquerétur ac perbíteret
squalé scabreque inlúvie et vastitúdine.

[Nonius, s. v. scabres : squalor (?) femin.]

VI.

Húnc Ceres, cibí ministra, frúgibus suís pórcet.

[Nonius, s. v. porcet = prohibet.]

VII.

Tam eum ad quem veniunt in hospitium lac humanum fellasse.

[Nonius, s. v. fellare.]

VIII.

Haec adventoribus accedunt : cellae, claves, claustra, carnaria, dolia.

[Nonius, s. v. dolia.]

habens
antepositam alimóniam, sedéns altus aliéno sumptu,
néque post respiciéns neque ante próspiciens, sed límus
      intra
límites culinae.

    [Nonius, s. v. limus = obtortus, i. e. with sidelong glance.]

X.

Alterum bene dormire 'super amphitapha bene molli.'
    [Nonius, s. v. amphitaphae, utrinque habentes villos.]

XI.

Quocirca oportet bonum civem legibus parere, et deos
colere, in patellam dare μικρὸν κρέας.

    [Nonius, s. v. patella.]

XII.

Non maledicere, pedem in focum non imponere, sacrificari.

    [Nonius, s. v. sacrificari.]

XIII.

Funere familiari commoto avito ac patrito more precabamur.

    [Nonius, s. v. patritum.]

MARCIPOR.

Marcipor, i. e. Marci puer, or Varro's own slave. It is difficult to decide whether the master is moralising to the slave, or the slave (as in Hor. *Sat.* 2. 7) lecturing the master. The general subject of the Satura is the vanity and extravagance of human wishes, exemplified in children and in men and women, who are as silly as children (I-III). The verses about the storm have been taken to refer to the dangers incurred by merchants in search of gain, and have been compared with the picture of the shipwrecked adventurer in Juvenal (*Sat.* 14. 290 foll.). But this is hardly compatible with the description of the soaring storks, blasted by lightning, and tumbling to the ground. It may therefore be better to see in this scene a reminiscence of the flight of Menippus, on a voyage of investigation, to the court of Zeus, as given by Lucian in the Icaromenippus, though the fate of the philosopher there was not so disastrous.

I.

Utri magis sunt pueri? hi pusilli pigri, qui exspectant nundinas [1], ut magister dimittat lusum?

[Nonius, *s. v.* lusus pro ludo.]

II.

Altera exorat patrem libram ocellatorum [2], altera virum semodium margaritarum.

[Nonius, *s. v.* margaritum.]

III.

Astrologi non sunt, qui conscribillarunt pingentes caelum?

[Nonius, *s. v.* conscribillavi.]

IV.

Repénte noctis circiter merídie,
cum píctus aër férvidis late ígnibus
caelí choréan ástricen osténderet.

[Nonius, *s. v.* meridiem = noctis mediam partem.]

nubés aquali frígido veló leves
caelí cavernas aúreas subdúxerant,
aquám vomentes ínferam mortálibus.

[Nonius, *s. v.* inferum.]

ventíque frigidó se ab axe erúperant,

---

[1] *nundinas*, sc. 'holidays.'
[2] some precious stone, with marks or dots like eyes.

phrenétici septéntrionum fílii,
secúm ferentes tégulas, ramós, syrus.

[Nonius, s. v. syrus (σύρειν) = scopas.]

at nós caduci naúfragi. ut cicóniae,
quarúm bipennis fúlminis plumás vapor
perussit, alto maésti in terram cécidimus.

[Nonius, s. v. bipennis.]

MARCOPOLIS (περὶ ἀρχῆς).

It is impossible to say whether the title of this Satura suggests a real and practicable commonwealth, such as Marcus (Varro) would wish it to be; or whether it is only an aspiration—a Νεφελοκοκκυγία after his own heart, as Mommsen calls it.—Anyhow, the point seems to lie in an elaborate analogy between the various arrangements of a properly organised city and the general economy of the human body (I). Though in the beginning of human society there may be a general equality, it is not long before the principle of the 'survival of the fittest' asserts itself (II, III).

I.

Sensus portae, venae hydragogiae, cloaca intestini.

[Nonius, s. v. intestini, masc.]

II.

Natura humanis omnia sunt paria.
Qui pote plus, urget pisces ut saepe minutos
  Magnus comest, ut avis enicat accipiter.

[Nonius, s. v. comest = comedit.]

III.

Némini Fortúna currum a cárcere emissum íntimó
lábi inoffensúm per aequor cándidum ad calcém sivit.

[Nonius, s. v. calx. masc.]

MODIUS.

This word, which properly means a dry measure of capacity, is used as the title of the Satura because it suggests a constant play on the words 'modus,' 'modicus,' 'modeste,' 'medioxime,' and the like. Varro apologises for the 'theatrical measure' of his treatise: which, however, need not be touched by his friend, and the writing can easily be sponged out (I, II). It is better to keep to a moderate amount of meat and drink (III); unlike the custom of those whose measure of living is high living (IV). This 'moderation' is the secret of life, and it is the text of the famous Delphic inscription (V, VI).

I.

Sed, ó Petrulle, né meum taxís librum
si té pepúgerit hic modús scaenátilis.
[Nonius, s. v. taxis = tetigeris.]

II.

Si díspliccbit, tám tibi latúm mare
parabit aliquam spongiam deletilem.
[Nonius, s. v. deletile = quod deleat.]

III.

... trimodiam amphoramque eundem temeti ac farris
modium.
[Nonius, s v. temetum.]

IV.

Et hoc interest inter Epicurum et ganeones nostros quibus modulus est vitae colina.
[Nonius, s. v. colina = coquina.]

V.

Non eos optime vixisse qui diutissime vixent, sed qui modestissime.
[Nonius, s. v. modestum a modico.]

VI.

Quid aliud est quod
  'Délphice canít columna lítteris suís ἄγαν
  μηθέν'
quam nos facere ad mortalem modum 'medioxime,' ut
quondam patres nostri loquebantur?

[Nonius, *s. v.* medioximum = mediocre.]

ὌΝΟΣ ΛΎΡΑΣ.

The proverb in full runs thus: ὄνος λύρας ἀκούων κινεῖ τὰ ὦτα, and the expression ὄνος λύρας is used for a stupid man, who has no appreciation of music. The Cynics generally looked down upon music, and Diogenes had a sneer for those who could tune a lyre, but were indifferent as to their soul being in a state of harmony. The Satura describes a contention between a devotee of music and one of its detractors. It may remind us of the way in which Zethus (in the Antiope of Euripides and Pacuvius) presses the claims of a practical life against his dreamy, music-loving brother Amphion. The prologue opens with Phonascus a professor, announcing himself and his accomplishments (I): music is natural to man (II): it is the harmony of the spheres which regulates the universe III) : workers sing over their daily toil (IV : the vast audience in a theatre is melted by the tender notes of the flute, or excited by more stirring tones (V) : the priests of Cybele can tame the lion with the sound of their cymbals, as the statue on Mt. Ida commemorates (VI) : how much nobler is such a profession than the coarse amusements of the huntsman! VII . To which the unmusical man replies, that after all it is an unprofitable art (VIII) ; and that we must admit as great a variety in the accomplishments of men, as we see in the colours of horses (IX).

I.

Phonáscus[1] adsum. vócis suscitábulum,
Cantántiumque gállus gallináceus.

[Nonius, *s. v.* suscitabulum.]

[1] Al. φωνασκία.

II.

Primum eam esse physicen, quod sit ἔμφυτος, ut ipsa vox, basis eius.

[Nonius, s. v. basis.]

III.

Quam móbilem divúm lyram Sol hármoge[1]
quadám gubernans mótibus diís veget.

[Nonius, s. v. diis : veget.]

IV.

Homines rusticos in vindemia incondita canere, sarcinatricis in machinis.

[Nonius, s. v. sarcinatrices.]

V.

Saépe totiús theatri tibiis cernó flectendo
Cómmutare méntes, erigi ánimos eorum ...

[Nonius, s. v. frigi : 1. erigi.]

VI.

Non vidisti simulacrum leonis ad Idam eo loco, ubi quondam, subito cum cum vidissent quadrupedem, Galli tympanis adeo fecerunt mansuem, ut tractarent manibus?

[Nonius, s. v. mansues, nom.]

VII.

Nempe aút sues silváticos in móntibus sectáris
Venábulo aut cervós, qui tibi malí nihil fecérunt,
Verrútis—a! artem praeclaram.

[Nonius, s. v. venabulum.]

VIII.

Iurgare coepit dicens:
'Quae scís, age qui in vulgúm vulgas artémque expromis inértem?'

[Nonius, s. v. vulgus, masc.]

---

[1] ἁρμογῇ = 'harmony.'

IX.

Equí colore díspares ítem nati :
hic bádius, iste gílvus, ille múrinus.

[Nonius, s. v. badius.]

PAPIAPAPAE (περὶ ἐγκωμίων).

The title seems to be only an exclamation expressive of wondering admiration. The Satura is directed against excessive praise, which is often given out of mere ignorance, as a man may mistake a 'bit of glass for an emerald' (I). Funeral orations are fulsome; they do not discriminate between the worthy and unworthy (II). The mincing compliments paid to a pretty woman are absurd in their extravagance III–VII. But there is another side to the picture—excessive dispraise. Some critics know how to pick holes in everything, but do not know how to give honour where honour is due (VIII, IX).

I.

Imperito nonnunquam concha videtur margarita,
vitrum smaragdos.

[Nonius, s. v. margaritum.]

II.

Qui potest laus videri vera, cum mortuus saepe furacissimus ac nequissimus civis iuxta ac Publius Africanus—?

[Nonius, s. v. iuxta = similiter.]

III.

Ante aúris nodo ex cróbyli subpárvuli
intórti emittebántur sex cicínnuli ;
oculís suppactulís nigelli púpuli
quantam hílaritatem sígnificantes ánimuli !

[Cp. inf. V.]

IV.

Quos cálliblepharo náturali pálpebrae
tinctae vallatos móbili septó tenent.

[Nonius, s. v. palpebrae.]

V.

rictus parvíssimus
ut réfrenato rísu roseo . . .

[III, V. Nonius, s. v. rictus hominis,.]

VI.

Lacúlla in mento impréssa Amoris dígitulo
vestígio demónstrat mollitúdinem.

[Nonius, s. v. mollitudinem.]

VII.

Collúm procerum fíctum levi mármore
regillae tunicae définitur púrpura.

[Nonius, regilla, dimin. a regia.]

VIII.

Omni ópstant in ministerio invidúm tabes.

[Nonius, s. v. invidum, gen.

IX.

Quare resides lingulaeae, optrectatores tui, iam nunc
murmurantes dicunt :

μωμήσεταί τις μᾶλλον ἢ μιμήσεται.

[Nonius, s. v. lingulacae, &c.]

PROMETHEUS LIBER.

ANTISTHENES, the Cynic philosopher, had already written a
dialogue between Prometheus and Hercules, in which Hercules
reproaches Prometheus for his ill-advised gift of fire to mortals,

which is interpreted to mean the fatal tendency to philosophic speculations.

This suggests that the interlocutors in this Satura may be Prometheus and Hercules. In the first part of it, Prometheus bewails his terrible tortures (I-V): in the second, Hercules taunts him with the deterioration of the human beings which he has animated; exhibiting the extravagant licentiousness of the young profligate with his dainty mistress, and the coarse, swinish life of the common citizen (VI, VII).

I.

Ego infelix nón queam
vim própulsare, atque ínimicum Orco inmittere?
nequíquam saepe aerátas manuis cómpedes
conór revellere.

[Nonius, s. v. compedes.]

II.

Sum utí subernus[1] córtex aut cacúmina
moriéntum in quérqueto arborum aritúdine.

[Nonius, s. v. cortex.]

III.

atque *ex artubus*
exsánguibus dolóre evirescát color.

[Nonius, s. v. evirescat.]

IV.

Mortális nemo exaúdit, sed late íncolens
Scythárum inhospitális campis vástitas.

[Nonius, s. v. vastitas = desertio. Cf. Aesch. P. V. 2, 21.]

V.

Levís mens nunquam sómnurnas imágines
adfátur, non umbrántur somno púpulae.

[Nonius, s. v. somnurnae = quae in somno videantur.]

---

[1] From *suber* = 'cork tree.' Al. *supernus*.

VI.

Chrysosandalos locat sibi amiculam de lacte et cera Tarentina quam apes Milesiae coegerint ex omnibus floribus lilantes, sine osse et nervis, sine pelle, sine pilis, puram putam, proceram, candidam, teneram, formosam.

[Nonius, *s. v.* putus.]

VII.

In tenebris ac suili vivunt, nisi non forum hara atque homines ibi plerique sues sunt existimandi.

[Nonius, *s. v.* hara = porcorum stabulum.]

QUINQUATRUS.

This festival of Minerva gives Varro an opportunity of dealing with those professions under the especial patronage of the goddess, and particularly that of the physician. 'Why,' asks one 'should I employ a doctor, and have to drink nauseous physic and reduce my strength?' I). In preference to this, he writes (in true medical style) a prescription for a good dose of wine, with no addition but pure water II, III). The doctor who draws the fluid from a dropsical patient is not as clever as an Etruscan inspector of conduits! (IV).

I.

Quid médico mi est opús? perpetuo absíntium ut bibám
  gravem
et cástoreum, levémque robur?

[Nonius, *s. v.* absintium, masc.]

II.

Cape hánc caducam Liberi mollém dapem
de frónde Bromia autúmnitatis úvidam.

[Nonius, *s. v.* autumnitas.]

III.

Quom lýmpham mélius é lacuna fóntium
adlátam nido pótili permísceat.

[Nonius, *s. v.* nidus, pro poculo.]

IV.

An hoc praestat Herophilus Diogeni, quod ille e ventre aquam mittit? hoc tu iactas? At hoc pacto utilior te Tuscus aquilex!

[Nonius, *s. v.* aquilex.]

SEXAGESSIS.

This word, which commonly means a sum of sixty *asses*, is here grotesquely used for 'a man of sixty years.' He is the Roman Rip van Winkle, who falls asleep at the age of ten and does not wake for half-a-century (I, II). Then he looks around and finds everything changed; himself not least, for he has a bristly beard like a hedgehog, and a great snout for a nose (III). 'So a pup changes to a dog, or a grain of corn to an ear' (IV). The ancient virtues have been banished from Rome, and their place is supplied by Impiety, Disloyalty and Impudence (V). No 'pious Aeneas' would 'carry' his father now-a-days; but every brat is ready to 'carry him off' by poison (VI). There is a regular sale of votes in the Comitia (VII); the judges make money out of the accused (VIII); there is only one law observed—'Give and take' (IX). Marcus deplores this detestable change, recalling the days of sobriety and steadiness (X); when men were not ready to rush into the decoy, like so many silly ducks (XI). The young Romans resent this protest, and proceed to illustrate in his person the proverb—'sexagenarios de ponte': which properly means that men of this age were barred from the voting-lobby (*pons*); but the joke lies in the other interpretation of the phrase, referring to the actual casting of old men from one of the bridges over the Tiber, as a relic of human sacrifice. See *s. v. depontani senes* (XII–XIV).

I.

O stúlta nostri péctoris dormítio

vigilábilis, quae mé puellum impúberem
cepísti!

[Nonius, s. v. puellus.]

II.

Romam regressus ibi nihil offendi quod ante annos
quinquaginta cum primum dormire coepi reliqui.

[Nonius, s. v. offendere = invenire.]

III.

Se circumspexe atque invenisse se. cum dormire
coepisset tam glaber quam Socrates, esse factum ericium
cum pilis albis, cum proboscide.

[Nonius, s. v. ericium.]

IV.

Sic canis fit é catello, sic e tritico spica.

[Nonius, s. v. spica.]

V.

In quarum locum subierunt inquilinae impietas, perfidia, impudicitia.

[Nonius, s. v. subire.]

VI.

Nunc quis patrem decem annorum natus non modo
aufert, sed tollit, nisi veneno?

[Nonius, s. v. tollere = occidere.]

VII.

Ubi tum comitia habebant, ibi nunc fit mercatus.

[Nonius, s. v. mercatus.]

VIII.

Avidus iudex reum ducit esse κοινὸν Ἑρμῆν.

[Nonius, s. v. ducere = existimare.]

IX.

Quod leges iubent, non faciunt : δὸς καὶ λαβέ fervit omnino.

[Nonius, s. v. fervit pro fervet.]

X.

Ergo tum Romae parce pureque pudentes
  vixere in patria : at nunc sumus in rutuba.

[Nonius, s. v. rutuba = perturbatio.]

XI.

Nequiquam is agilipénnis anates trémipedas,
buxeis cum rostris pecudes in palúdibus
de nócte nigra ad lúmina lampadís sequens.

[Nonius, s. v. pecudes = non solum quadrupedes.]

XII.

Senibus[1] crassis homulli non videmus quid fiat?

[Nonius, s. v. crassus = stultus.]

XIII.

Acciti sumus, ut depontaremur : murmur fit ferus.

[Nonius, s. v. murmur, masc.]

XIV.

Vix ecfatus erat, cum more maiorum ultro casnares
arripiunt, de ponte in Tiberim deturbant.

[Nonius, s. v. casnares = seniles.]

---

[1] Al. *sensibus*.

EX LIBRO IMAGINUM.

Varro wrote fifteen books of *Imagines* or *Hebdomades*. The first book contained 14, and each of the other fourteen books 49 biographies of distinguished Greeks and Romans, illustrated with portraits. The following fragments are preserved.

1.
DEMETRIUS.

Hic Demetrius est, tot aera[1] nanctus
quot lucis habet annus absolutus.

[Nonius, s. v. luces = dies.]

II.
HOMER.

Capélla Homeri cándida haec tumulum índicat,
quod hác Ietae[2] mórtuo faciúnt sacra.

[Aul. Gell. 3. 11.]

III.
NAEVIUS.

Inmórtalés mortáles | si forét fas flére,
flerént divaé Camenae | Naévium poétam.
itáque póstquam est Orci | tráditús thesaúro,
oblíti súnt Romae | loquiér linguá latína.

[Aul. Gell. 1. 24.]

---

[1] *aera*, if the reading be right, must mean bronze statues.

[2] *Ietae*, the inhabitants of the island of Ios, one of the places which claimed to be the birthplace of Homer.

IV.

PACUVIUS.

Tamenétsi, adulescens, próperas, te hoc saxúm rogat
aspícias ut se, deínde quod scriptum ést legas.
hic súnt poetae Pácuvi Marcí sita
ossa. hóc volebam néscius ne essés. vale.

[AUL. GELL. *l. c.*]

V.

PLAUTUS.

Postquam est mortem aptus Plautus, comoedia luget,
scaena est deserta, dein risus, ludus, iocusque
et numeri innumeri simul omnes conlacrumarunt.

[AUL. GELL. *l. c.*]

VI.

SEPTEM SAPIENTES.

'Optimus est,' Cleobulus ait, 'modus,' incola Lindi;
ex Ephyra Periandre doces 'cuncta emeditanda';
'tempus nosce' inquit Mitylenis Pittacus ortus;
'plures esse malos' Bias autumat ille Prieneus;
Milesiusque Thales 'sponsori damna' minatur;
'nosce' inquit 'tete' Chilon Lacedaemone cretus;
Cecropiusque Solon 'ne quid nimis' induperabit.

[HYGINUS, *Fab.* 221.]

[I have followed Bährens in grouping all these epigrams under Varro's name, as, at least, convenient; but the authorship of several is uncertain.]

M. T. CICERO.

(106-43 A.C.)

For a brief period the dictum of Plutarch (*Vit. Cic.* c. 2) was really true—that Cicero was the first poet as well as the first orator of his time. It was only true till Lucretius and Catullus came into the field. In spite of the abuse and ridicule[1] which was heaped upon the poetical compositions of Cicero for excessive vanity and expressions in questionable taste, the fact remains that the fruits of Cicero's leisure hours mark a distinct advance in Latin poetry, and a real development of the hexameter, which made the perfect Virgilian rhythm distinctly more possible.

His *Marius* is a tribute from one citizen of Arpinum to another. Cicero was still young when he wrote it: and there is something in the boldness of the man who could choose such a subject under the dictatorship of Sulla that may remind us of his famous defence of Roscius of Ameria. But the date of the poem is very doubtful.

The scene is laid at Arpinum. We see Marius beneath the famous oak (Arpinatium, Mariana quercus, Cic. *De Legg.* 1. 1), encouraged by a favourable omen:—

MARIUS.

I.

Hic Iovis altisoni subito pinnata satelles
arboris e trunco serpentis saucia morsu
subrigit, ipsa feris transfigens unguibus, anguem
semianimum et varia graviter cervice micantem;
quem se intorquentem lanians rostroque cruentans,
iam satiata animos, iam duros ulta dolores,

[1] Cp. Senec. rhet. *Controv.* 3. praef.; Senec. phil. *De Ira*, 3. 37; *Epist.* 106; Tacit. *Dial. de Orat.* 21; Juv. *Sat.* 10. 121 foll.; Martial, *Epig.* 2. 89, &c.

abicit efflantem et laceratum adfligit in unda.
seque obitu a solis nitidos convertit ad ortus.
hanc ubi praepetibus pinnis lapsuque volantem
conspexit Marius, divini numinis augur,
faustaque signa suae laudis reditusque notavit,
partibus intonuit caeli pater ipse sinistris :
sic aquilae clarum firmavit Iuppiter omen.

    [Cic. *De Div.* 1. 48. Cp. Hom. *Il.* 12. 200; Verg. *Aen.* 11. 751.]

LIMON.

Λειμών i. e. the *Meadow*; (ἐστὶ δὲ ποικίλων περιοχή, a sort of album of different 'cullings.')

Tu quoque, qui solus lecto sermone, Terenti,
conversum expressumque Latina voce Menandrum
in medium nobis sedatis motibus effers,
quiddam come loquens atque omnia dulcia dicens.

    [Sueton. *Vit. Terent.*]

DE CONSULATU SUO.

[For nearly twenty-six years Cicero's muse was silent. But after his return from exile he resumed his poetical studies; partly as an alleviation of his own anxiety, and partly as a means of keeping up in the minds of his countrymen the memory of his splendid services, on which he set so much store. The *De Consulatu suo* was the work of his forty-seventh year; the *De Temporibus suis* of his fiftieth.

The *De Consulatu* consisted of three books, of which the second was connected with the name of the Muse Urania; the third with Calliope. The first book is only known to us from a note of Servius on Verg. *Ecl.* 8. 106, which tells us the story of Terentia's sacrifice: how that when the fire had died down and she was about to pour in the libation, the flame shot up again from the ashes, thus foretelling that Cicero would be made Consul that very year.]

The two verses may be filled up as follows:—

I

Aspice: corripuit tremulis altaria flammis
sponte sua, dum ferre moror, cinis ipse. Bonum sit!
[Servius, *l. c.*]

II.

(Urania addresses Cicero.)

Principio aetherio flammatus Iuppiter igni
vertitur et totum conlustrat lumine mundum,
menteque divina caelum terrasque petessit.
quae penitus sensus hominum vitasque retentat,
aetheris aeterni saepta atque inclusa cavernis.
et si stellarum motus cursusque vagantes
nosse velis, qua sint signorum in sede locatae,
(quae verbo e falsis Graiorum vocibus errant,
re vera certo lapsu spatioque feruntur),
omnia iam cernes divina mente notata.
nam primum astrorum volucris te consule motus
concursusque gravi stellarum ardore micantis
tu quoque, cum tumulos Albano in monte nivalis
lustrasti, et lacte mactasti lacte Latinas,[1]
vidisti et claro tremulos ardore cometas;
multaque misceri nocturna caede putasti,
quod ferme dirum in tempus cecidere Latinae,
cum claram speciem concreto lumine luna
abdidit et subito stellanti nocte perempta est.
quid vero Phoebi fax, tristis nuntia belli,

[1] *Latinas*, sc. ferias. A sacrifice to Iuppiter Latiaris on the Alban Mount, held at times appointed by the magistrates (f. *conceptirae*). Besides the common sacrifice of an ox, the towns which had a share in the Alban sanctuary sent gifts of *milk* (*lacte*) &c.

quae, magnum ad columen[1], flammato ardore volabat,
praecipitis caeli partis obitusque potissens :
aut cum terribili perculsus fulmine civis
luce serenanti[2] vitalia lumina liquit?
aut cum se gravido tremefecit corpore tellus?
iam vero variae nocturno tempore visae
terribiles formae bellum motusque monebant,
multaque per terras vates oracla furenti
pectore fundebant tristia minitantia casus ;
atque ea quae lapsu tandem cecidere vetusto,
haec fore perpetuis signis clarisque frequentans
ipse deum genitor caelo terrisque canebat.
nunc ea Torquato quae quondam et consule[3] Cotta
Lydius ediderat Tyrrhenae gentis haruspex,
omnia fixa tuus glomerans determinat annus.
nam pater altitonans stellanti nixus Olympo
ipse suos quondam tumulos ac templa petivit
et Capitolinis iniecit sedibus ignis.
tum species ex aere vetus venerataque Nattae[4]
concidit elapsaeque vetusto numine leges,
et divom simulacra peremit fulminis ardor.
hic silvestris erat Romani nominis altrix
Martia[5], quae parvos Mavortis semine natos
uberibus gravidis vitali rore rigabat :
quae tum cum pueris flammato fulminis ictu
concidit atque avulsa pedum vestigia liquit.
tum quis non artis scripta ac monumenta volutans

[1] *ad columen* : perhaps, 'like a column.'
[2] *serenanti* : it was 'a bolt from the blue.'
[3] *consule*, B. C. 65.
[4] *Nattae species*. See Cic. *De Div.* 2. 21 'Nattae statua et aera legum de caelo tacta.'
[5] *Martia*, sc. lupa, Liv. 10. 27.

voces tristificas chartis promebat Etruscis?
omnes civili generosa stirpe profectam
volvier ingentem cladem pestemque monebant,
tum legum exitium constanti voce ferebant,
templa deumque adeo flammis urbemque iubebant
eripere, et stragem horribilem caedemque vereri;
atque haec fixa gravi fato ac fundata teneri,
ni post, excelsum ad columen formata decore,
sancta Iovis spécies claros spectaret in ortus:
tum fore ut occultos populus sanctusque senatus
cernere conatus posset, si solis ad ortum
conversa inde patrum sedes populique videret,
haec tardata diu species multumque morata
consule te tandem celsa est in sede locata;
atque una fixi ac signati temporis hora
Iuppiter excelsa clarabat sceptra corona.
et clades patriae flamma ferroque parata
vocibus Allobrogum patribus populoque patebat.
rite igitur veteres, quorum monumenta tenetis,
qui populos urbisque modo ac virtute regebant,
rite etiam vestri, quorum pietasque fidesque
praestitit ac longe vicit sapientia cunctos,
praecipue coluere vigenti numine divos.
haec adeo penitus cura videre sagaci,
otia qui studiis laeti tenuere decoris
inque Academia umbrifera nitidoque Lyceo
fuderunt claras fecundi pectoris artis.
e quibus ereptum, primo iam a flore iuventae,
te patria in media virtutum mole locavit.
tu tamen anxiferas curas requiete relaxans,
quod patria vacat, hic studiis nobisque sacrasti.

[Cic. *De Div.* I. 11-13.]

III.

(Calliope addresses Cicero.)

Interea cursus, quos prima in parte iuventae
quosque adeo consul virtute animoque petisti,
hos retine atque auge famam laudesque bonorum.

[Cic. *Ad Att.* 2. 3. 3.]

EX GRAECIS CONVERSA.

ILIAS.

I.

Ferte, viri, et duros animo tolerate labores.
auguris ut nostri Calchantis fata queamus
scire ratosne habeant an vanos pectoris orsus.
namque omnes memori portentum mente retentant,
qui non funestis liquerunt lumina fatis.
Argolicis primum ut vestita est classibus Aulis.
quae Priamo cladem et Troiae pestemque ferebant,
nos circum latices gelidos fumantibus aris,
aurigeris divom placantes numina tauris,
sub platano umbrifera, fons unde emanat aquai,
vidimus inmani specie tortuque draconem
terribilem, Iovis ut pulsu penetraret ab ara;
qui platani in ramo foliorum tegmine saeptos
corripuit pullos; quos cum consumeret octo,
nona super tremulo genetrix clangore volabat,
cui ferus inmani laniavit viscera morsu.
hunc ubi tam teneros volucris matremque peremit,

qui luci ediderat genitor Saturnius, idem
abdidit[1], et duro firmavit tegmina saxo.
nos autem timidi stantes mirabile monstrum
vidimus in mediis divom versarier aris.
tum Calchas haec est fidenti voce locutus:
'quidnam torpentes subito obstipuistis, Achivi?
nobis haec portenta deum dedit ipse creator
tarda et sera nimis, sed fama ac laude perenni,
nam quot avis taetro mactatas dente videtis,
tot nos ad Troiam belli exanclabimus annos,
quae decumo cadet, et poena satiabit Achivos.'
edidit haec Calchas, quae iam matura videtis.

[Cic. De Div. 2. 30; cp. Hom. Il. 2. 299 foll.]

II.

Qui miser in campis maerens errabat Aleis,
ipse suum cor edens, hominum vestigia vitans.

[Cic. Tusc. Disp. 3. 26; cp. Hom. Il. 6. 201 foll.]

III.

ODYSSEA.

O decus Argolicum, quin puppim flectis, Ulixes,
auribus ut nostros possis agnoscere cantus?
nam nemo haec unquam est transvectus caerula cursu
quin prius adstiterit vocum dulcedine captus,
post, variis avido satiatus pectore Musis,
doctior ad patrias lapsus pervenerit oras.
nos grave certamen belli clademque tenemus

---

[1] *abdidit.* This implies that Cicero read in *Il.* 2. 318 ἀίζηλον, i. e. ἀίδηλον, the lect. of Aristarchus, and not ἀρίζηλον as MSS.

Graecia quam Troiae divino numine vexit,
omniaque e latis rerum vestigia terris.
   [Cic. De Fin. 5. 18; cp. Hom. Od. 12. 184 foll.]

IV.
EX AESCHYLO.

Titánum[1] soboles, sócia nostri sánguinis,
generáta Caelo, aspícite religatum ásperis
vinctúmque saxis, návem ut horrisonó freto
noctém paventes tímidi adnectunt návitae.
Satúrnius me síc infixit Iúppiter,
Iovísque numen Múlcibri adscivít manus.
hos ílle cuneos fábrica crudeli ínserens
perrúpit artus; quá miser sollértia
transvérberatus cástrum hoc Furiarum íncolo.
iam tértio me quóque funestó die
tristi ádvolatu adúncis lacerans únguibus
Iovis satelles pástu dilaniát fero.
tum iécore opimo fárta et satiata ádfatim
clangórem fundit vástum, et sublime ávolans
pinnáta cauda nóstrum adulat sánguinem.
cum véro adesum inflátu renovatum ést iecur,
tum rúrsus tactros ávida se ad pastús refert.
sic húnc custodem maésti cruciatús alo,
qui mé perenni vívum foedat misería.
namque út videtis vínclis constrictús Iovis
arcére nequeo díram volucrem a péctore.
sic me ipse viduus[2] péstis excipio ánxias,

---

[1] *Titanum.* The Titans formed the Chorus in the Προμηθεὺς Λυό-
μενος of Aeschylus, from which this passage is translated.

[2] If *viduus* is to be joined with *me* (cp. 'viduus pharetra' Hor. Od.
I. 10. 12) render, 'meis viribus destitutus.' Kühner joins *excipio
me pestis anxias* = ipse mihi paro pestem.

amóre mortis términum anquiréns mali ;
sed lónge a leto númine aspellór Iovis.
atque haéc vetusta, saéclis glomerata hórridis,
luctífica clades nóstro infixa est córpori,
e quó liquatae sólis ardore éxcidunt
guttaé, quae saxa adsídue instillant Caúcasi.

[Cic. *Tusc. Disp.* 2. 10.]

V.

EX SOPHOCLE.

O múlta dictu grávia, perpessu áspera,
quae córpore exancláta atque animo[1] pértuli!
nec míhi Iunonis térror implacábilis,
nec tántum invexit trístis[2] Eurystheús mali
quantúm una vecors Oénei partu édita.
haec me ínretivit véste furiali ínscium,
quae láteri inhaerens morsu lacerat víscera
urguénsque graviter púlmonum haurit spíritus ;
iam décolorem[3] sánguinem omnem exsórbuit.
sic córpus clade horríbili absumptum extábuit,
ipse ílligatus péste interimor téxtili.
hos nón hostilis déxtra, non Terra édita
molés Gigantum, nón biformato ínpetu
Centaúrus ictus córpori inflixít meo,
non Gráia vis, non bárbara ulla inmánitas,
non saéva terris géns relegata ultimis,
quas péragrans undique ómnem efferitatem éxpuli :

---

[1] *animo.* In the original, Soph. *Trach.* 1047, the corresponding word is νώτοισι. Perhaps Cicero read στέρνοισι (cp. Trach. 1090) and misunderstood it.

[2] *tristis,* i. e. στυγνός.

[3] *decolorem,* a mistaken translation of χλωρόν.

sed féminea vir, féminea interimór manu.
O náte, vere hoc nómen usurpá patri!
ne me óccidentem mátris superet cáritas.
huc árripe ad me mánibus abstractám piis.
iam cérnam mene an íllam potiorém putes.
perge, aúde, nate! illácrima patris péstibus!
miserére! gentes nóstras flebunt míserias.
heu! vírginalem me óre ploratum édere,
quem vídit nemo ulli íngemiscentém malo!
sic féminata[1] vírtus adflicta óccidit.
accéde, nate, adsíste, miserandum ádspice
evíscerati córpus laceratúm patris!
vidéte, cuncti, túque, caelestúm sator,
iace, óbsecro, in me vím coruscam fúlminis!
nunc, núnc dolorum anxíferi torquent vértices,
nunc sérpit ardor. O ánte victricés manus!
o péctora, o terga, ó lacertorúm tori!
vestróne pressu quóndam Nemeaeús leo
frendéns efflavit gráviter extremum hálitum?
haec déxtra Lernam taétra mactata éxcetra,[2]
pacávit[3]; haec bicórporem afflixít manum;
Erymánthiam haec vastíficam abiecit béluam;
haec é Tartarea ténebrica abstractúm plaga
tricípitem eduxit, Hydra generatúm canem;
haec ínteremit tórtu multiplicábili
dracónem, auriferam obtútu adservantem árborem.
multa ália victrix nóstra lustravít manus,
nec quísquam e nostris spólia cepit laúdibus.

     [Cic. *Tusc. Disp.* 2. 8, 9; Soph. *Trach.* 1046 foll.]

[1] *feminata.* Soph. *Trach.* 1075 νῦν δ' ἐκ τοιούτου θῆλυς εὕρημαι τάλας.
[2] *excetra,* apparently a corrupt form of ἔχιδνα.
[3] *pacavit.* Cp. Verg. *Aen.* 6. 804.

VI.
EX EURIPIDE.
I.
Iurávi lingua, méntem iniurátám gero.
[Cic. *De Off*. 3. 29; Eur. *Hippol*. 612.]

II.
Nam sí violandum est iús, regnandi grátia
violándum est: aliis rébus pietatém colas.
[Cic. *De Off*. 3. 21; Eur. *Phoen*. 524.]

III.
Nam nós decebat coétus celebrantís domum
lugére, ubi esset áliquis in lucem éditus,
humánae vitae vária reputantís mala:
at quí labores mórte finissét gravis,
hunc ómni amicos laúde et laetítia éxsequi.
[Cic. *Tusc. Disp*. 1. 48; Eur. *Cresphont*. fr. 13.]

INCERTAE SEDIS FRAGMENTA.
I.
Quorum luxuries fortunam ac censa perédit.
[Nonius, *s. v.* censum *neutr*.]

II.
Cedant arma togae, concedat laurea laudi [1].
[Cic. *De Off*. 1. 77. &c.]

III.
O fortunatam natam me consule Romam!
[Juv. *Sat*. 10. 122. &c.]

---
[1] *laudi*. Al. *linguae*.

IV.

In montes patrios et ad incunabula nostra
pergam.

[Cic. *Ad Att.* 2. 15. 3.]

EPIGRAMMA.

[On the last day of December, B. C. 45, the consul Q. Fabius Maximus having died suddenly, Caesar made C. Caninius Rebilus consul for the few remaining hours of the day.]

Vigilántem habemus cónsulem Caninium,
qui in cónsulatu sómnum non vidit suo.

[Macrob. *Sat.* 2. 3. 6.]

EX VARIIS.

I.

Mors mea ne careat lacrimis : linquamus amicis
maerorem, ut celebrent funera cum gemitu.

[Cic. *Tusc. Disp.* 1. 49 ; Solon, frag. 21.]

II.

Croesus Halyn penetrans magnam pervertet opum vim.

[Cic. *De Div.* 2. 56 ; see Hdt. 1. 53.]

III.

Dic, hospes, Spartae nos te hic vidisse iacentis,
dum sanctis patriae legibus obsequimur.

[Cic. *Tusc. Disp.* 1. 42 ; Simonid. *ap. Hdt.* 7. 228.]

DECIMUS LABERIUS.

(Circ. 105-43 A.C.)

MIMUS.

The Mime, which originally came to Rome from Magna Graecia, was at first only a 'ballet divertissement,' without song or dialogue. It received a new impulse in the time of Sulla; and under Julius Caesar it reached its zenith of literary perfection at the hands of Decimus Laberius, a Roman knight. The titles of forty-four of his Mimes are preserved. The distinguishing peculiarity of the Mime was the disuse of masks, and the performance of female parts by women. The stock characters of the Atellane do not appear in the Mime; otherwise, the plots were not dissimilar. But the Mime had its own set of regular characters—the stupid husband; the faithless wife; the confidential slave; the *soubrette*, in her short mantle (ricinium, which gave the alternative title of *fabula riciniata* to the Mime.

[For a general idea of the quality of these plays we may refer to Ovid[1]:

Quid si scripsissem mimos obscena iocantes,
    qui semper vetiti crimen amoris habent;
in quibus assidue cultus procedit adulter,
    verbaque dat stulto callida nupta viro?
nubilis hos virgo matronaque virque puerque
    spectat, et e magna parte senatus adest.
nec satis incestis temerari vocibus aures;
    assuescant oculi multa pudenda pati;
cumque fefellit amans aliqua novitate maritum,
    plauditur, et magno palma favore datur.]

The remains of the named plays of Laberius are very slight.

[1] *Trist.* 2. 497 foll.

I.

ALEXANDREA.

A promise on oath to pay is a temporary cure for debt.

Quíd est ius iurandum ? émplastrum acris álieni . . .

[Aul. Gell. 16. 7. 14.]

II.

BELONISTRIA.

A seller of needles. Apparently a parody on the Hippolytus.

domina nóstra privignúm suum
amát efflictim.

[Nonius, s. v. efflictim = vehementer.]

III.

EPHEBUS.

A quarrel in Olympus over the fate of Rome.

Licéntiam ac libídinem ut tollám petis
togátae stirpis.
Idcírco ope nostra dílatatum est dóminium
togátae gentis.

[Macrob. Sat. 6. 5. 15.]

IV.

FULLO.

A picture of a bare-legged, spindle-shanked man, treading cloth in the water.

. . . utrum tu húnc gruem Baleáricum an hominém putas
ésse ?

[Aul. Gell. 17. 36.]

V.

NECYOMANTIA.

Perhaps a sneering allusion to the intention attributed to Julius Caesar to authorise polygamy, and to increase the police force.

Duás uxores? hércle hoc plus negóti est, inquit, cóctio:
séx aediles víderat.

[AUL. GLLL. 16. 7. 12.]

VI.

RESTIO.

How a father would blind himself, rather than see his prodigal son's enjoyment.

Demócritus Abderítes physicus philosophus
clipeúm constituit cóntra exortum Hyperíonis,
oculós effodere ut pósset splendore aéreo.
ita rádiis solis áciem effodit lúminis,
malís bene esse né videret cívibus.
sic égo fulgentis splendorem pecúniae
volo elucificare éxitum aetatís meae,
ne in ré bona esse vídeam nequam fílium.

[AUL. GELL. 10. 17.]

VII.

VIRGO.

How I fell in love like a cockroach into a basin.

Amóre cecidi tamquam blatta in pélvim.

[NONIUS, s. v. pelvis.]

VIII.

The story about Caesar, Laberius, and his rival Publilius Syrus, is thus given by Macrobius (Sat. 2. 7): 'Laberium asperae libertatis equitem Romanum Caesar quingentis milibus invitavit ut prodiret in scaenam et ipse ageret mimos quos scriptitabat. Sed potestas non solum si invitet, sed etiam si supplicet, cogit : unde se et Laberius a Caesare coactum in prologo testatur his versibus :

Necéssitas, cuius cúrsus transvérsi ímpetum
voluérunt multi effúgere, pauci pótuerunt,
quo mé detrusit paéne extremis sénsibus !
quem núlla ambitio, núlla umquam largítio,
nullús timor, vis núlla, nulla auctóritas
movére potuit ín iuventa dé statu :
ecce in senecta ut fácile labefecít loco
viri éxcellentis ménte clemente édita
summíssa placide blándiloquens orátio !
etenim ípsi di negáre cui nil pótuerunt
hominém me denegáre quis possét pati ?
ego bís tricenis ánnis actis síne nota
equés Romanus é Lare egressús meo
domúm revertar mímus. nimirum hóc die
unó plus vixi míhi quam vivendúm fuit.
Fortúna, inmoderata ín bono aeque atque ín malo,
si tíbi erat libitum lítterarum laúdibus
flórens cacumen nóstrae famae frángere,
cur cúm vigebam mémbris praeviridántibus,
satisfácere populo et táli cum poterám viro,
non mé flexibilem cóncurvasti ut cárperes ?
nuncíne me deicis ? quó ? quid ad scaenam ádfero ?
decórem formae an dígnitatem córporis,
anímí virtutem an vócis iucundaé sonum ?
ut hédera serpens víres arboreás necat
ita mé vetustas ámplexu annorum énecat :
sepúlchri similis níl nisi nomen rétineo.

In ipsa quoque actione subinde se qua poterat ulciscebatur, inducto habitu Syri, qui velut flagris caesus praecipientique se similis exclamabat :

Porró, Quirites, libertatem pérdimus.

Et paulo post adiecit :

Nécesse est multos tímeat quem multi timent.

Quo dicto universitas populi ad solum Caesarem oculos et ora convertit, notantes inpotentiam eius hac dicacitate lapidatam. Ob haec in Publilium vertit favorem.'

Laberius was adjudged by Caesar to have been unsuccessful : as the dictator himself phrased it, 'favente tibi me victus es, Laberi, a Syro.' He then gave the prize to Publilius Syrus, and to Laberius a sum of five hundred sestertia, with a golden ring ; thus restoring to him the equestrian rank, which he had lost by appearing on the stage. Laberius, though crushed in spirit, took his defeat very well ; and, as Macrobius *l. c.* goes on to say, 'sequenti statim commissione mimo novo interiecit hos versus :

'Non póssunt primi esse ómnes omni in témpore.
summum ád gradum cum cláritatis véneris
consístes aegre, níctu citius décidas.
cecidi égo, cadet qui séquitur : laus est pública.'

M. FURIUS BIBACULUS.

(Nat. 103 A.C.)

LUDICRA.

P. VALERIUS CATO, a native of Cisalpine Gaul, had been robbed of his patrimony at the time of the Sullan proscriptions, and it is possible that the *Lydia* or *Dirae* (which has been doubtfully ascribed to him) deals with this grievance. Bibaculus in these fragments alludes to Cato's grammatical and poetical studies (I) ; to his debts, which all his cleverness could not 'clear up,' and which forced him to sell his villa at Tusculum (II) ; and to his poverty-stricken old age in a miserable hut (III).

I.

Cato grammaticus, Latina Siren,
qui solus legit[1] et facit poetas.

[SUETON. *De Gramm.* 109.]

II.

Catonis modo, Galle, Tusculanum
tota creditor urbe venditabat.
mirati sumus unicum magistrum,
summum grammaticum, optimum poetam,
omnes solvere[2] poss~ quaestiones,
unum deficere expedire nomen :
en cor Zenodoti[3], en iecur Cratetis.

[SUETON. *l. c.*]

---

[1] *legit*, perhaps 'reads aloud,' and so make a reputation for them.

[2] *solvere*. The point of the epigram turns on the double meaning of '*solvere*' = 'pay,' or 'solve'; as applied to a 'debt' or a 'difficulty' : and similarly of '*nomen expedire*,' meaning 'to elucidate an expression' or 'to clear off a debt.'

[3] *Zenodotus* and *Crates*, famous Homeric critics of the Alexandrine period.

III.

Si quis forte mei domum Catonis,
depictas minio assulas, et illos
custodis videt hortulos Priapi,
miratur quibus ille disciplinis
tantam sit sapientiam assecutus,
quem tres cauliculi, selibra farris,
racemi duo tegula sub una
ad summam prope nutriant senectam.

[Sueton. *l. c.*]

ANNALES.

Book I.

(On Caesar's Gallic War.)

I.

Interea Oceani linquens Aurora cubile.

[Macrob. *Sat.* 6. 1. 3.]

II.

Ille gravi subito deiectus vulnere habenas
misit equi. lapsusque in humum defluxit et armis
reddidit aeratis sonitum.

[Macrob. *Sat.* 6. 4. 10.]

Book IV.

Pressatur pede pes, mucro mucrone, viro vir.

[Macrob. *Sat.* 6. 3. 5.]

Book X.

Rumoresque serunt varios et multa requirunt.

[Macrob. *Sat.* 6. i. 33]

Book XI.

I.

Nomine quemque ciet : dictorum tempus adesse
commemorat.
[Macrob. Sat. 6. 1. 34.]

II.

Confirmat dictis simul atque exsuscitat acris
ad bellandum animos, relicitque ad praelia mentes.
[Macrob. l. c.]

EX LIBRIS INCERTIS.

I.

Iuppiter hibernas cana nive conspuit Alpes.
[Porphyr. ad Hor. Sat. 2. 5. 40.]

II.

Hic qua ducebant vastae divortia fossae.
[Schol. Veron. ad Verg. Aen. 9. 793.]

C. IULIUS CAESAR.

(100-44 A.C.)

IUDICIUM DE TERENTIO POETA.

Tu quoque tu in summis, o dimidiate Menander,
poneris, et merito, puri sermonis amator.
lenibus atque utinam scriptis adiuncta foret vis
comica, ut aequato virtus polleret honore
cum Graecis, neve hac despectus parte iaceres!
unum hoc maceror ac doleo tibi deesse, Terenti.

P. TERENTIUS VARRO ATACINUS.

(Fl. 50 A.C.)

ARGONAUTAE.

A FREE version of the Ἀργοναυτικά of Apollonius Rhodius. Four books are ascribed to Varro.

Book I.

I.

Ecce venit Danai multis *celebrata propago;*
namque satus Clytio, Lerni quem Naubolus ex se,
Lernum Naupliades Proteus, sed Nauplion edit
filia *Amymone Europae Danaique superbi.*
[SCHOL. VERON. ad *Verg. Aen.* 2. 82; see AP. RHOD. I. 133 foll.]

II.

Tiphyn *at* aurigam celeris fecere carinae.
[CHARIS. 272 K.; see AP. RHOD. I. 400 foll.]

III.

Quos magno Anchiale partus adducta dolore
et geminis capiens tellurem Oaxida palmis[1]
edidit in Dicta.
[SERV. ad *Verg. Ecl.* I. 66; see AP. RHOD. I. 1129.]

[1] ἀμφοτέρῃσι δραξαμένη γαίης Οἰαξίδος. Ap. Rhod. *l. c.*

Book II.

I.

Te nunc Coryciae[1] tendentem spicula nymphae
hortantes 'o Phoebe' et 'ieie' conclamarunt.
[GR. L. K. 7. 332 ; see AP. RHOD. 2. 711.]

II.

Frigidus et silvis aquilo[2] decussit honorem.
[SERV. ad Verg. Georg. 2. 400 ; see AP. RHOD. 2. 1098 foll.]

Book III.

I.

Desierant[3] latrare canes urbesque silebant :
omnia noctis erant placida composta quiete.
[SENECA, Rhet. p. 313 K. ; see AP. RHOD. 3. 749 foll.

II.

Cuius ut aspexit torta caput angue revinctum.
[CHARIS. 90 K ; see AP. RHOD. 3. 1214 foll.]

Book IV.

I.

Tum te flagranti deiectum fulmine Phaethon[4].
[QUINT. Inst. 1. 5. 17 de syllabarum συναιρέσει.]

---

[1] Πολλὰ δὲ Κωρύκιαι Νύμφαι, Πλείστοιο θύγατρες, | θαρσύνεσκον ἔπεσσιν, Ἰήιε κεκληγυῖαι. Ap. Rhod. l. c.

[2] Βορέαο μένος . . . ἐν οὔρεσι φύλλ' ἐτίνασσεν. Ap. Rhod. l. c

[3] Οὐδὲ κυνῶν ὑλακὴ ἔτ' ἀνὰ πτόλιν, οὐ θρόος ἦεν | ἠχήεις· σιγὴ δὲ μελαινομένην ἔχεν ὀρφνην. Ap. Rhod. l. c.

[4] Ἔνθα ποτ' αἰθαλόεντι τυπεὶς πρὸς στέρνα κεραυνῷ | ἡμιδαὴς Φαέθων πέσεν ἅρματος Ἡελίοιο. Ap. Rhod. 4. 597 foll.

II.

Semianimesque micant oculi lumenque requirunt[1].

[Serv. ad Verg. Aen. 10 396.]

CHOROGRAPHIA.

(Imitated from the work of Alexander of Ephesus.)

I.

Vidit et aetherio mundum torquerier axe
et septem aeternis sonitum dare vocibus orbes[2]
nitentes aliis alios, quae maxima divis
laetitiast. at tunc longe gratissima Phoebi
dextera consimiles meditatur reddere voces.

[Mar. Victor. 60 K.]

II.

Ergo inter solis stationem et sidera septem
exporrecta iacet tellus; huic extima fluctu
Oceani, interior Neptuno cingitur ora.

[Priscian, 1. 100 II. s. v. extimus.]

III.

Europam Libyamque rapax ubi dividit unda.

[Cic. Tusc. Disp. 1. 20.]

EPHEMERIS.

(The following lines, translated from Aratus, have been closely imitated, or borrowed, by Virgil, *Georg.* 1. 375 foll.)

---

[1] Said by Servius to have been taken directly from Ennius by Varro.

[2] Cp. Cic. Somn. Scip. 4: 'Quis est qui complet aures meas tantus et tam dulcis sonus? Hic est, inquit ille, qui intervallis coniunctus imparibus, sed tamen pro rata parte distinctis, impulsu et motu ipsorum orbium conficitur, et acuta cum gravibus temperans varios aequabiliter concentus efficit.'

Tum liceat pelagi volucres tardaeque paludis
cernere inexpleto studio certare lavandi,
et velut insolitum pennis infundere rorem;
aut arguta lacus circumvolitavit hirundo,
et bos suspiciens caelum (mirabile visu)
naribus aërium patulis decerpsit odorem;
nec tenuis formica cavis non evehit ova.
                      [SERV. *ad Verg. Georg.* I. 375.]

PUBLILIUS SYRUS.

(Fl. 50 A C.)

MIMUS.

A specimen of an unnamed passage from Publilius Syrus is given in Petronius (55):

Luxúriae rictu Mártis marcent moénia.
tuó palato claúsus pavo páscitur
plumáto amictus aúreo Babylónico,
gallína tibi Numídica, tibi gallús spado:
cicónia etiam, gráta, peregrina hóspita
pietáticultrix grácilipes crotalístria
avis, éxul hiemis, titulus tepídi témporis,
nequítiae nidum in cáccabo fecít modo.
quo márgarita cára tibi, bacam Índicam,
smarágdum ad quam rem víridem, pretiosúm vitrum,
quo Cárchedonios óptas ignes lápideos,
nisi út scintilles? próbitas est carbúnculus.
an út matrona ornáta phaleris pélagiis
tollát pedes indómita in strato extráneo?
aequum ést induere núptam ventum téxtilem,
palám prostare núdam in nebula línea?

In spite of the licentious character of the Mimes, and the unrestrained merriment which marked them, there was always an undercurrent of something better; which showed itself in those shrewd maxims of worldly wisdom and even of high morality, which the industry of later ages has culled from the Mimes. The principal collection goes by the name of PUBLILII SYRI SENTENTIAE; of which the following lines are typical specimens.

SENTENTIAE.

I. Ab álio expectes álteri quod féceris.
II. Aliénum aes homini ingénuo acerba est sérvitus.
III. Amáre et sapere víx deo concéditur.
IV. Avárus nisi cum móritur nil recté facit.
V. Animo imperabit sápiens, stultus sérviet.
VI. Bonitátis verba imitári maior málitia est.
VII. Bis interimitur qui suis armis perit.
VIII. Bene víxit is qui pótuit cum volúit mori.
IX. Cotídie damnatus qui sempér timet.
X. Crimén relinquit vítae qui mortem áppetit.
XI. Didicére flere féminae ad mendácium.
XII. Discórdia fit cárior concórdia.
XIII. Etiám celeritas in desiderió mora est.
XIV. Effúgere cupiditátem regnum est víncere.
XV. Fortúna vitrea est: túm cum splendet frángitur
XVI. Gravíssimum est impérium consuetúdinis.
XVII. Homo éxtra corpus ést suum cum iráscitur.
XVIII. Honésta turpitúdo est pro causá bona.
XIX. Herédis fletus sub persona rísus est.
XX. In núllum avarus bónus est, in se péssimus.
XXI. Inópiae desunt pauca, avaritiae ómnia.
XXII. Iniúriarum rémedium est oblívio.
XXIII. Inértia est labóris excusátio.
XXIV. Legém nocens verétur, fortunam ínnocens.
XXV. Locis remotis qui latet lex ést sibi.
XXVI. Male víncit quem post paénitet victóriae.
XXVII. Malús quicumque in poéna est praesidium ést bonis.
XXVIII. Nil péccent oculi si ánimus oculis ímperet.
XXIX. Numquám periclum síne periclo víncitur.

xxx.	Non túrpis est cicátrix quam virtús parit.
xxxi.	Occásio recéptus difficilés habet.
xxxii.	Pudór dimissus númquam redit in grátiam.
xxxiii.	Probó beneficium quí dat ex parte áccipit.
xxxiv.	Qui dócte servit pártem dominatús tenet.
xxxv.	Quidquíd fit cum virtúte fit cum glória.
xxxvi.	Rapere ést accipere quód non possis réddere.
xxxvii.	Rubórem amico excútere amicum est pérdere.
xxxviii.	Spina étiam grata est éx qua spectatúr rosa.
xxxix.	Solét sequi Laus cúm viam fecít Labor.
xl.	Sat mágna usura est pró beneficio mémoria.
xli.	Tacitúrnitas stulto hómini pro sapiéntia est.
xlii.	Tam deést avaro quód habet quam quod nón habet.
xliii.	Ubi fáta peccant hóminum consilia éxcidunt.
xliv.	Ubi péccat aetas maíor male discít minor.
xlv.	Ubi níl timetur quód timeatur náscitur.
xlvi.	Ubi ínnocens formídat damnat iúdicem.
xlvii.	Virúm bonum natúra non ordó facit.
xlviii.	Veterém ferendo iniúriam invités novam.
xlix.	Volúptas tacita métus est magis quam gaúdium.
l.	Vultu án natura sápiens sis, multum ínterest.

C. HELVIUS CINNA.

(Fl. 50 A.C.)

Cinna was a close friend of Catullus (*sodalis*, Cat. 10. 30), and had been with him in Bithynia. His gentile name, Helvius, explains his long sojourn among the Cenumani. A visit to his old haunts is here alluded to.

LUDICRA.

At nunc me Cenumana per salicta
bigis raeda rapit citata nanis.[1]

[Aul. Gell. 19 13.]

PROPEMPTICON POLLIONIS.

This seems to have been a guide-book in the form of a poem, to describe for the young Asinius Pollio the outline of a journey he was about to take from Brundisium, via Corcyra, to Actium, and so along the coasts of Greece into the interior of that country. It was probably modelled on the *Propempticon* of the Bithynian Parthenios.

I.

Nec tam donorum ingentes mirabere acervos
innumerabilibus congestos undique saeclis
iam inde a Belidis natalique urbis ab anno,
Cecropis atque alta Tyrii iam ab origine Cadmi.

[Charis. 124 K.]

[1] *nanis*: this word seems to have been used for a kind of small cob.

II.

Lucida cum fulgent summi carchesia[1] mali.
[Isidor. 19. 2. 10.]

III.

Atque anquina[2] regat stabilem fortissima cursum.
[Isidor. 19. 4. 7.]

IV.

Atque imitata nives lucens legitur crystallus.
[Schol. ad Iuv. Sat. 6. 155.]

ZMYRNA.

This poem ⌈quem libellum decem annis elimavit Serv. ad Verg. Ecl. 9. 35⌉ dealt with the passion of Zmyrna Myrrha, for her father Cinyras.

Te matutinus flentem conspexit Eous,
et flentem paulo vidit post Hesperus idem.
[Serv. ad Verg. Georg. 1. 288.]

EPIGRAMMA.

(He seems to have brought from Bithynia a copy of the *Diosemia* of Aratus, inscribed on mallow leaves.)

Haec tibi Arateis multum vigilata lucernis
    carmina, quis ignes novimus aetherios,
levis in aridulo malvae descripta libello
    Prusiaca vexi munera navicula.
[Isidor. 6. 12.]

---

[1] *carchesia*: 'summa pars mali, id est foramina quae summo malo funes recipiunt' Nonius, 546. 13.

[2] *anquina*: 'funis quo ad malum antenna constringitur' (Isidor. l. c.).

POPULARES VERSUS.

I.

Ribaldry of the soldiery at Caesar's triumph after the Gallic War, on the model of the old songs sung by the troops, making jokes at their officers (Livy 4. 20, 53; 5. 49; 7. 10, 38; 10. 30; 28. 9).

Gállias Caesár subégit, Nícomedes Caésarem:
ecce Caesar nunc triumphat, qui subegit Gállias,
Nícomedes nón triumphat, qui subegit Caésarem.

[Sueton. d. Iul. 49.]

II.

The introduction of Gauls into the Senate.

Gállos Caesar in triumphum dúcit, idem in cúriam:
Gálli bracas déposuérunt, látum clavum súmpserunt.

[Sueton. d. Iul. 80.]

III.

The difference between Caesar and Brutus.

Brútus, quia regés eiecit, cónsul primus fáctus est:
híc, quia consulés eiecit, réx postremo fáctus est.

[Sueton. ib.]

IV.

Cp. Vell. Patere. 2. 67: 'Lepidus Paulus fratrem proscripserat; nec Planco gratia defuit ad inpetrandum ut frater eius Plancus Plotius proscriberetur; eoque inter iocos militaris qui currum Lepidi Plancique secuti erant ... usurpabant hunc versum:

Dé germanis nón de Gallis dúo triumphant cónsules.'

V.

Ventidius Bassus, who had once made his living by looking after mules, was elected consul, and these lines were sung about the city:

Concúrrite omnes aúgures, haruspices
porténtum inusitátum conflatum ést recens;
nam múlos qui fricábat consul fáctus est.

[AUL. GELL. 15. 4.]

NOTE ON I.—MUNRO (Crit. and Elucid. of Catullus, pp. 76-79 reminds us that the occasion of a Triumph when a man seemed to stand on the highest pinnacle of glory, was just the moment when jealous Fortune must be appeased, and the effect of the Evil Eye averted. 'The greater the General was, and the more adored by his soldiers, the greater would be the sacrifice demanded by Fortuna, and the more ribald the fun in honour of their much-loved General. Caesar has grievously suffered for this. . . . In the days of Suetonius and Dio Cassius people had forgotten that in Julius' time the abuse meant little or nothing; and these two writers have taken literally what soldiers said in boisterous good humour.'

C. LICINIUS MACER CALVUS.

(82-47 A.C.)

The friend (and, sometimes, the butt) of Catullus. A man perhaps more eminent as a barrister than as a poet.

EPITHALAMIA.

Et leges sanctas docuit et cara iugavit
corpora conubiis et magnas condidit urbes.
[SERV. ad Verg. Aen. 4. 58, de Cerere.]

IO.

I.

A virgo infelix, herbis pasceris amaris!
[SERV. ad Verg. Ed. 6. 47.]

II.

Mens mea dira sibi praedicens omina vecors.
[PROBUS, 234 K. s. v. sibī.]

III.

Cum gravis ingenti conivere pupula somno . . .
[PRISCIAN, 1. 479 K. s. v. conivēre]

IV.

Frigida iam celeri superata est Bistonis ora.
[PROBUS, 226 K.]

V.

Sol quoque perpetuos meminit requiescere cursus.

[SERV. ad Verg. Ecl. 8. 4.]

LUDICRA.

I.

(Alluding to Q. Curius, a notorious gambler.)

Et talis Curius pereruditus.

[ASCON. 84 K.]

II.

(Hermogenes Tigellius offered for sale as a Sardinian slave.)

Sardi Tigelli putidum venit caput.

[PORPHYR. ad Hor. Sat. 1. 3. 1.]

L. VARIUS RUFUS.

(74-14 A.C.).

DE MORTE.

(This Epic by Varius, the friend of Virgil, is commonly supposed to refer to the violent death of Caesar.)

I.

Vendidit hic Latium populis agrosque Quiritum
eripuit: fixit leges pretio atque refixit.
           [Macrob. *Sat.* 6. 1. 39; see Verg. *Aen.* 6. 621.]

II.

Incubet ut Tyriis atque ex solido bibat auro.
           [Macrob. *Sat.* 6. 1. 40.]

III.

Quem non ille sinit lentae moderator habenae
qua velit ire, sed angusto prius orbe coercens
insultare docet campis fingitque morando.
           [Macrob. *Sat.* 6. 2. 19.]

IV.

Ceu canis umbrosam lustrans Gortynia vallem,
si veteris potuit cervae deprendere lustra,
saevit in absentem et circum vestigia lustrans
aethera per nitidum tenues sectatur odores;
non amnes illam medii, non ardua tardant,
perdita nec serae meminit decedere nocti.
           [Macrob. *Sat.* 6. 2. 20; see Verg. *Ecl.* 8. 88.]

M. TULLIUS LAUREA.

(Fl. 40 A.C.)

EPIGRAMMA.

SEE Pliny, *N. H.* 31. § 7: 'huius (*Academiae, Villae Ciceronianae*) in parte prima exiguo post obitum ipsius (Ciceronis), Antistio Vetere possidente, eruperunt fontes calidi perquam salubres oculis, celebrati carmine Laureae Tullii, qui fuit e libertis eius':

Quo tua, Romanae vindex clarissime linguae,
   silva loco melius surgere iussa viret,
atque Academiae celebratam nomine villam
   nunc reparat cultu sub potiore Vetus:
hoc en iam apparent lymphae non ante repertae,
   languida quae infuso lumina rore levant.
nimirum locus ipse sui Ciceronis honori
   hoc dedit, hac fontes cum patefecit ope,
ut, quoniam totum legitur sine fine per orbem
   sint plures oculis quae medeantur aquae.

[PLINY, *l. c.*]

THE END.

CLARENDON PRESS BOOKS

LATIN AND GREEK

Grammars and Exercise Books

Extra fcap 8vo

Mr. J. B. Allen's Elementary Series

Rudimenta Latina. Comprising accidence and exercises of a very elementary character for the use of beginners. 2s.

An Elementary Latin Grammar. 266th thousand. 2s. 6d.

A First Latin Exercise Book. Eighth edition. 2s. 6d.

A Second Latin Exercise Book. Second edition. 3s. 6d.

Key (see note p. 35) to both Exercise Books. 5s. net.

An Elementary Greek Grammar. Containing accidence and elementary syntax. 3s.

Mr. J. B. Allen's Latin Readers

With notes, maps, vocabularies and English exercises; stiff covers, 1s. 6d. each. These books are of the same and not of graduated difficulty.

Lives from Cornelius Nepos.
Tales of Early Rome.
Tales of the Roman Republic, Part I.
Tales of the Roman Republic, Part II.
} Adapted from the Text of Livy.

Other Latin Readers, etc

Tales of the Civil War, edited by W. D. Lowe. 1s. 6d.

Scenes from the Life of Hannibal. Selected from Livy. Edited by W. D. Lowe. 1s. 6d.

Extracts from Cicero, with notes, by Henry Walford. In three Parts. Third edition. Part I. Anecdotes from Grecian and Roman History. 1s. 6d. Part II. Omens and Dreams: Beauties of Nature. 1s. 6d. Part III. Rome's Rule of her Provinces. 1s. 6d. Parts I–III, 4s. 6d.

Extracts from Livy, with notes and maps, by H. Lee-Warner. New edition. Part I. The Caudine Disaster. Part II. Hannibal's Campaign in Italy. Part III, by H. Lee-Warner and T. W. Gould. The Macedonian War. 1s. 6d. each.

A First Latin Reader, by T. J. Nunns. Third edition. 2s.

An Introduction to Latin Syntax, by W. S. Gibson. 2s.

Mr. C. S. Jerram's Series

Reddenda Minora; or easy passages, Latin and Greek, for unseen translation. For the use of lower forms. Sixth edition, revised and enlarged. 1s. 6d.

Anglice Reddenda; or extracts, Latin and Greek, for unseen translation. First Series. Fifth edition. 2s. 6d. Also Latin extracts (First and Second Series), 2s. 6d.; Greek extracts, 3s. Vol. I, Latin, 2s. 6d.; Vol. II, Greek, 3s. Second Series. New edition. 3s. Third Series. 3s.

Greek Readers and Primers

Greek Reader. Selected and adapted with English notes from Professor von Wilamowitz-Moellendorff's *Griechisches Lesebuch*, by E. C. MARCHANT. Crown 8vo. 2 vols., each (with or without Vocabulary), 2s.

Selections from Plutarch's Life of Caesar. Crown 8vo, large type. Edited with notes by R. L. A. DU PONTET. 2s.

Greek Readers; Easy, by EVELYN ABBOTT. In stiff covers. 2s. **First Reader,** by W. G. RUSHBROOKE. Third edition. 2s. 6d. **Second Reader,** by A. M. BELL. Second edition. 3s. **Specimens of Greek Dialects;** being a Fourth Greek Reader. With introductions, etc, by W. W. MERRY. 4s. 6d. **Selections from Homer and the Greek Dramatists;** being a Fifth Greek Reader. With explanatory notes and introductions to the study of Greek Epic and Dramatic Poetry, by EVELYN ABBOTT. 4s. 6d.

A Greek Testament Primer. For the use of students beginning Greek, by E. MILLER. Second edition. Paper covers, 2s.; cloth, 3s. 6d.

Xenophon (see p. 43)

Easy Selections, with a vocabulary, notes, illustrations carefully chosen from coins, casts and ancient statues, and map, by J. S. PHILLPOTTS and C. S. JERRAM. Third edition. 3s. 6d.

Selections, with notes, illustrations, and maps, by J. S. PHILLPOTTS. Fifth ed. 3s. 6d. Key (see p. 35) to §§ 1-3, 2s. 6d. net.

A Greek Primer, for the use of beginners in that language. By the Right Rev. CHARLES WORDSWORTH. Eighty-sixth thousand. 1s. 6d. Graecae Grammaticae Rudimenta. Nineteenth edition. 4s.

An Introduction to the Comparative Grammar of Greek and Latin. By J. E. KING and C. COOKSON. Extra fcap 8vo. 5s. 6d.

Latin Dictionaries

A Latin Dictionary. Founded on Andrews's edition of Freund's Latin Dictionary. Revised, enlarged, and in great part rewritten, by CHARLTON T. LEWIS and CHARLES SHORT. 4to. 25s.

A School Latin Dictionary. By C. T. LEWIS. 4to. 12s. 6d.

Elementary Latin Dictionary. By C. T. LEWIS. Square 8vo. 7s. 6d.

Greek Dictionaries

A Greek-English Lexicon. By H. G. LIDDELL and ROBERT SCOTT. Eighth edition, revised. 4to. 36s.

An Intermediate Greek Lexicon. By the same. 12s. 6d.

An Abridged Greek Lexicon. By the same. 7s. 6d.

LATIN AND GREEK PROSE

Latin and Greek Prose Composition

Mr. J. Y. Sargent's Course. Extra fcap 8vo

Primer of Latin Prose Composition. 2s. 6d.

Passages for Translation into Latin Prose. Eighth edition. 2s. 6d. Key (see note below) to the eighth edition, 5s. net.

Primer of Greek Prose. 3s. 6d. Key (see note below) 5s. net.

Passages for Translation into Greek Prose. 3s.

Exemplaria Graeca. Select Greek versions of the above. 3s.

Other Prose Composition Books. Extra fcap 8vo

Ramsay's Latin Prose Composition. Fourth edition.
Vol. I: Syntax and Exercises. 4s. 6d. Or Part 1, First Year's Course, 1s. 6d.; Part 2, Second Year's Course, 1s. 6d.; Part 3, Syntax and Appendix, 2s. 6d. Key (see note below) to the volume, 5s. net.
Vol. II: Passages for Translation. 4s. 6d.

Jerram's Graece Reddenda. Being exercises for Greek Prose. 2s. 6d.

Unseen Translation

Jerram's Reddenda Minora and Anglice Reddenda. See p. 33.

Fox and Bromley's Models and Exercises in Unseen Translation. Revised edition. Extra fcap 8vo. 5s. 6d. A Key (see note below) giving references for the passages contained in the above, 6d. net.

Latin and Greek Verse

Lee-Warner's Helps and Exercises for Latin Elegiacs. 3s. 6d. Key (see note below) 4s. 6d. net.

Rouse's Demonstrations in Latin Elegiac Verse. Crown 8vo. 4s. 6d. (Exercises and versions.)

Laurence's Helps and Exercises for Greek Iambic Verse. 3s. 6d. Key (see note below) 5s. net.

Sargent's Models and Materials for Greek Iambic Verse. 4s. 6d. Key (see note below) 5s. net.

Nova Anthologia Oxoniensis. Edited by Robinson Ellis and A. D. Godley. Crown 8vo buckram extra, 6s. net; on India paper, 7s. 6d. net.

Musa Clauda. Being translations into Latin Elegiac Verse, by S. G. Owen and J. S. Phillimore. Crown 8vo, boards, 3s. 6d.

Latin Prose Versions. Contributed by various Scholars, edited by G. G. Ramsay. Extra fcap 8vo, 5s.

NOTE AS TO KEYS

Application for all Keys to be made direct to the Secretary, Clarendon Press, Oxford. Keys can be obtained by teachers, or bona fide private students, on application to the Secretary, Clarendon Press, Oxford.

CLARENDON PRESS BOOKS

Annotated editions of Latin Authors

For Oxford Classical Texts see p. 41; for Oxford Translations, p. 21.

Aetna. A critical recension of the Text, with prolegomena, translation, commentary, and index verborum. By ROBINSON ELLIS. Crown 8vo. 7s. 6d. net.

Avianus, The Fables. With prolegomena, critical apparatus, commentary, etc. By ROBINSON ELLIS. 8vo. 8s. 6d.

Caesar, De Bello Gallico, I–VII. In two crown 8vo volumes. By ST. G. STOCK. Vol. I, Introduction, 5s.; Vol. II, Text and Notes, 6s.

    The Gallic War. By C. E. MOBERLY. Second edition. With maps. Books I–III, 2s.; III–V, 2s. 6d.; VI–VIII, 3s. 6d.

    The Civil War. New edition. By the same editor. 3s. 6d.

Catulli Veronensis Liber rec. ROBINSON ELLIS. Second edition, with notes and appendices. 8vo. 21s. net.

    Commentary. By the same. Second edition. 8vo. 18s. net.

    Carmina Selecta. Text only, for Schools. 3s. 6d.

Cicero, de Amicitia. By ST. GEORGE STOCK. 3s.

    de Senectute. By L. HUXLEY. 2s.

    in Catilinam. By E. A. UPCOTT. Third edition. 2s. 6d.

    in Q. Caecilium Divinatio and in C. Verrem Actio Prima. By J. R. KING. Limp, 1s. 6d.

    pro Cluentio. By G. G. RAMSAY. Second ed. 3s. 6d.

    pro Marcello, pro Ligario, pro Rege Deiotaro. By W. Y. FAUSSET. Second edition. 2s. 6d.

    pro Milone. By A. C. CLARK. 8vo. 8s. 6d. By A. B. POYNTON. Second edition. Crown 8vo. 2s. 6d.

    Philippics, I, II, III, V, VII. By J. R. KING. Revised by A. C. CLARK. 3s. 6d.

    pro Roscio. By ST. GEORGE STOCK. 3s. 6d.

    Select Orations, viz. in Verrem Actio Prima, de Imperio Gn. Pompeii, pro Archia, Philippica IX. By J. R. KING. Second edition. 2s. 6d.

    Select Letters. With introductions, notes, and appendices. By A. WATSON. Fourth edition. 8vo. 18s. Text only of the large edition. By the same. Third edition. Extra fcap 8vo. 4s.

    Selected Letters. By C. E. PRICHARD and E. R. BERNARD. Second edition. 3s.

    De Oratore Libri Tres. With introduction and notes. By A. S. WILKINS. 8vo. 18s. Or separately, Book I. Third edition. 7s. 6d. Book II. Second edition. 5s. Book III. 6s.

LATIN AUTHORS

Horace, Odes, Carmen Saeculare, and Epodes. By E. C. Wickham. 8vo. Third edition. 12s. Crown 8vo. Second edition. 6s.

Selected Odes. By the same. 2nd ed. 2s. Odes, Book I. 2s.

Satires, Epistles, De Arte Poetica. By the same. Crown 8vo. 6s.

Text only: miniature Oxford edition. On writing-paper for MS notes, 3s. net; on Oxford India paper, roan, 4s. 6d. net.

Iuvenalis ad satiram sextam additi versus xxxvi exscr. E. O. Winstedt. With a facsimile. In wrapper, 2s. 6d. net.

Thirteen Satires. By C. H. Pearson and Herbert A. Strong. Second edition. Crown 8vo. 9s.

Livy, Book I. By Sir J. R. Seeley. Third edition. 8vo. 6s.

Books V-VII. By A. R. Cluer. Revised by P. E. Matheson. 5s. Separately: Book V, 2s. 6d.; Book VI, 2s.; Book VII, 2s.

Books XXI-XXIII. By M. T. Tatham. Second edition, enlarged. 5s. Separately: Book XXI, 2s. 6d.; Book XXII, 2s. 6d.

Lucretius, Book V (783-1457). Edited, with Notes for a Fifth Form, by W. D. Lowe. Crown 8vo. 2s.

Noctes Manilianae. Being elucidations of Manilius, with some conjectural emendations of Aratea. By Robinson Ellis. Crown 8vo. 6s.

Martialis Epigrammata Selecta (W. M. Lindsay's Text and critical notes). Crown 8vo. 3s. 6d. On India paper. 5s.

Books I-VI, VII-XII. Edited by R. T. Bridge and E. D. C. Lake, each 3s. 6d. Notes only, each 2s.

Nepos. By Oscar Browning. Third edition, revised by W. R. Inge. 3s.

Nonius Marcellus, de compendiosa doctrina I-III. Edited, with introduction and critical apparatus, by J. H. Onions. 8vo. 10s. 6d.

Ovid, Heroides, with the Greek translations of Planudes. Edited by Arthur Palmer. 8vo. With a facsimile. 21s.

Ibis. With scholia and commentary. By Robinson Ellis. 8vo. 10s. 6d.

Metamorphoses, Book III. Edited by M. Cartwright. Crown 8vo. 2s. With or without vocabulary. **Book XI.** Edited by G. A. T. Davies. Crown 8vo. 2s. With or without vocabulary.

Tristia. Edited by S. G. Owen. 8vo. 16s. Extra fcap 8vo. Third edition. Book I, 3s. 6d. Book III, 2s.

Selections, with an Appendix on the Roman Calendar by W. Ramsay. By G. G. Ramsay. Third edition. 5s. 6d.

Persius, The Satires. With a translation and commentary, by John Conington. Edited by Henry Nettleship. Third edition. 8vo. 8s. 6d.

Plautus, Captivi. By Wallace M. Lindsay. Second edition. 2s. 6d.

Mostellaria. By E. A. Sonnenschein. Second edition. Fcap 8vo. Text interleaved. 4s. 6d.

Rudens. By the same. 8vo. 8s. 6d. **Editio minor,** Text and Appendix on Metre interleaved. Second edition. 4s. 6d.

Trinummus. By C. E. Freeman and A. Sloman. Third edition. 3s.

Plauti Codex Turnebi. By W. M. Lindsay. 8vo. 21s. net.

CLARENDON PRESS BOOKS

Pliny, Selected Letters. By C. E. Prichard and E. R. Bernard. Third edition. 3s.

Propertius. Index Verborum. By J. S. Phillimore. Crown 8vo. 4s. 6d. net. Translation by the same. Extra fcap 8vo. 3s. 6d. net.
    Selections. See Tibullus.

Quintilian, Institutionis Oratoriae Lib. X. By W. Peterson. 8vo. 12s. 6d. School edition. By the same. Extra fcap 8vo. Second edition. 3s. 6d.

Sallust. By W. W. Capes. Second edition. 4s. 6d.

Scriptores Latini Rei Metricae. Edited by T. Gaisford. 8vo. 5s.

Selections from the less known Latin Poets. By North Pinder. 7s. 6d.

Tacitus. Edited, with introductions and notes, by H. Furneaux. 8vo.

    Annals. Books I–VI. Second ed. 18s. Books XI–XVI. Second edition, revised by H. F. Pelham and C. D. Fisher. 21s.

    Annals. (Text only.) Crown 8vo. 6s.

    Annals, Books I–IV. Second edition. 5s. Book I. Limp, 2s. Books XIII–XVI (abridged from Furneaux's 8vo edition). By H. Pitman. 4s. 6d.

    De Germania. Vita Agricolae. 6s. 6d. each.

    Dialogus de Oratoribus. Edited, with introduction and notes, by W. Peterson. 8vo. 10s. 6d. net.

Terence, Adelphi. By A. Sloman. Second edition. 3s.
    Andria. By C. E. Freeman and A. Sloman. Second edition. 3s.
    Phormio. By A. Sloman. Second edition. 3s.
    'Famulus.' By J. Sargeaunt and A. G. S. Raynor. 2s.

Tibullus and Propertius, Selections. By G. G. Ramsay. Third edition. 6s.

Velleius Paterculus, libri duo ad M. Vinicium. By Robinson Ellis. Crown 8vo. 6s.

Virgil. By T. L. Papillon and A. E. Haigh. Two volumes. Crown 8vo. Cloth, 6s. each; or stiff covers, 3s. 6d. each.

    Text only (including the minor works emended by R. Ellis). Miniature Oxford edition. By the same editors. 32mo. On writing-paper, 3s. net; on Oxford India paper, roan, 4s. 6d. net.

    Aeneid, Books I–III, IV–VI, VII–IX, X–XII. By the same editors. 2s. each part. Book IX, by A. E. Haigh, 1s. 6d.; in two parts, 2s.

    Bucolics and Georgics. By the same editors. 2s. 6d.

    Bucolics. 2s. 6d. Georgics, Books I, II, 2s. 6d. Books III, IV, 2s. 6d. Aeneid, Book I. Limp cloth, 1s. 6d. All by C. S. Jerram.

LATIN

Latin Works of Reference

Lewis and Short's Latin Dictionaries. See p. 34.

The Latin Language, being an historical account of Latin Sounds, Stems, and Flexions. By W. M. LINDSAY. 8vo. 21s.

Selected Fragments of Roman Poetry. Edited, with introduction and notes, by W. W. MERRY. Second edition. Crown 8vo. 6s. 6d.

Fragments and Specimens of Early Latin. With introductions and notes. By J. WORDSWORTH. 8vo. 18s.

Selections from the less known Latin Poets. By NORTH PINDER. 8vo. 7s. 6d.

Latin Historical Inscriptions, illustrating the history of the Early Empire. By G. McN. RUSHFORTH. 8vo. 10s. net.

Scheller's Latin Dictionary. Revised and translated into English by J. L. RIDDLE. Folio. 21s. net.

Professor Nettleship's Books

Contributions to Latin Lexicography. 8vo. 21s.

Lectures and Essays. Second Series. Edited by F. HAVERFIELD. With portrait and memoir. Crown 8vo. 7s. 6d. (The first series is out of print.)

The Roman Satura. 8vo. Sewed. 1s.

Ancient Lives of Vergil. 8vo. Sewed. 2s.

Professor Sellar's Books

Roman Poets of the Republic. Third edition. Crown 8vo. 10s.

Roman Poets of the Augustan Age. Crown 8vo. viz.: **Virgil.** Third edition. 9s., and **Horace and the Elegiac Poets,** with a memoir of the Author, by ANDREW LANG. Second edition. 7s. 6d.

(A limited number of copies of the first edition of *Horace*, containing a portrait of the Author, can still be obtained in Demy 8vo, price 14s.)

Post-Augustan Poetry from Seneca to Juvenal. By H. E. BUTLER. 8vo. 8s. 6d. net.

The Principles of Sound and Inflexion, as illustrated in the Greek and Latin Languages. By J. E. KING and C. COOKSON. 8vo. 18s.

Manual of Comparative Philology. By T. L. PAPILLON. Third edition. Crown 8vo. 6s.

Fontes Prosae Numerosae collegit A. C. CLARK. 8vo. 4s. 6d. net.

Professor Ellis's Lectures

8vo, each 1s. net. Published by Mr. Frowde.

Juvenal, The New Fragments.—Phaedrus, The Fables.—The Correspondence of Fronto and M. Aurelius.—Catullus in the Fourteenth Century.—A Bodleian MS of Copa, Moretum, and other Poems of the Appendix Vergiliana. (Cr. 8vo.)—The Elegiac in Maecenatem.—The Annalist Licinianus, with an Appendix of Emendations of the Text.

CLARENDON PRESS BOOKS

OXFORD CLASSICAL TEXTS

The prices given of copies on ordinary paper are for copies bound in limp cloth; uncut copies may be had in paper covers at 6d. less per volume (1s. less for those priced from 6s. in cloth). All volumes are also on sale interleaved with writing-paper and bound in stout cloth; prices on application.

Greek

Aeschylus. A. SIDGWICK. 3s. 6d. (India paper, 4s. 6d.)

Antoninus. J. H. LEOPOLD. 3s. (India paper, 4s.)

Apollonius Rhodius. R. C. SEATON. 3s. (India paper, 4s.)

Aristophanes. F. W. HALL, W. M. GELDART. (India paper, 8s. 6d.)
    I. Ach., Eq., Nub., Vesp., Pax, Aves. 3s. 6d. (India paper, 4s. 6d.)
    II. Lys., Thesm., Ran., Eccl., Plut., fr. 3s. 6d. (India paper, 4s. 6d.)

Bucolici Graeci. U. VON WILAMOWITZ-MOELLENDORFF. 3s. (India paper, 4s.)

Demosthenes. S. H. BUTCHER. (India paper, 12s. 6d.)
    I. Orationes I–XIX. 4s. 6d. II. i. Orationes XX–XXVI. 3s. 6d.

Euripides. G. G. A. MURRAY. (India paper, Vols. I–III, 12s. 6d.; Vols. I–II, 9s.; Vol. III, 4s. 6d.)
    I. Cyc., Alc., Med., Heracl., Hip., Andr., Hec. 3s. 6d.
    II. Suppl., Herc., Ion, Tro., El., I. T. 3s. 6d.
    III. Hel., Phoen., Or., Bacch., Iph. Aul., Rh. 3s. 6d.

Hellenica Oxyrhynchia cum Theopompi et Cratippi fragmentis. B. P. GRENFELL, A. S. HUNT. 4s. 6d.

Herodotus. K. HUDE. (India paper, 12s. 6d.)
    Vol. I (Books I–IV). 4s. 6d. Vol. II (Books V–IX). 4s. 6d.

Homer, 3s. per volume.
    Iliad. (Vols. I and II.) D. B. MONRO, T. W. ALLEN. (India paper, 7s.)
    Odyssey. (Vols. III and IV.) T. W. ALLEN. (India paper, 6s.)

Hyperides. F. G. KENYON. 3s. 6d.

Longinus. A. O. PRICKARD. 2s. 6d.

Plato. J. BURNET. Vols. I–III, 6s. each (India paper, 7s. each). Vol. IV. 7s. (India paper, 8s. 6d.) Vol. V. 8s. (India paper, 10s. 6d.)
    I. Euth., Apol., Crit., Ph.; Crat., Tht., Soph., Polit.
    II. Par., Phil., Symp., Phdr.; Alc. I, II, Hipp., Am.
    III. Thg., Chrm., Lch., Lys.; Euthd., Prot., Gorg., Men.; Hp., Io, Mnx.
    IV. Clit., Rep., Tim., Critias. Also Republic, separately, 6s.; on quarto writing-paper, 10s. 6d.
    V. Minos, Leges, Epinomis, Epistulae. Definitiones, Spuria.
        First and fifth tetralogies separately, paper covers, 2s. each.

Theophrasti Characteres. H. DIELS. 3s. 6d.

Thucydides. H. STUART JONES. (India paper, 8s. 6d.)
    I. Books 1–4. II. Books 5–8. 3s. 6d. each.

Xenophon. E. C. MARCHANT. Vols. I–III. (India Paper, 12s. 6d.)
    I. Historia Graeca. 3s.
    II. Libri Socratici. 3s. 6d.
    III. Anabasis. 3s.
    IV. Cyropaedia. [In the press.

OXFORD CLASSICAL TEXTS

Latin

Asconius. A. C. Clark. 3s. 6d.

Caesar, Commentarii. R. L. A. Du Pontet. (India paper, 7s.)
Bellum Gallicum. 2s. 6d. Bellum Civile. 3s.

Catullus. R. Ellis. 2s. 6d. (With Tibullus and Propertius, on India paper, 8s. 6d.)

Cicero, Epistulae. L. C. Purser. (India paper, 21s.)
  I. Epp. ad Fam. 6s.; II. ad Att., Pars i (1–8), Pars ii (9–16), 4s. 6d. each;
  III. ad Q. F., ad M. Brut., Fragm. 3s.

  Orationes. (Rosc. Am. etc, Mil. etc, Verrinae, India paper, 18s. 6d.)
    Rosc. Am., I. Pomp., Clu., Cat., Mur., Cael. A. C. Clark. 3s.
    Pro Milone, Caesarianae, Philippicae. A. C. Clark. 3s.
    Verrinae. W. Peterson. 4s.
    Quinct., Rosc. Com., Caec., Leg. Agr., Rab. Perduell., Flacc., Pis., Rab. Post. A. C. Clark. 3s.

  Rhetorica. A. S. Wilkins. (India paper, 7s. 6d.)
    I. De Oratore. 3s. II. Brutus, etc. 3s. 6d.

Horace. E. C. Wickham. 3s. (India paper, 4s. 6d.)

Lucretius. C. Bailey. 3s. (India paper, 4s.)

Martial. W. M. Lindsay. 6s. (India paper, 7s. 6d.)

Nepos. E. O. Winstedt. 2s.

Persius and Juvenal. S. G. Owen. 3s. (India paper, 4s.)

Plautus. W. M. Lindsay. (India paper, 16s.)
  I. Amph.—Merc. II. Miles—fragm. 6s. each.

Propertius. J. S. Phillimore. 3s. (India paper, see Catullus.)

Statius. (Complete on India paper. 10s. 6d.)
    Silvae. J. S. Phillimore. 3s. 6d.
    Thebais and Achilleis. H. W. Garrod. 6s.

Tacitus, Opera Minora. H. Furneaux. 2s.
    Annales. C. D. Fisher. 6s. (India paper, 7s.)

Terence. R. Y. Tyrrell. 3s. 6d. (India paper, 5s.)

Tibullus. J. P. Postgate. 2s. (India paper, see Catullus.)

Vergil. F. A. Hirtzel. 3s. 6d. (India paper, 4s. 6d.)

Appendix Vergiliana. R. Ellis. 4s.

CLARENDON PRESS BOOKS

Annotated Greek Classics

For Oxford Classical Texts, see p. 40; for Oxford Translations, p. 21.

Extra fcap 8vo

Aeschylus. By ARTHUR SIDGWICK. New editions with the text of the Oxford Classical Texts.
> Agamemnon. Sixth edition revised. 3s. Choephoroi. New edition revised. 3s. Eumenides. Third edition. 3s. Persae. 3s. Septem contra Thebas. 3s.
> Prometheus Vinctus. By A. O. PRICKARD. Fourth edition. 2s.

Aristophanes. By W. W. MERRY.
> Acharnians. Fifth edition. 3s. Birds. Fourth edition. 3s. 6d.
> Clouds. Second edition. 3s. Frogs. Fifth edition. 3s.
> Knights. Second edition. 3s. Peace. 3s. 6d.
> Wasps. Second edition. 3s. 6d.

Cebes, Tabula. By C. S. JERRAM. Stiff covers, 1s. 6d.; cloth, 2s. 6d.

Demosthenes. By EVELYN ABBOTT and P. E. MATHESON.
> Against Philip. Vol. I: Philippic I, Olynthiacs I-III. Fourth edition. 3s. Vol. II: De Pace, Philippic II, de Chersoneso, Philippic III. 4s. 6d. Philippics I-III (reprinted from above). 2s. 6d.
> On the Crown. 3s. 6d.
> Against Meidias. By J. R. KING. Crown 8vo. 3s. 6d.

Euripides.
> Alcestis. By C. S. JERRAM. Fifth edition. 2s. 6d. Bacchae. By A. H. CRUICKSHANK. 3s. 6d. Cyclops. By W. E. LONG. 2s. 6d. Hecuba. By C. B. HEBERDEN. 2s. 6d. Helena. By C. S. JERRAM. Second edition. 3s. Heracleidae. By C. S. JERRAM. 3s. Ion. By C. S. JERRAM. 3s. Iphigenia in Tauris. By C. S. JERRAM. New edition revised. 3s. Medea. By C. B. HEBERDEN. Third edition. 2s.

Herodotus, Book IX. By EVELYN ABBOTT. 3s.
> Selections. With a map. By W. W. MERRY. 2s. 6d.

Homer, Iliad. By D. B. MONRO. I-XII. With a brief Homeric Grammar. Fifth edition. 6s. Book I, with the Homeric Grammar, separately. Third edition. 1s. 6d. XIII-XXIV. Fourth edition. 6s.
> Book III (for beginners), by M. T. TATHAM. 1s. 6d. Book XXI. By HERBERT HAILSTONE. 1s. 6d.

Homer, Odyssey. By W. W. MERRY.
> I-XII. Sixty-sixth thousand. 5s. Books I and II, separately, each 1s. 6d. Books VI and VII. 1s. 6d. Books VII-XII. 3s.
> XIII-XXIV. Sixteenth thousand. 5s. Books XIII-XVIII. 3s. Books XIX-XXIV. 3s.

ANNOTATED GREEK CLASSICS

Lucian, Vera Historia. By C. S. Jerram. Second edition. 1s. 6d.

Dialogues prepared for Schools. By W. H. D. Rouse. Text 2s., Notes in Greek 2s.

Lysias, Epitaphios. By F. J. Snell. 2s.

Plato. By St. George Stock. Euthyphro. 2s. 6d. Apology. Ed. 3. 2s. 6d. Crito. 2s. Meno. Ed. 3. 2s. 6d. Ion. 2s. 6d.

Euthydemus. With revised text, introduction, notes, and indices, by E. H. Gifford. Crown 8vo. 3s. 6d.

Menexenus. By J. A. Shawyer. Crown 8vo. 2s.

Selections. By J. Purves with preface by B. Jowett. 2nd ed. 5s.

Plutarch, Lives of the Gracchi. By G. E. Underhill. Crown 8vo. 4s. 6d.

Coriolanus (for Junior Students). With introduction and notes. 2s.

Sophocles. By Lewis Campbell and Evelyn Abbott. New and revised edition. Two volumes: Vol. I text 4s. 6d.; Vol. II notes 6s.

Or singly 2s. each (text and notes), Ajax, Antigone, Electra, Oedipus Coloneus, Oedipus Tyrannus, Philoctetes, Trachiniae.

Scenes from Sophocles, edited by C. E. Laurence. With illustrations. 1s. 6d. each. (1) Ajax. (2) Antigone.

Select Fragments of the Greek Comic Poets. By A. W. Pickard-Cambridge. Crown 8vo. 5s.

Golden Treasury of Ancient Greek Poetry. By Sir R. S. Wright. Second edition. Revised by E. Abbott. Extra fcap 8vo. 10s. 6d.

Golden Treasury of Greek Prose. By Sir R. S. Wright and J. E. L. Shadwell. Extra fcap 8vo. 4s. 6d.

Theocritus. By H. Kynaston. Fifth edition. 4s. 6d.

Thucydides. Book III. By H. F. Fox. Crown 8vo. 3s. 6d. Book IV. By T. R. Mills. With an introductory essay by H. S. Jones. Crown 8vo. 3s. 6d. Notes only, 2s. 6d.

Xenophon. (See also p. 34.)

Anabasis. Each of the first four Books is now issued in uniform cloth binding at 1s. 6d. Each volume contains introduction, text, notes, and a full vocabulary to the Anabasis. Book I. By J. Marshall. Book II. By C. S. Jerram. Books III and IV. By J. Marshall. Books III, IV, 3s. Vocabulary to the Anabasis, by J. Marshall. 1s.

Cyropaedia, Book I. 2s. Books IV and V. 2s. 6d. By C. Bigg.

Hellenica, Books I, II. By G. E. Underhill. 3s.

Memorabilia. By J. Marshall. 4s. 6d.

Editions etc of Greek Authors mostly with English notes

Appian, Book I. Edited with map and appendix on Pompey's passage of the Alps, by J. L. STRACHAN-DAVIDSON. Crown 8vo. 3s. 6d.

Aristophanes, A Concordance to. By H. DUNBAR. 4to. £1 1s. net.

Aristotle.

    The Poetics. A revised Greek text, with critical introduction, English translation and commentary, by I. BYWATER. 8vo. 16s. net.

    De Arte Poetica Liber recognovit I. BYWATER. Post 8vo. 1s. 6d.

    Ethica Nicomachea recognovit breviqve adnotatione critica instruxit I. BYWATER. On 4to paper, for marginal notes. 10s. 6d. Also in crown 8vo. 3s. 6d.

    Contributions to the Textual Criticism of Aristotle's Nicomachean Ethics. By I. BYWATER. Stiff cover. 2s. 6d.

    Notes on the Nicomachean Ethics. By J. A. STEWART. 2 vols. Post 8vo. £1 12s.

    The English Manuscripts of the Nicomachean Ethics. By J. A. STEWART. Crown 4to. 3s. 6d. net.

    Selecta ex Organo Capitula: in usum Scholarum Academicarum. Crown 8vo, stiff covers. 3s. 6d.

    The Politics, with introduction, notes, etc, by W. L. NEWMAN. 4 vols. Medium 8vo. 14s. net per volume.

    The Politics, translated into English, with introduction, notes, and indices, by B. JOWETT. Medium 8vo. Vol. I, 10s. net; Vol. II, 8s. 6d. net.

    Aristotelian Studies. On the Structure of the Seventh Book of the Nicomachean Ethics. By J. COOK WILSON. 8vo. 5s.

    On the History of the Aristotelian Writings. By R. SHUTE. 8vo. 7s. 6d.

    Physics, Book VII. With introduction by R. SHUTE. 2s. net.

    The Works of Aristotle. Translated into English under the Editorship of J. A. SMITH and W. D. ROSS. 8vo.

        Parva Naturalia. By J. I. BEARE and G. R. T. ROSS. 3s. 6d. net.

        De Lineis Insecabilibus. By H. H. JOACHIM. 2s. 6d. net.

        Metaphysica. (Vol. VIII.) By W. D. ROSS. 7s. 6d. net.

        De Mirabilibus Auscultationibus. By L. D. DOWDALL. 2s. net.

        Historia Animalium. (Vol. IV.) By D'ARCY W. THOMPSON. (In the press.)

        De Generatione Animalium. By A. PLATT. (In the press.)

Aristoxenus. Edited, with introduction, music, translation, and notes, by H. S. MACRAN. Crown 8vo. 10s. 6d. net.

GREEK AUTHORS

Demosthenes and Aeschines on the Crown. With introductory essays and notes, by G. A. Simcox and W. H. Simcox. 8vo. 12s.

Heracliti Ephesii Reliquiae. Edited by I. Bywater, with Diogenes Laertius' Life of Heraclitus, etc. 8vo. 6s.

Herodas. Edited, with full introduction and notes, by J. Arbuthnot Nairn. With facsimiles of the fragments and other illustrations. 8vo. 12s. 6d. net.

Herodotus, Books V and VI. Terpsichore and Erato. Edited, with notes and appendices, by E. Abbott. With two maps. Post 8vo. 6s.

Homer, A Concordance to the Odyssey and Hymns; and to the Parallel Passages in the Iliad, Odyssey, and Hymns. By H. Dunbar. 4to. £1 1s. net.

    Odyssey. Books I-XII. Edited, with English notes, appendices, etc, by W. W. Merry and J. Riddell. Second edition. 8vo. 16s.

    Books XIII-XXIV. Edited, with English notes, appendices, and illustrations, by D. B. Monro. 8vo. 16s.

    Hymni Homerici codicibus denuo collatis recensuit A. Goodwin. Small folio. With four plates. £1 1s. net.

    Scholia Graeca in Iliadem. Edited by W. Dindorf, after a new collation of the Venetian MSS by D. B. Monro. 4 vols. 8vo. £2 10s. net. See also p. 47.

    Opera et Reliquiae, recensuit D. B. Monro. Crown 8vo, on India paper. 10s. 6d. net. 'The Oxford Homer.'

    Homerica. Emendations and Elucidations of the Odyssey. By T. L. Agar. 8vo. 11s. net.

Index Andocideus, Lycurgeus, Dinarcheus, confectus ab A. L. Forman. 8vo. 7s. 6d. net.

Menander's Γεωργός, the Geneva Fragment, with text, translation, and notes, by B. P. Grenfell and A. S. Hunt. 8vo, stiff covers. 1s. 6d.

Νόμος Ῥοδίων Ναυτικός. The Rhodian Sea-Law. Edited, with introduction, translation, and commentary, by W. Ashburner. 8vo. 18s. net.

Plato, Philebus. Edited by E. Poste. 8vo. 7s. 6d.

    Republic. Edited, with notes and essays, by B. Jowett and L. Campbell. In three volumes. Medium 8vo, cloth. £2 2s.

    Sophistes and Politicus. Edited by L. Campbell. 8vo. 10s. 6d. net.

    Theaetetus. Edited by L. Campbell. 2nd ed. 8vo. 10s. 6d. net.

    The Dialogues, translated into English, with analyses and introductions, by B. Jowett. Third edition. Five volumes, medium 8vo. £4 4s. In half-morocco, £5. *The Subject-Index to the second edition of the Dialogues,* by E. Abbott, separately. 8vo, cloth. 2s. 6d.

    The Republic, translated into English, by B. Jowett. Third edition. Medium 8vo. 12s. 6d. Half-roan, 14s.

    Selections from Jowett's translation, with introductions by M. J. Knight. Two volumes. Crown 8vo. 12s.

Polybius, Selections. Edited by J. L. Strachan-Davidson. With maps. Medium 8vo, buckram. 21s.

CLARENDON PRESS BOOKS

Sophocles, The Plays and Fragments. Edited by L. CAMPBELL.
Vol. I: Oedipus Tyrannus. Oedipus Coloneus. Antigone. 8vo. 16s.
Vol. II: Ajax. Electra. Trachiniae. Philoctetes. Fragments. 8vo. 16s.

Strabo, Selections. With an introduction on Strabo's Life and Works. By H. F. TOZER. With maps and plans. Post 8vo, cloth. 12s.

Thucydides. Translated into English by B. JOWETT. Second edition, revised. 2 vols. 8vo. 15s.
Vol. I: Essay on Inscriptions, and Books I-III.
Vol. II: Books IV-VIII, and Historical Index.

Xenophon, Hellenica. Edited, with introduction and appendices, by G. E. UNDERHILL. Crown 8vo. 7s. 6d. Also with the Oxford Text by E. C. MARCHANT, one volume. 7s. 6d. net.

Older Clarendon Press Editions of Greek Authors

The Greek texts in fine and generally large type; the Scholia (and some of the texts) have not appeared in any later editions. The annotations are in Latin.

Aeschinem et Isocratem, Scholia Graeca in, edidit G. DINDORFIUS. 8vo. 4s.

Aeschylus ex rec. G. DINDORFII. Tragoediae et Fragmenta. Second edition. 8vo. 5s. 6d. Annotationes. Partes II. 8vo. 10s.
Quae supersunt in codice Laurentiano typis descripta edidit R. MERKEL. Small folio. £1 1s. net.

Apsinis et Longini Rhetorica recensuit JOH. BAKIUS. 8vo. 3s.

Aristophanes ex rec. G. DINDORFII. Comoediae et Fragmenta. Tomi II. 8vo. 11s. Annotationes. Partes II. 8vo. 11s. Scholia Graeca. Partes III. 8vo. £1. J. Caravellae Index. 8vo. 3s.

Aristoteles ex recensione IMMANUELIS BEKKERI. Accedunt Indices Sylburgiani. Tomi I-XI. 8vo.
The nine volumes in print (I (Organon) and IX (Ethica) are out of print) may be had separately, price 5s. 6d. each.

Choerobosci Dictata in Theodosii Canones, necnon Epimerismi in Psalmos edidit THOMAS GAISFORD. Tomi III. 8vo. 15s.

Demosthenes ex recensione G. DINDORFII. Tomi IX. 8vo. £2 6s.
Separately: Textus, £1 1s. Annotationes, 15s. Scholia, 10s.

Etymologicon Magnum. Edited by T. GAISFORD. Folio. Out of print.

Euripides ex rec. G. DINDORFII. Fragoediae et Fragmenta. Tomi II. 8vo. 10s. Annotationes. Partes II. 8vo. 10s. Scholia Graeca. Tomi IV. 8vo. £1 16s. Alcestis. 8vo. 2s. 6d.

GREEK AUTHORS

Harpocrationis Lexicon ex recensione G. Dindorfii. Tomi II. 8vo. 21s. net.

Hephaestionis Enchiridion, Terentianus Maurus, Proclus, etc. edidit T. Gaisford. Tomi II. 12s. 6d. net.

Homerus
    Ilias, cum brevi annotatione C. G. Heynii. Accedunt Scholia minora. Tomi II. 8vo. 15s.
    Ilias. Ex rec. G. Dindorfii. 8vo. 5s. 6d.
    Scholia Graeca in Iliadem. See p. 45.
    Scholia Graeca in Iliadem Townleyana recensuit Ernestus Maass. 2 vols. 8vo. £1 16s.
    Odyssea. Ex rec. G. Dindorfii. 8vo. 5s. 6d.
    Scholia Graeca in Odysseam ed. G. Dindorfius. Tomi II. 8vo. 15s. 6d.
    Seberi Index in Homerum. 8vo. 6s. 6d.

Oratores Attici ex recensione Bekkeri: Vol. III. Isaeus, Æschines, Lycurgus, etc. 8vo. 7s. Vols. I and II are out of print.

Paroemiographi Graeci edidit T. Gaisford. Out of print.

Index Graecitatis Platonicae confecit T. Mitchell. 1832. 2 vols. 8vo. 5s.

Plotinus edidit F. Creuzer. Tomi III. 4to. 42s. net.

Plutarchi Moralia edidit D. Wyttenbach. Accedit Index Graecitatis. Tomi VIII. Partes XV. 8vo, cloth. £3 10s. net.

Sophoclis Tragoediae et Fragmenta. Ex recensione et cum commentariis G. Dindorfii. Third edition. 2 vols. Fcap 8vo. £1 1s.
    Each Play separately, limp, 1s.; text only, 6d.; text on writing-paper, 8s.
        Tragoediae et Fragmenta cum annotationibus G. Dindorfii. Tomi II. 8vo. 10s.
        The text, Vol. I, 5s. 6d. The notes, Vol. II, 4s. 6d.

Stobaei Florilegium ad MSS fidem emendavit et supplevit T. Gaisford. Tomi IV. 8vo. £3 3s. net.
        Eclogarum Physicarum et Ethicarum libri duo: accedit Hieroclis Commentarius in aurea carmina Pythagoreorum. Recensuit T. Gaisford. Tomi II. 8vo. 11s.

Suidae Lexicon. Edited by T. Gaisford. Three vols. Folio. Large paper copies, £6 6s. net. (A few copies remain.)

Xenophon. Ex rec. et cum annotatt. L. Dindorfii.
    Historia Graeca. Second edition. 8vo. 10s. 6d.
    Expeditio Cyri. Second edition. 8vo. 10s. 6d.
    Institutio Cyri. 8vo. 10s. 6d.
    Memorabilia Socratis. 8vo. 7s. 6d.
    Opuscula Politica Equestria et Venatica cum Arriani Libello de Venatione. 8vo. 10s. 6d.

CLARENDON PRESS BOOKS

Greek Literature

The Attic Theatre. By A. E. Haigh. Third edition, revised and in part rewritten by A. W. Pickard-Cambridge. Illustrated. 8vo. 10s. 6d. net. A few copies of the second edition can still be obtained.

The Tragic Drama of the Greeks. By A. E. Haigh. With illustrations. 8vo. 10s. 6d. net.

Ancient Classical Drama. By R. G. Moulton. Ed. 2. Cr. 8vo. 8s. 6d.

Modes of Ancient Greek Music. By D. B. Monro. 15s. net. (For Aristoxenus, see p. 44.)

The Rise of the Greek Epic. By Gilbert Murray. 8vo. 7s. 6d. net.

The Interpretation of Greek Literature. An Inaugural Lecture by Gilbert Murray. 8vo. 1s. net.

Greek Historical Writing and Apollo. Two Lectures by U. von Wilamowitz-Moellendorff. Translation by Gilbert Murray. 8vo. 2s. net.

The Erasmian Pronunciation of Greek. A Lecture by I. Bywater. 8vo. 1s. net (published by Mr. Frowde).

The Value of Byzantine and Modern Greek. A Lecture by S. Menardos. 8vo. 1s. net.

Ionia and the East. By D. G. Hogarth. 8vo. With a map. 3s. 6d. net.

Coins and Inscriptions

Historia Numorum. A Manual of Greek Numismatics. By Barclay V. Head. [Second edition in the press.]

A Manual of Greek Historical Inscriptions. By E. L. Hicks. New edition, revised by G. F. Hill. 8vo. 10s. 6d. net.

The Inscriptions of Cos. By W. R. Paton & E. L. Hicks. Ry. 8vo. £1 8s.

A Grammar of the Homeric Dialect. By D. B. Monro. 8vo. Ed. 2, 14s.

The Sounds and Inflections of Greek Dialects (Ionic). By H. W. Smyth. 8vo. £1 4s.

A Glossary of Greek Birds. By D'Arcy W. Thompson, C.B. 8vo. 10s. n.

Practical Introduction to Greek Accentuation. By H. W. Chandler. 8vo. 2nd ed. 10s. 6d. Also an abridgement. Ext. fcap 8vo. 2s. 6d.

Palaeography: Papyri

Catalogus Codicum Graecorum Sinaiticorum. Scripsit V. Gardthausen. With facsimiles. 8vo, linen. £1 5s. net.

On abbreviations in Greek MSS. By T. W. Allen. Royal 8vo. 5s.

An Alexandrian erotic fragment and other Greek papyri, chiefly Ptolemaic. Edited by B. P. Grenfell. Small 4to. 8s. 6d. net.

New classical fragments and other papyri. Edited by B. P. Grenfell and A. S. Hunt. 12s. 6d. net.

Revenue laws of Ptolemy Philadelphus. Edited by B. P. Grenfell and J. P. Mahaffy. £1 11s. 6d. net.

Palaeography of Greek papyri, by F. G. Kenyon. 8vo. 10s. 6d.

www.ingramcontent.com/pod-product-compliance
Lightning Source LLC
Chambersburg PA
CBHW032118230426
43672CB00009B/1775